AF897618

Politics and Economic Development in Nigeria

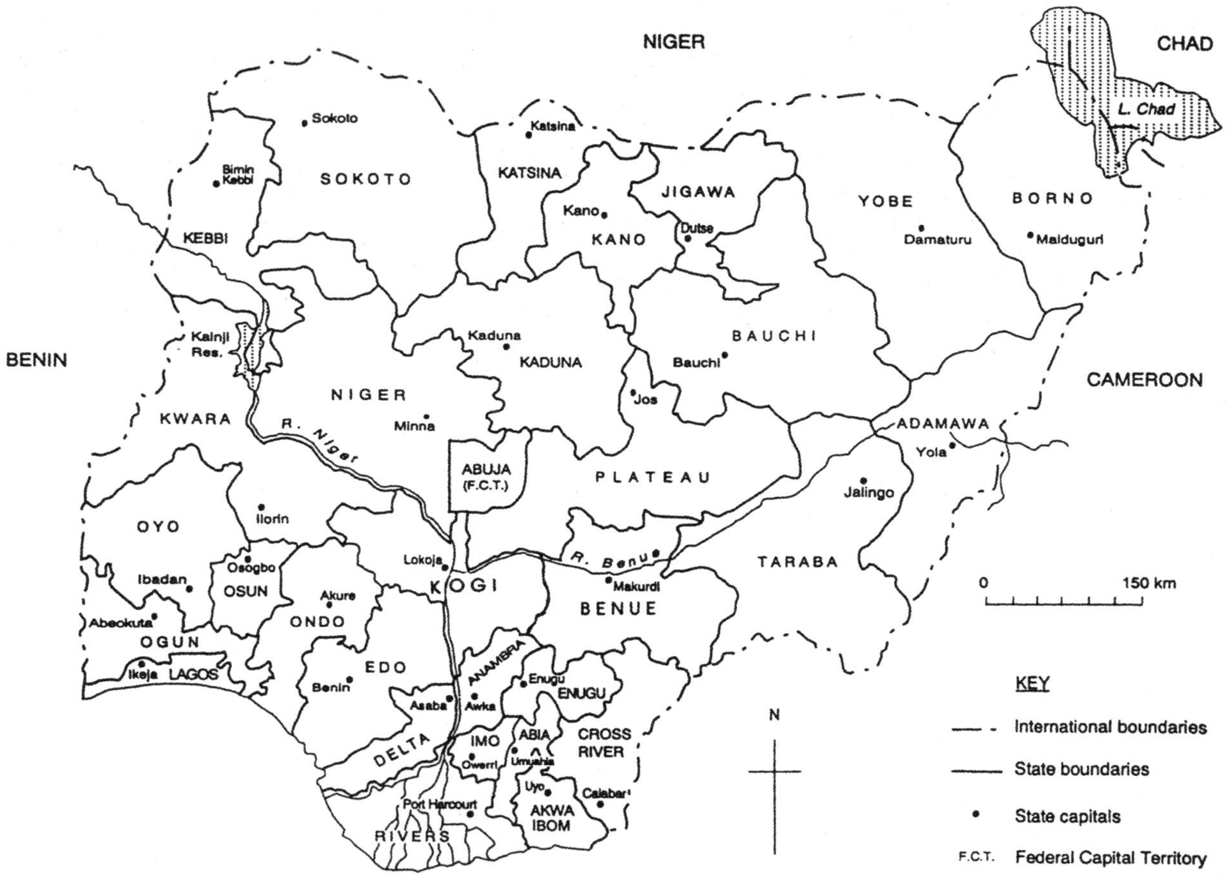

Nigeria: Political Divisions. At the time of writing, no official map of the thirty states was available. Boundaries should be treated as rough approximations.

African Modernization and Development Series

Paul Lovejoy, Series Editor

Politics and Economic Development in Nigeria, Updated Edition,
Tom Forrest

Pawnship in Africa: Debt and Bondage in Historical Perspective,
edited by Toyin Falola and Paul E. Lovejoy

African Refugees: Development Aid and Repatriation,
edited by Howard Adelman and John Sorenson

Slavery and South Africa: Captive Labor on the Dutch Frontier,
edited by Elizabeth A. Eldredge and Fred Morton

Democracy and Socialism in Africa,
edited by Robin Cohen and Harry Goulbourne

The Precarious Balance: State and Society in Africa,
edited by Donald Rothchild and Naomi Chazan

Politics and Economic Development in Nigeria
Updated Edition

Tom Forrest

Routledge
Taylor & Francis Group
LONDON AND NEW YORK

First published 1995 by Westview Press

Published 2019 by Routledge
52 Vanderbilt Avenue, New York, NY 10017
2 Park Square, Milton Park, Abingdon, Oxon OX14 4RN

Routledge is an imprint of the Taylor & Francis Group, an informa business

Copyright © 1993, 1995 Taylor & Francis

All rights reserved. No part of this book may be reprinted or reproduced or utilised in any form or by any electronic, mechanical, or other means, now known or hereafter invented, including photocopying and recording, or in any information storage or retrieval system, without permission in writing from the publishers.

Notice:
Product or corporate names may be trademarks or registered trademarks, and are used only for identification and explanation without intent to infringe.

Library of Congress Cataloging-in-Publication Data
Forrest, Tom (Tom G.)
Politics and economic development in Nigeria / Tom Forrest. — Updated ed.
p. cm. — (African modernization and development series)
Includes bibliographical references and index.
1. Nigeria—Economic policy. 2. Nigeria—Politics and government—1960– 3. Industrial policy—Nigeria. 4. Military government—Nigeria. 5. Federal government—Nigeria. I. Title. II. Series.
HC1055.F67 1995
338.9669—dc20 95-37941
CIP

ISBN 13: 978-0-367-28362-9 (hbk)
ISBN 13: 978-0-367-29908-8 (pbk)

Contents

Illustrations

Maps

Tables

Acknowledgements

My original interest in the political economy of Nigeria developed when I taught at Ahmadu Bello University, Zaria. I owe a large debt to former colleagues and students at that institution. In Oxford, Tajuddeen Abdulraheem and Tony Akinola were always willing to share with me their vast knowledge of Nigerian politics. At the Queen Elizabeth House Library, Gill Short and Bob Townsend were a constant help. In London, Patrick Smith, Richard Synge, and Tony Berrett assisted me in various ways. Tajuddeen Abdulraheem, Yakubu Aliyu, Sara Berry, Tom Biersteker, Tabitha Kanogo, Mathew Lockwood, Otto Marenin, Susan Martin, 'Bayo Olukoshi, John Peel, Ken Swindell, Nick Van Hear, Gavin Williams, and Alhaji Mahmood Yakubu commented on various chapters. I thank them and take full responsibility for the final product.

Tom Forrest
Oxford

Abbreviations

ABN	Association for a Better Nigeria
ADGN	Association for Democracy and Good Governance in Nigeria
ADPs	Agricultural Development Projects
AFRC	Armed Forces Ruling Council
AG	Action Group
APMEPU	Agricultural Projects Monitoring Evaluation and Planning Unit
ASUU	Academic Staff Union of Universities
b/d	barrels per day
CAN	Christian Association of Nigeria
CD	Campaign for Democracy
CDC	Constitution Drafting Committee
CDHR	Committee for the Defense of Human Rights
CFA	Communauté Financière Africaine
CLO	Civil Liberties Organisation
CU	Christian Union
DFRRI	Directorate of Foods, Roads, and Rural Infrastructure
DPA	Distributable Pool Account
ECGD	Export Credits Guarantee Department
ECOMOG	ECOWAS Ceasefire and Monitoring Group
ECOWAS	Economic Community of West African States
FEDECO	Federal Electoral Commission
FESTAC	Festival of Black Arts and Culture
FRCN	Federal Radio Corporation of Nigeria
GDP	Gross Domestic Product
GFSA	Gani Fawehinmi Solidarity Association
GNPP	Great Nigeria People's Party
IMF	International Monetary Fund
ING	Interim National Government
ITT	International Telephone and Telegraph
JAMB	Joint Admission and Matriculation Board
JNI	Jama'atu Nasril Islam
LBA	Licenced Buying Agent

MAMSER	Mass Mobilisation for Self-reliance, Social Justice, and Economic Recovery
MAN	Manufacturers Association of Nigeria
MOSOP	Movement for the Survival of the Ogoni People
MPLA	Movimento Popular de Liberticão de Angola
NADECO	National Democratic Coalition
NADL	National Association of Democratic Lawyers
NANS	National Association of Nigerian Students
NCF	National Consultative Forum
NCNC	National Convention of Nigerian Citizens
NEC	Nigerian Electoral Commission
NEPA	Nigerian Electric Power Authority
NEPU	Northern Elements Progressive Union
NIDB	Nigerian Industrial Development Bank
NIIA	Nigerian Institute of International Affairs
NLC	Nigerian Labour Congress
NNDC	New Nigeria Development Company
NNDP	Nigerian National Democratic Party
NNOC	Nigerian National Oil Corporation
NNPC	Nigerian National Petroleum Corporation
NNSC	Nigerian National Supply Company
NPC	Northern People's Congress
NPN	National Party of Nigeria
NPP	Nigerian People's Party
NRC	National Republican Convention
NSO	National Security Organisation
NUJ	Nigerian Union of Journalists
NUPENG	National Union of Petroleum and Natural Gas Workers
OAU	Organisation of African Unity
OIC	Organisation of Islamic Conference
OMATA	Onitsha Market Traders Association
OMPADEC	Oil Mineral Producing Areas Development Commission
OPEC	Organisation of Petroleum Exporting Countries
PENGASSAN	Petroleum and Natural Gas Senior Staff Association
PLO	Presidential Liaison Officer
PNP	"Party of National Patronage"
PRODA	Products Development Agency
PRP	People's Redemption Party
RBDA	River Basin Development Authority
SAP	Structural Adjustment Programme
SCM	Student Christian Movement
SDP	Social Democratic Party
SFEM	Second Tier Foreign Exchange Market

SMC	Supreme Military Council
SU	Scripture Union
UAC	United Africa Company
UBA	United Bank for Africa
UPE	Universal Primary Education
UPN	Unity Party of Nigeria
UTC	Union Trading Company
WAI	War Against Indiscipline
WIN	Women in Nigeria

1

Introduction

Recent images of Africa in the West have depicted the continent in the throes of great political instability and economic stagnation or decline.[1] A corrupt and authoritarian leadership, personal rule, ineffective government, poor policies, and unproductive patterns of accumulation are variously held to blame. Applied to Nigeria, these images seem exaggerated and too general. Although state policies have often been inefficient, inconsistent, and wasteful, there is a long-term capitalist dynamic at work. The federal system of government has evolved, and the pattern of political competition has kept strongly authoritarian rule at bay. In the struggle to govern a recent colonial creation of great complexity and create a national identity, there have been some achievements; and I will argue that the prospects for material progress are not as gloomy as the perpetual talk of crisis implies.

The study is focussed largely, though not exclusively, at the level of national politics and the macroeconomy. In both major sections, a chronological approach is used. The study begins in Part 1 with a historical introduction to Nigeria's political economy. Part 2 (Chapters 3–6) contains an account of contemporary political development in Nigeria since 1970, when a civil war that had lasted for thirty months ended with the defeat of secessionist Biafra. Major issues and conflicts in Nigerian politics, the dynamics of regime change, and the challenges that have arisen from ethnic, religious, and regional divisions are identified. The political, ideological, and social context within which state power has been exercised and the federal system of government has evolved is examined.

In Part 3 (Chapters 7–10), the focus is on the evolution of economic policy, economic institutions, and economic performance. These issues are examined in relation to the overall priorities and capacities of the state under different regimes and to the longer term dynamics of capitalist development.

The division into parts reflects the fact that political and economic aspects of Nigerian society can be separated analytically. Such a separation helps to clarify their character and the nature of their interaction. Both economy and politics are rooted in common social relations and historical experiences, and the division is not meant to imply the existence of separate spheres of activity. A measure of independence can be given to political activity and institutions. Thus the manner in which political power is mobilised, competed for, and shared affects the political demands that find expression. Economic forces, on the other hand, find expression in local patterns of capital accumulation and class alignment, in the character of the productive classes, in the changing fiscal basis of the state, and in the power of international capital.

Often it is the two-way interaction between political and economic forces that is important in shaping the direction of development and public policies through time. A few instances will help to make this clear.

1. The Marketing Boards, which originated out of the need for wartime controls and the growth of monopoly in the export trade, became instruments of taxation. They also became important political institutions at the centre of regional party power. In turn, they shaped the extent and form of government economic intervention, allowing scope for the exercise of bureaucratic power and the growth of state patronage.
2. The strength of distributive issues that have made up much of the substance of political debate and controversy and affected the allocation of resources is not explicable without reference to the evolution of the federal system and the structure of political competition. Study of the dynamic impact of large oil revenues demonstrates how the distribution of a centralised revenue from above affects political incentives and the focus of political competition. At the same time, low levels of taxation weakened political participation, discouraged a concern with policy issues, and tended to undermine financial responsibility at all levels.
3. The impact of large oil revenues on economic strategy and management in the 1970s was shaped by existing political conditions. In turn, the timing and form of the subsequent reform and reversal of policy in the 1980s under reduced oil revenues was conditioned by political forces.

Perspectives on the State, Class, and Community

State institutions and the exercise of state power are important for a number of reasons. First, there is the general role of the state in providing the conditions for capitalist development through the rule of law and protection of property relations. Beyond that, the state intervenes to regulate and manage the economy. It also intervenes in production and redistributes resources and structures the economy through the system of revenue allocation and institutions like the Marketing Boards. In analysing the orientation of the state and the conduct of economic policy, I have tried to avoid functional or instrumental approaches that would reduce the state to a mere organ of capital or an instrument of a ruling class. At the level of policy, such approaches tend to leave out the political dynamics that shape policy over time and ignore the economic consequences of particular policies. The state may establish some of the conditions that are favourable to capitalist development while simultaneously failing to establish others. The state may face contradictory tasks involving, on the one hand, the need to sustain and promote the process of accumulation and, on the other, the need to legitimate power and counter uneven development by allocating resources through the federal system to the less advantaged areas.[2]

Second, state institutions play a role in the creation of social order, mediating conflicting interests and providing a basis for the exercise of political authority and capital accumulation. This coercive role depends on power relations and hence the political configuration. By origin, the Nigerian state was a state of colonial conquest and an instrument of subjugation that forced many different nationalities to live together in a single territorial unit. This origin was not conducive to the development of a close identification with the state or to the growth of a legitimate authority at the centre. Loyalties were very often focussed on communities of origin. The state, or more accurately, the government, was often perceived as remote and alien. It came to be seen as a purveyor of services and employment that belonged to no one. Without a strong sense of nationhood or citizenship, the state was seen as vulnerable to private and sectional interests. A just distribution of state resources was therefore of paramount concern.

Far from being a fixed functional or structural category, the state has evolved over time. In response to economic demands and political creativity, new state functions and responsibilities have emerged, and the federal system of government has evolved (for example, breakdown of the regional structure with the creation of new states, changes in the system of revenue allocation, new financial responsibilities and controls, growth of security and surveillance functions). In turn, the structure of the state institutions has shaped political conflict.[3]

Despite a trend to administrative and financial centralisation, political authority has been weak and fragmented. Bureaucratic power has not been heavily entrenched, and governments have generally not attempted to incorporate sources of opposition within the state apparatus. On occasion, the struggle by private interests for state resources has helped to undermine the legitimacy of governments and erode the authority of the state. The state then appears to be highly fragmented and corrupted from within and without. This competition for access to the state has been heightened by the large amount of oil revenues directly available to the state and by the weakness of a class of taxpayers who might otherwise have limited the demands made on the state and pressed for public accountability.

In the 1970s weak government combined with centralised oil revenues opened up a serious imbalance between political authority and financial responsibility within the federal system. State governments, which had considerable autonomy, received a large proportion of their revenues from the federal centre. This situation encouraged financial irresponsibility and set up strong forces for the creation of new states.

There is no suggestion that the state is the key to understanding social and economic change in Nigeria. Arguably the state has been given too much centrality in recent writing. This perspective arises partly from instrumental, developmental views that attach great importance to state policy, often without showing its effect. Much economic activity is not the result of state policy in a proximate, causal sense. The importance attached to the state also derives from an emphasis on resource allocation by the state and on access to the state as the main avenue to wealth and social mobility. In the literature, political and economic power at the level of the state are sometimes fused together in the all-embracing notion of ruling-class formation or domination.[4] Politics is then seen as a struggle between a ruling class and subordinate classes and as a competition between ruling-class fractions over access to state resources.

Recent perspectives shift the emphasis to the relation between the state and civil society in Africa.[5] A period of "incorporation" of society by the state is followed by the "disengagement" of the society from the state under conditions of economic deterioration and state crisis. However, the division between state and civil society and between public and private domains is a very imprecise one, and this reading of shifts in power relations between the state and civil society does not fit my interpretation. It fails to relate changes in state power to political conditions and to social forces within civil society that penetrate and enmesh the state. In Nigeria, the expansion of state activity, on the one hand, was not associated with a strong state, and it derived in part from pressures within civil society. State "withdrawal," on the other hand, was linked to the existence of a stronger political authority at the centre, as was the case with the introduction and implementation of the Structural Adjustment Programme (SAP).

Despite the spread of capitalist relations involving state, local, and foreign private capital and the limited creation of a domestic capitalist class, capitalism is not a dominant force in the political process. Those who derive their power from the temporary occupation of state office or access to the state do not constitute a coherent ruling class that is bourgeois or national in orientation.[6] Nor do they necessarily act in the interests of a capitalist class. Lacking independent sources of wealth, some may aspire to build up more independent property bases outside the state that will advance their individual, family, and community interests. To this end, they may engage in corruption and primary forms of capital accumulation that tend to erode the distinction between private and public spheres of activity.

Those who hold state power are not specifically bourgeois in their culture or political orientation. In office, they bring with them identities and political orientations formed in a broader field that includes their home communities and local political arenas. Their culture is to a large extent derived from ethnic traditions and religious affiliations that are contingent in relation to the basic economic determinants of class position.

The coherence and strength of ruling groups has varied with the extent of external threats, with alliances between groups like the military, civil servants, businesspeople and politicians, and with the extent of coalitions between various sectional interests. Power and status have shifted between groups, and alliances have proved unstable. The large population of the country, combined with its cultural diversity, has given rise to powerful subnational identities that have contributed to political divisions and set limits to central political control. The military have the advantage of a relatively strong corporate organisation and force of arms, but they incur the envy of other groups in the civil population and are themselves subject to strong pressures and demands from various constituencies.

Politics

Patron-client ties provide much of the social fabric for informal and party politics in Nigeria. Patronage flows along personal networks based on kinship, marriage, community, ethnic associations, old school ties, social clubs, and religious affiliations. These multiple networks are effective relations of power that wealthy individuals or those in positions of authority can use to mobilise support from below. Those below can use the networks as channels to lobby for all manner of support from patrons higher up in the hierarchy. The hierarchy extends from the village and clan to wider communities and then to the state governments and on to "representatives" at the federal level whose role is often recognised by taking traditional titles in their home communities. In this way, clientage acts as a channel for political participation, social mobility, and economic advancement at local and national levels. These vertical ties are quite consistent with processes of class formation, though they tend to weaken collective class actions.

Broader patterns of political mobilisation and alignment that build on clientilist networks have often followed ethnic lines. At times of mass electoral politics, ethnic identities have generally proved stronger than those of religion or class. The prime concern of communities and broader ethnicities has been to secure adequate representation at higher levels in the administrative and governmental hierarchy so that they are not at a disadvantage in the competition to obtain material benefits and to influence state policy. In a bid to regulate this competition and provide a basis for sharing power between the various constituencies, the 1979 constitution introduced the principle of federal character, which was a way of distributing public patronage in appointments and state expenditures. One result of the mass of particular and personal demands on those who hold state office, together with the absence of strong class alignments in agricultural or industrial production, has been the dominance of distributive demands in matters of policy.

Some authors have characterised Nigerian politics or the state as prebendal and patrimonial.[7] Although these perspectives capture aspects of Nigeria's political economy, they do not give the whole picture. They tend to draw the links between political behaviour, the state, and private accumulation too tightly. They have in common an emphasis on state regulation of the economy and state control over the opportunities for private accumulation (via contract, licence, office, and corruption). Accumulation takes unproductive forms. Political competition is focussed on access to state resources. The administrative and economic functions of the state are undermined and personalised, and state policies and institutions become incoherent, inefficient, and wasteful.

These views, in the first place, do not allow for the capacity of those who exercise state power to respond to economic crises and sustain accumulation over time through policy and institutional reforms and new political initiatives. Second, they do not give adequate recognition to the existence of social and political space that is more or less autonomous of the state and where, for example, individuals can pursue long-term strategies of private accumulation. Finally, these perspectives tend to neglect forms of political conflict that are not focussed on the struggle for material benefits and access to state power.

There is, for example a tradition of democratic struggle against the abuse of state power in Nigeria that goes back to the nationalist movement. The fight for individual rights, for the freedom of the press, and for public accountability is a continuing one. Though often subject to threat and harassment, the Nigerian press has generally played a major part in checking the abuses of those in power. Lawyers, writers, students, intellectuals, professional associations, and organised labour have all on occasion played prominent roles.

An approach based on the competition for material benefits also leaves out of account nationalism, ideological divisions between parties, collective action by trade unions, and shifts in attitudes and ideology. It cannot comprehend the politics of centralisation, local autonomy, and uneven development. At a more local level, it ignores many forms of popular protest like peasant resistance to the alienation of land and urban protests that have often been directed against the police and the military. It cannot comprehend the 'Yan Tatsine riots as religious protests directed against the gross materialism of the oil boom in the northern states. Nor can it account for the anticorruption campaign of the Buhari regime or the politics of resistance to the Structural Adjustment Programme after its introduction in 1986. This study attempts to bring together these various elements of Nigerian politics.

There is a further theme—the alternation of military and civil government and its relation to the economy. Is there a relationship between political authority and capitalist development in the long term? Despite twenty years of military rule in Nigeria, tendencies towards authoritarian government have generally been resisted. Military governments have remained relatively open. Compared to military regimes in Latin America and elsewhere in Africa, there has been a low degree of state coercion and domination. Twice military regimes have initiated programmes to return the country to civil rule. Under civil rule, moves towards one-party rule have been undermined by lack of purposeful government and corruption.

Perhaps the main difference between military and civil regimes lies in the capacity for political and economic reform under military government. Practically all reforms have been carried out under the military. The major exception was the creation of the Mid-West Region in 1963 under civil rule. The capacity for reform stems from the ability of the military to insulate state institutions and government more effectively from external pressures, allowing stronger management of conflicting interests and more effective government and economic control. However, this argument cannot be taken very far. The latter days of the military under the Gowon government showed an acute loss of economic and political control that brought about the downfall of the government. Since that time, the military have become increasingly professionalised and have extended their involvement in civil politics and political reform, attempting to create a presidential system of government.

In general, changes of government and regime since independence have not been associated with changes in economic policy or strategy, which has shown considerable continuity. The major exception was the coming to power of the Babangida government in 1985, which marked a shift in strategy towards more reliance on private enterprise and market forces. At the same time, the government announced an elaborate transition programme to return the country to civil rule by 1992. How are these programmes related? From a neoliberal market perspective,[8] moves to reduce the concentration of power in the hands of an authoritarian military government and reforms aimed at economic liberalisation might appear to have common origins and to reinforce one another. From this perspective, the "withdrawal" of the state will release entrepreneurial capacities and promote bourgeois democracy as well. I argue that the assumptions behind such doctrines are mistaken and that the two programmes have different, conflicting sets of forces behind them. There is no necessary compatibility between economic reforms that require stronger political control and civilian politics that will bring greater participation in politics.

Capitalist Development

The colonial trade economy experienced a rapid expansion of peasant commodity production. With foreign monopolies controlling much of the trade and finance, there was little opportunity for accumulation by indigenous capital beyond domestic commercial activity, property investment, and transport. In the late colonial period, financial surpluses extracted from agriculture through the marketing board system were used to support the onset of large-scale industry as foreign capital shifted from trade to industry. Later, oil replaced commodity exports as the major source of government revenue and foreign exchange. Its very abundance created severe fiscal imbalances and distributive pressures that tended to undermine any longer-term state strategies.

International capital penetrated the economy, attracted by the large size of the market. Capitalist relations of production were extended, and foreign capital entrenched itself with the support of those in control of the Nigerian state. Foreign companies then became more domesticated through the advance of Nigerian middle-level and senior-level management and local ownership.

The strategy of reliance on foreign capital initially contributed to rapid industrial growth. But import-substituting industrialisation was import- and capital-intensive and contributed to balance-of-payments problems. Oil revenues allowed this constraint to be temporarily relaxed. They also encouraged greater state investment. Much of this state industry was unproductive and did little to raise indigenous technical capacity from its low level or to accelerate structural change towards intermediate and basic industry. Very limited use was made of oil and associated gases as a source of energy or raw materials for domestic industry.

The Nigerian market has not proved consistently attractive to foreign direct investment. Foreign capital has often been more concerned to realise profits in hard currencies through trade, transfer pricing, and loans. Yet it would be an error to interpret recent limited flows of new foreign investment as evidence of a trend towards the marginalisation or looser integration of Nigeria in the world economy. The view from the major centres of economic power can be misleading.[9] The prospects for further capitalist development in Nigeria do not depend primarily on foreign direct investment. Recent changes favourable to capitalist development include improvements in the communications infrastructure, advances by local capital, deregulation and dynamism in the financial sector, the emergence of national business associations, and a shift in the ideological climate as state resources have declined and international pressures for reform intensified.

There has been a tendency for private Nigerian capital to be seen as subordinate to the public sector and foreign corporate interests. It has, nevertheless, advanced in scale, corporate organisation, and managerial and technical capabilities and in the range of its investment.[10] There has been a gradual shift from commerce to industry in some parts of the country. There has also been a strong movement into the financial sector and some advance into large-scale agriculture, where the commoditisation of labour and land has deepened. This capitalist group is not an auxiliary comprador class. It is an active component of capital that has grown partly through collaboration with foreign capital, partly in competition with it, and partly independently.

It is commonly held that indigenous patterns of accumulation have taken largely unproductive forms. This view is often linked to a stress on political forms of accumulation via the state, on statism, and on the arbitrariness and unpredictability of a patrimonial state. This emphasis is misplaced. There are long-term trajectories of private accumulation in Nigeria that are relatively independent of the state. They deserve more recognition.

Despite the dominance of foreign capital in several sectors of the economy (including oil), weak external economic management, the buildup of external debt, and pressure from international institutions, Nigerian rulers have on occasion shown autonomy in the pursuit of national economic interests. Geopolitical rivalry between imperialist powers and competition between foreign companies can create the potential for bargaining and leverage (for example, the enforced divestment of the indigenisation decrees and the nationalisation of British Petroleum). Moreover, the weight of the Nigerian market and industrial production in turn places the economies of neighbouring countries in a subordinate position with large unofficial flows of goods, labour, and currency in both directions. These economic flows and the existence of mineral deposits underpin Nigeria's geopolitical interest in the West African subregion. Nigeria's position as an economic power has risen within the region. This power was exercised by the Nigerian military in the Liberian conflict where a leading role in peacekeeping in 1990 led to direct military engagement in 1992.

Organisation

Chapter 2 provides a historical introduction to Nigeria's political economy. It covers the terminal decade of colonial rule and the first years of independence. Under colonial rule, the growth of a regional tripartite system of government left a political vacuum at the centre. With the gradual transfer of power to Nigerian politicians, a political mobilisation of vigorous subnationalisms was accentuated by uneven development and by fear of political domination at the centre. This led eventually to an attempt by the Eastern Region to secede from the federation.

The period from the end of the civil war in 1970 to 1979 is covered in Chapter 3. With the breakdown of the old regional centres of power, an alliance of the military and civil servants tried to use federal power to increase national integration, enhance national control of the economy, and promote structural changes in the economy. I examine in some detail the loss of political and economic control that undermined the Gowon regime. The Murtala-Obasanjo government released a more radical brand of nationalism. It speeded up reforms and embarked on a successful programme to return the country to civil rule. Many new initiatives were undertaken in this decade, including changes in the system of revenue allocation and the creation of new states, that had the effect of increasing the dependence of the states on federal finances while at the same time creating a more even distribution of revenue. The civil service was purged, the trade unions reformed, and a new system of local government introduced. In 1979, the new civilian government of President Shehu Shagari took power.

In Chapter 4, I attempt to explain why the Second Republic (1979–1983) combined formally democratic institutions with ineffective government and an economic crisis. The nature of the National Party of Nigeria (NPN), the ruling party, is examined in detail. It is argued that the party was formed with the express purpose of distributing patronage on a national basis. Distributive concerns dominated over policy issues, and the main axis of political conflict was between the centre and those states controlled by the opposition parties. Clientilist politics and the demands of those intent on pursuing wealth through political connection sapped the authority of the state. Corruption accelerated and the management of the economy became subordinate to political objectives. The rule of the politicians created a profound disillusionment with those who held public office and contributed to a deep economic crisis.

The return of the military is treated in Chapters 5 and 6. I examine the authoritarian tendencies in the short period of correction and discipline under the Buhari government (1984–1985). I then assess the first five years of the Babangida government (1985–1990) that ousted the Buhari regime. I look at how challenges to authority have been met and the institutional reforms that have been introduced. I attempt to explain the rise to prominence of religious identities and their relation to political divisions. I also examine the forces behind the transition programme that was intended to return the country to civil rule by 1992 and ask whether the substance of politics is likely to change with attempts by the military to engineer changes from above.

Chapter 7 covers economic changes in the period from 1970 to 1979. Immediately after the war, attempts were made in the Second Plan to promote structural changes in industry and secure greater national control of the economy through local ownership. These strategies were weakened by a lack of priority and loss of macroeconomic control. The basic accounting and budgeting functions of the state were poorly developed and the sudden surge of oil revenues undermined accountability in the public sector. Many state-sponsored projects turned out to be costly failures. The state played an ambiguous role, neither taking a leading part in promoting economic growth nor supporting private enterprise effectively.

Oil was a source of great economic instability. As a centralised rental income, it created strong pressures to maximise state revenues and expenditures. The massive increase in government expenditures and imports quickly brought about a balance-of-payments crisis. Yet existing policies, which included the appreciation of the exchange rate, were maintained and led to a rapid increase in the external debt.

What was the dynamic impact of oil on agriculture and industry? Some economists have used the term "Dutch disease" to describe the adverse effect of windfall foreign exchange earnings on domestic production.[11] I argue that this is not a particularly useful concept in the case of Nigeria, because the logic only really fits agricultural exports and oil had many other important economic consequences like the loss of macroeconomic control, the growth of foreign debt, and the expansion of the public sector.

The disastrous impact of civil rule on economic affairs is examined in Chapter 8. No consistent policies emerged as the management of the economy was subordinated to the political imperative of retaining power. Economic management, policymaking, and implementation were all exposed to the political pressures for state patronage, competition for rents, and distributive demands. Capital flight and corruption gathered new momentum from a second surge in oil revenues.

Chapter 9 is devoted entirely to agricultural policy and is intended as a corrective to commonly held views. Contrary to the influential arguments of some, agrarian policies in Nigeria have not been especially detrimental to the interests of the majority of farmers.[12] More generally, the extent to which policy has been responsible for performance and the extent of the agrarian crisis have been exaggerated. Large oil revenues were not responsible for an agrarian crisis caused by loss of labour from agriculture and the appreciation of the exchange rate. No single economic mechanism can be generalised for the whole country.

Chapter 10 looks at the economic reforms associated with the Structural Adjustment Programme. They were introduced in 1986 by the Babangida regime, which was favourable to the strategies promoted by the World Bank and the International Monetary Fund (IMF). Through deregulation, privatisation, and changes in relative prices, the reforms attempt to encourage private enterprise and market forces and restructure the basis for capital accumulation. A number of questions are addressed: Why did the reforms come so late and how were they introduced? How extensive are the reforms and how have they been shaped by domestic opposition? What are their short- and medium-term economic consequences? How might economic reforms and demands of economic management be reconciled with the politics of civil rule? What challenges do they pose to national economic strategies in the long run? Finally, how are the reforms related to other long-term features of Nigeria's political economy?

A final chapter examines the failure of the transition to civil rule and the persistence of military rule. In light of the long-term weakness of economic management, policy instability, and the demise of the Structural Adjustment Programme, it takes a more sombre view of the prospects for economic growth. A central issue before the country is whether or not a degree of political coherence and legitimacy at the centre that would allow effective economic management and more productive use of resources can again be established.

Notes

A note on currency: until January 1973, the unit of currency was the Nigerian pound (£). The naira (N) was then introduced at the rate of one naira (N1) = $1.52. The value of the naira then fluctuated, reaching an annual average value of N1 = $1.83 in 1980. Subsequently the naira depreciated and was devalued sharply after 1986. By mid-1995, N1 = $0.012 ($1 = N80).

1. R. Sandbrook, *The Politics of Africa's Economic Stagnation* (Cambridge: Cambridge University Press, 1985).
2. C. Offe, *Contradictions of the Welfare State* (London: Hutchinson, 1984).
3. Held emphasises the importance of institutional arrangements and the state's

capacity to influence social and political development. D. Held, *Political Theory and the Modern State* (Oxford: Polity Press, 1989).

4. For a critique of state-as-class approaches, see J. Forrest, "The Contemporary African State: A 'Ruling Class'?" *Review of African Political Economy* 38 (April 1987), pp. 64–71.

5. See D. Rothchild and N. Chazan, eds., *The Precarious Balance: State and Society in Africa* (Boulder: Westview Press, 1988).

6. My view differs from that of Bjorn Beckman, who sees a ruling class that is both bourgeois and national in orientation. Beckman's position is related to his overall view of the state as the organ of capital and his emphasis on the two long-run processes of capitalist state formation and bourgeois class formation. I find his analysis too general, too aggregated, and too fully determined by the logic of capital.

B. Beckman, "Neocolonialism, Capitalism and the State in Nigeria," in H. Bernstein and B. Campbell, eds., *Contradictions of Accumulation in Africa* (Beverly Hills, Calif.: Sage, 1985); B. Beckman, "The Post-Colonial State: Crisis and Reconstruction," *Institute of Development Studies Bulletin* (Sussex), 19/4 (1988), pp. 26–34.

7. R. A. Joseph, *Democracy and Prebendal Politics in Nigeria: The Rise and Fall of the Second Republic* (Cambridge: Cambridge University Press, 1987); T. M. Callaghy, "The State as Lame Leviathan: The Patrimonial Administrative State in Africa," in Z. Ergas, ed., *The African State in Transition* (London: Macmillan, 1987); T. M. Callaghy, "The State and the Development of Capitalism in Africa: Theoretical, Historical and Comparative Reflections," in D. Rothchild and N. Chazan, eds., *The Precarious Balance: State and Society in Africa* (Boulder: Westview Press, 1988).

8. See M. R. Friedman, *Capitalism and Freedom* (Chicago: University of Chicago Press, 1962).

9. It usually fails to take account of investment by existing foreign companies and the activities of Indian, Lebanese, and indigenous companies.

10. T. G. Forrest, "The Advance of African Capital: The Growth of Nigerian Private Enterprise," in F. Stewart, S. Lall, and S. M. Wangwe, eds., *Alternative Development Strategies in Sub-Saharan Africa* (London: Macmillan, 1992).

11. W. M. Corden, "Booming Sector and Dutch Disease Economics: Survey and Consolidation," in W. M. Corden, ed., *Protection, Growth and Trade: Essays in International Economics* (Oxford: Basil Blackwell, 1985).

12. R. H. Bates, *Markets and States in Tropical Africa: The Political Basis of Agricultural Policies* (Berkeley: University of California Press, 1981).

PART ONE

State, Society, and Economy

2

State, Society, and Economy: Historical Background

Federal Structure, Regions, and Unequal Development

Although in theory colonial Nigeria was ruled by the British as a single political unit, in practice the administrations of the units were distinct and independent. There was no central representative institution or unifying political focus.[1] After World War II, under pressure from nationalist politicians, constitutional developments led to a truly federal system of government in which the regions had considerable autonomy.

In 1954, Nigeria became a federation of three regions (Northern, Western, and Eastern). The centre had responsibility for foreign relations, defence, the police, overall aspects of finance and trade policy, and major forms of transport and communications. The regions had responsibility for primary and secondary education, agriculture, public health, and local government. They could undertake their own initiatives in spending and public works. The judiciary, the public service commission, and institutions like the Marketing Boards were regionalised. Responsibility for economic development, together with higher education and labour matters, was shared between the centre and the regions.

The federal structure reflected the wide cultural and political differences between the country's three largest ethno-linguistic groups—the Igbo, Yoruba, and Hausa-Fulani, which constituted the majority of the population in the Eastern, Western, and Northern regions, respectively (see Table 2.1). Within each region, the majority group tended to exercise political dominance over numerous other smaller ethnic groups.

Through the regional system of separate administrations and the use of local authority structures, the British divided and ruled. In this way, cultural and linguistic differences were emphasised and communal sentiments encouraged.[2] Local systems of authority were upheld, provided they did not conflict with commercial expansion and administrative convenience.[3] The policy of indirect rule strengthened and centralised existing forms of leadership and authority. In the north, the emirate structure

TABLE 2.1 Geographical Distribution of Principal Ethnic Groups of Nigeria in the Early 1950s

Ethnic Group and Region of Origin	*Lagos Township*	*Western Region*	*Eastern Region*	*Northern Region*	*Total*	*Percentage of Population of Nigeria*
Western groups						
Yoruba	195,974	4,302,401	11,377	536,109[b]	5,045,861	16.6
Edo	5,708	446,444	4,027	11,938	468,177	1.5
Others	5,051	486,902	a	a	491,953	
Total	206,733	5,235,747	15,404	548,047	6,005,931	
Eastern groups						
Ibo	31,887	342,335[c]	4,916,736	166,910[d]	5,457,868	17.9
Ibibio-Efik	4,505	5,265	809,387	12,759	831,916	2.7
Ijaw	3,925	79,079[e]	258,962	a	341,966	1.1
Others	a	a	1,038,117	a	1,038,117	
Total	40,317	426,679	7,023,202	179,669	7,669,867	
Northern groups						
Hausa	3,847	41,374	10,288	5,488,446	5,543,955	18.2
Fulani	285	6,858	757	3,022,581	3,030,481	9.9
Kanuri	148	1,170	2,151	1,298,306	1,301,775	4.2
Nupe	444	6,980	2,811	348,979	359,214	1.1
Tiv	805	2,428	5,121[f]	772,771	781,125	2.5
Others	202	4,110	a	5,051,380	5,055,692	
Total	5,731	62,920	21,128	15,982,463	16,072,242	
Other groups	14,626	356,680	151,228	101,874	624,408	
Grand total	267,407	6,082,026	7,210,962	16,812,053	30,372,488	

[a]Exact number not known; included in "Other groups."
[b]Of this number, about 480,000 constitute a border minority in the Northern Region.
[c]Of this number, about 285,000 constitute a border minority in the Western Region.
[d]Of this number, about 40,000 constitute a border minority in the Northern Region.
[e]Of this number, about 65,000 constitute a border minority in the Western Region.
[f]Of this number, about 4,500 constitute a border minority in the Eastern Region.

Sources: Population Census of the Western Region of Nigeria, 1952 (Lagos: Government Statistician, 1953–1954); *Population Census of the Northern Region of Nigeria, 1952* (Lagos: Government Statistician, 1952–1953), pp. 26–29; *Population Census of the Eastern Region of Nigeria, 1953,* Bulletin No. 1 (Lagos: Government Statistician, 1954), pp. 18–19. As found in J. S. Coleman, *Nigeria: Background to Nationalism* (Berkeley: University of California Press, 1958), p. 15. Copyright © 1958, The Regents of the University of California. Reprinted with permission.

of the most powerful political entity, the Sokoto caliphate, a Muslim community of thirty emirates, was kept intact and formed the basis of local government. The British tried to extend the emirate model of indirect rule to the administration of "pagan" areas. In the 1950s, attempts were made to reform the Native Authority system, but emirs and chiefs remained the most powerful figures, acting as crucial power brokers between the British and a new generation of political leaders.

The premier of the Northern Region, Ahmadu Bello, the Sardauna of Sokoto, used the authority structure of the caliphate, with its "gateways" (loyal notables) who acted as intermediaries between the centre and outlying areas to hold the Northern Region together.[4] This political system worked well with the emirates, though relations with Kano proved difficult. It was less successful on the southern fringes of the Muslim emirate north where the Sardauna tried to consolidate Northern Regional unity and a northern identity in the face of efforts to break up the region by supporters of a Middle Belt state. Here, there was a series of minority ethnic groups stretching from present day Gongola state in the east through to Bauchi, Plateau, Benue, Kwara, Kaduna, and Niger states to the west. It was in this Middle Belt area that the bulk of the non-Muslim populations of the north, including Christians, was located.

The Christian populations were originally built up as a result of the activity of foreign missionaries, who provided schools and health facilities. For a time, Western education and Christianity were synonymous. The Sardauna made alliances with some Christian leaders and co-opted them. Yet the Tiv, the largest of the Middle Belt communities, never accepted the political and cultural domination that its members perceived in the attempt to create a unified north.[5] They rejected the centralised system of local administration imposed on them from above and the attempt to incorporate them within the ruling regional party. Their opposition led eventually to violent resistance and the army was sent into Tivland in 1960 and 1964 to pacify the area.

The vicissitudes of local government and traditional authority under colonial rule are well demonstrated in Igboland. Here, the British could find no centralised authority to incorporate and administer. At first, they tried unsuccessfully to create a class of local chiefs.[6] The imposition of the warrant chiefs was very unpopular. Resentment against them, together with opposition to the introduction of direct taxation, led in 1929 to the Women's Riot, which brought their regime to an end. The government then tried to get back to what were said to be the traditional authorities of the Igbo by creating native authorities and native courts.[7] This system appeared at first to be a more satisfactory solution; but although the clan was a valid basis for cultural and ritual cooperation among its members, it was not a valid basis for political and administrative action. Each Igbo village group or town was in fact autonomous. Also, the clan unit was too small to be viable. The government then decided to de-emphasise traditional rights to headship and emphasise proven ability and popular acceptability. It also compelled clans to amalgamate into larger adminstrative units.

Ethnic identities were to a large extent created, widened, and shaped under colonial rule. Villages, towns, and communities were incorporated into larger administrative units and a wider political space. John Peel has described the process of creating and adopting an identity among the Yoruba:

> The vast bulk of peoples who now know themselves as Yoruba ... did not do so in 1900. Originally the word referred to only one Yoruba grouping, the Oyo. Yoruba ethnic identity began to be adopted by other groups (e.g. Ilesha, Egba, Ijebu, Ekiti, Ondo) from the 1920s, as migration, cash-cropping, education, and conversion to the world religions drew more people into a Nigeria-wide sphere of social relations. From the late 1930s, when nationalism really began to get underway, the Yoruba began to shape themselves politically against other "tribes," especially the Igbo in the political crucible of Lagos.[8]

Culture was an essential part of this ethnic politics. For the "Yoruba" parties it was *olaju*, or "enlightenment," a complex of development values rooted in Christianity and Western education.

Thus it was within the regional framework of administration that political mobilisation began to create powerful subnationalisms built up on hierarchies of communities. Support was mobilised from below as communities struggled to secure representation and access to resources at higher levels in the state machinery. At the same time, upward pressure was brought to bear on the colonial power by nationalists who retained strong links with their home communities. When the British departed, it was in the competition for power and office in the political vaccuum of the federal arena that the appeal to ethnicity was strongest.

The balance of initiative was with the regions rather than the federal government. The weakness of the federal centre in the 1950s and early 1960s was clearly reflected in the strength of regional institutions like the Marketing Boards and development corporations and in the general conduct of economic policy. In spite of the growing strength of the centre in financial matters and the establishment of a number of unitary institutions, the struggle for regional advantage could frustrate the centre and render it powerless.

The independence of the regions was offset to some extent by interregional trade and migration. It was estimated conservatively that interregional trade was worth £64 million in 1964, or 14 percent of the value of exports.[9] According to these estimates, the Northern Region de-

TABLE 2.2 Size and Population of Nigeria by Region

Region	Size (square miles)	1952–1953 Census (1,000)	1963 Census (1,000)	1985 Projection (1,000)	1991 Census (1,000)
Northern	281,782	16,835	29,809	51,238	46,883
Western	30,095	4,595	10,266	16,307	11,915
Mid-western	15,281	1,492	2,536	4,359	4,730
Eastern	29,484	7,215	12,394	21,304	18,922
Lagos	27	267	665	2,920	5,685
Abuja	—	—	—	—	379
	356,669	30,404	55,670	96,128	88,514

Notes: From 1964 to present, all official population figures are projections based on the 1963 census. The 1991 census results are provisional. They indicate a significant downward revision of the population.

The 1991 figure for Lagos includes areas that were formerly part of the Western Region. The Federal Capital Territory of Abuja was created from an area that was formerly part of the Northern region.

Source: For 1952–1953 and 1963, *Annual Abstract of Statistics* (Lagos: Federal Office of Statistics, 1964); for 1985, *Digest of Statistics* (Lagos: Federal Office of Statistics, December 1985); for 1991, *Newswatch Magazine*, Lagos, 30 March 1992.

rived most financial benefit from this trade, running a substantial trade surplus with the other regions. It was also dependent on access to southern ports for the export of agricultural produce, mainly cotton and groundnuts. The east, with its economic base in palm produce, contained a large food-deficit area and was more reliant on out-migration to reduce the pressure on the land and provide a flow of remittances from employment and trade.[10] The Northern Region was larger in population and area than the other regions combined (see Table 2.2). It was also the poorest region.

The richest region was the west, by virtue of cocoa production, early access to Western education, the location of much of the industrial development, and the presence of Lagos, the capital and major port.[11] The west, too, was favoured after 1954 by the system of revenue allocation, in that the principle of regional derivation applied to agricultural produce and certain imported commodities was prominent.[12] Boosted by large cocoa revenues, the Western Region took over 38 percent of the statutory revenue allocation in 1954/55 (see Table 2.3). There was thus a considerable disparity in the financial resources available to the regions.

The distribution of educational enrollment also showed a pattern of highly unequal development. In 1959, 90 percent of primary and secondary school enrollment was concentrated in the southern regions.[13] These regions had been exposed to Western education by Christian missions

TABLE 2.3 Shares of Statutory Revenue Allocation (percentage)

Area	*1948/49*	*1954/55*	*1966/67*	*1970/71*	*1976/77*	*1985*
Northern Region/States	40.7	34.7	35.3	41.0	47.1	52.4
Eastern Region/States	34.6	27.0	29.8	26.7	24.2	22.0
Western Region/States	24.7	38.3	34.9[a]	32.3	28.7	25.6

[a]Includes 13.8 percent for Mid-Western state that was created in 1963/64.

Source: A. O. Phillips, "Three Decades of Inter-Governmental Financial Relationships in the Federation of Nigeria," paper presented at Conference on Intergovernmental Relations in Nigeria, University of Ife, 1979; and Central Bank of Nigeria, *Annual Report* (1985).

from an early date, whereas in the north, which was predominantly Muslim (see Table 2.4), much of the schooling took the form of Koranic teaching. As Nigerian politicians gained power in the regions, so political pressures for the rapid expansion of education became overwhelming. In the 1950s, the gap between north and south widened as a result of new education programmes in the south.[14] In 1952, the government of the Western Region announced a universal, free, and compulsory system of primary education to be introduced in 1955. The Eastern Region soon followed with its own proposals for a programme to be introduced in 1957. By 1960, the southern regions were directing over 40 percent of their annual recurrent expenditures to education.

The pattern of educational imbalance sowed the seeds of tension between the north and south and led to efforts to bridge the gap. Within the Northern Region, immigrants from the southern regions provided much of the semiskilled labour as clerks and artisans. These immigrant communities prospered and competed effectively with local traders. To take one example, the Kano Sabon Gari market, which was dominated by Igbos, came in the early 1960s to surpass the older Kano city market in terms of the number of traders, volume of turnover, and average profit.[15] This pressure on jobs and markets led to local resentment that could easily be manipulated by politicians.

At the federal level, the civil service and senior positions in the army and police were dominated by southerners. This was a major factor in efforts by northerners to slow down the movement to independence—with British cooperation—for fear of southern domination. In the 1950s and 1960s, the Northern government, responding to these disparities, embarked on a concerted policy of northernisation of the public service and corporations at the regional and federal levels and of business enterprises in the north. This policy, which affected traders, artisans and professionals alike, was a major point of difference between northerners and southerners. Southerners resented the fact that they could only obtain employment in the north on short-term contracts.

TABLE 2.4 Religious Affiliation by Region, 1952 and 1963[a]

	Percent Muslim		*Percent Christian*		*Percent Other*	
Region	*1952*	*1963*	*1952*	*1963*	*1952*	*1963*
North	73.0	71.7	2.7	9.7	24.3	18.6
West	32.8	43.4	36.9	48.7	30.3	7.9
East	0.6	0.3	46.2	77.2	50.2	22.5
Lagos	41.0	44.3	53.0	54.6	2.0[b]	1.1
Mid-West	—	4.2	—	54.9	—	40.9
Total Country	44.4	49.0	22.0	34.0	33.6	17.0

[a]Since 1963 all official population figures are projections based on the 1963 census and estimated annual rates of increase.
[b]Plus 4 percent other

Source: Nigerian Census, 1952; *Nigeria Yearbook,* 1969 (Lagos: Times Press, 1970), p. 193. As found in J. N. Paden, *Religion and Political Culture in Kano* (Berkeley: University of California Press, 1973), p. 44. Copyright © 1973, The Regents of the University of California. Reprinted with permission.

Capital and Class

Strong class identities and alignments around agricultural or industrial production had not materialised in Nigeria by the time of Independence in 1960. Nigerian private capital was small scale—concentrated largely in commerce, residential property, and finance—and fragmented and regional in outlook. Locally, there were pockets of agricultural or landed wealth, as in the large farms controlled by the Muslim aristocracy in the northern emirates and the medium-scale cocoa and rubber farms in the south. Through their control of local government and patronage systems, traditional rulers in both the Northern Region and the Western Region exercised a great deal of power over land matters. Yet it was small farmers who dominated the rural economy and provided the vast bulk of the export produce. This meant that agricultural interests were not sharply defined, coherently organised, or powerfully promoted within the government.

Polly Hill argued that the general absence of agrarian hierarchy in precolonial West Africa was due to the lack of differential and transmittable rights over farmland.[16] The fact that land was plentiful and that the great majority of households were not prevented by poverty from actively undertaking cultivation was also important. The individual right to cultivate on a usufructuary basis derived from membership in a corporate landholding lineage or from position as a resident member of a rural community.

In Nigeria, the colonial period saw a large expansion of crops for export and food crops supported by the development of road and railway infrastructure, accompanied by the development of new areas of crop specialisation, population migration, and the reorientation of internal trade patterns. Most production was carried out on a small scale and depended on family labour, kin, or clients. Wage labour, usually temporary and seasonal, drew on labourers from other farm households and was difficult to attract and retain. Rich and powerful families were able to secure the services of various forms of unfree labour but it was always difficult to recruit and discipline.[17] In general, no clear class divisions between rich and poor farmers or between farmers and labourers emerged within rural communities in response to commercialisation and the commoditisation of land and labour. Access to resources and strategies of accumulation were very often dependent on ties of kinship, lineage, and friendship and on reciprocal ties of clientage. Community identities were strong, shaping economic participation and conditioning social differentiation. A distinct peasantry, landed gentry, or class of capitalist farmers did not emerge.

Capitalist agriculture did not take root during the colonial period. The colonial government generally resisted attempts to establish plantations for fear of the political consequences of widespread land alienation had made a political alliance with the traditional authorities who controlled the land. Taxation, the mobilisation of labour for public works, and the acquisition of land for government and commercial purposes had priority, and these concerns in themselves created considerable opposition. There were doubts, too, about the efficiency of plantations by comparison with smallholder agriculture in West African circumstances. Early plantations had a very poor record. The smallholder policy could draw support from ideas about colonial trusteeship in Africa that involved the protection of African communities and land rights from large-scale private appropriation of land.

The expansion of cocoa, a perennial crop, led to permanent transmittable rights over cocoa trees (but not land) and the development of tenancy and sharecropping. No class of capitalist farmers, cocoa gentry, or self-reproducing peasant households emerged. According to Sara Berry, the possibilities of accumulation in the colonial period were limited by problems of labour supervision, by the absence of economies of scale in agriculture, by the foreign trading and banking monopolies, and by colonial subordination.[18] Small prosperous farmers tended to diversify their assets rather than acquire large farms. The best opportunities for accumulation were not in agriculture but in trade, the professions, and civil service.

Berry has stressed that power and wealth were sought in a political and legal context, in that seniority and patronage played a large part in underpinning relations of production. The spread of cocoa and colonial rule did not undermine these relations of dependence and control and often strengthened them, affecting access to land and labour and the organisation of production. For example, accumulators had to act as patrons to retain and recruit labour, a situation that did not necessarily promote efficiency. It also meant that resources had to be used in establishing positions of patronage and supporting wider kin groups. In these ways, tendencies towards more capitalistic forms of accumulation, access to resources through the market, and rights in private property were checked. Peel has shown how the rise of a cocoa gentry in Ilesha was thwarted by the continued dominance of urban power and status and by the attractions of commercial and bureaucratic careers that persuaded farmers to educate their sons and take them out of farming.[19]

Some parallels have been drawn by Susan Martin from her work in the Ngwa region of Igboland where yam and oil palm production were the core activities during the colonial period.[20] There was limited commercialisation of land and labour. Senior men and warrant chiefs who did acquire wealth did not invest in plantations or contrive to consolidate their wealth in other ways. At death, property was very often dispersed. There was a proprietary interest in controlling land and gaining power over labour that often inhibited sustained investment in agriculture. In an area where population densities were high, the costs of land acquisition were very high, and there were limited technical opportunities for investment in production. Those among the younger men who had capital to invest tended to put it into trade.

In the 1950s, the areas where Nigerian private capital was present on a significant scale included commerce (imports, wholesaling, retailing, and the produce trade), real estate, transporting, construction, rubber processing, saw milling and wood products, tire retreading, bakeries, printing, and shoe making. Transporting created big businesses in every locality. In southwestern Nigeria in the 1930s, transport and cocoa-trading interests found political expression in the nationalism of the Nigerian Youth Movement. Among the most well-known transporters in the 1950s were Alhaji Sani Marshal of Kano, I. O. Ajanaku of Ilesha, and Sir Odumegwu Ojukwu of Nnewi. In this field—as in the retail, wholesale, and produce trades—there was sharp competition with Lebanese businesspeople, which led to hostility and restrictions on their immigration.[21] Landed property and urban real estate provided enormous attractions, and those owners of larger businesses who could get access to bank credit established residential estates. Landed property was the most secure store of wealth as well as collateral with which to finance other activities like trade.

The monopolistic structure of the import trade began to break down in the 1950s with increased competition and a larger market. Nigerian traders increased their share of the trade from 5 percent in 1949 to about 20 percent by 1963.[22] In 1958, two of the large foreign trading companies, the United Africa Company (UAC) and John Holt, withdrew from general importing as a result of intense competition, and they both provided their former Nigerian customers with clearance, warehousing, and credit facilities to avoid any major dislocation.[23] Assisted in this manner, Nigerian wholesalers were able to become importers on their own account. The foreign trading companies also withdrew from the produce trade in the 1950s. Internally the establishment of new industries like the Kaduna textile companies and the Nigerian Tobacco Company opened up new opportunities for local distributors. Some textile distributors in Kaduna later established enterprises in Kano and moved into the manufacture of textiles.[24] Nigerian businesspeople also set up enterprises after gaining management experience with the foreign trading companies.[25]

Many reasons have been given for the slow emergence of a Nigerian capitalist class. Sometimes a foreshortened time perspective is adopted, and the limited advance made by Nigerian capital by the time of independence is not recognized. Foremost among the complaints of the nationalists was the economic power of the foreign trading companies, which periodically combined in market-sharing arrangements to force out newcomers and prevent new entrants. In 1949, six old, established foreign trading companies, which were party to a market-sharing agreement, accounted for 70 percent of imported trade goods.[26] On the export side, where buying syndicates were common, the top six companies accounted for over 70 percent of the value of nonmineral exports.[27] The colonial banking monopolies, which advanced credit to foreign enterprise and discriminated against Nigerian businesspeople, also aroused hostility. The colonial government generally promoted trade as a means of increasing its revenues and did nothing to challenge the market power of the foreign merchants or to encourage local industry. Others have traced a history of comprador activity going back to the slave trade.[28] Bob Shenton has argued that merchant capital in northern Nigeria during the colonial period sought to preserve preexisting forms of surplus appropriation rather than transform them and develop the forces of production.[29] Indigenous capital expanded in the export trade but was subsumed by European merchant capital. The preference of the educated elite for careers in the civil service and professions and the siphoning away of local capital through the marketing board system after 1945 have also been cited.[30] The lack of managerial capacities appropriate to larger, more corporate forms of enterprise and manufacture is an additional explanation.[31] More recently, Berry has argued, with respect to small-scale Yoruba enterprises, that the political and social context has been such as to encourage unproductive social forms of investment.[32]

The 1950s saw the coincidence of a weak and fragmented local capitalist class and the gradual transfer of state power to Nigerian politicians and civil servants who had considerable funds at their disposal to expand the scope of state economic activity and patronage. What was the relationship between Nigerian businesspeople, foreign capital, politicians, and civil servants? The largest indigenous businesspeople supported an extension of state activity as a means of bypassing the expatriate banks and companies and getting access to credit and contracts.[33] Although this effort undoubtedly opened up new opportunities for political accumulation and new avenues of state support for indigenous businesspeople, it may also have adversely affected the advance of local capital and blunted economic nationalism. It is not clear that much of the capital gained from these sources was converted into productive enterprise or that existing enterprises necessarily stood to gain from the new relationship between government and indigenous business. Energies were diverted away from production towards obtaining patronage and state contracts. Political considerations were paramount.[34] The business elite, self-employed men of substance, were closely identified with the governing parties. Leading businesspeople were also attracted to positions of economic and political power in new state institutions. Some took up representative positions that were opened up by constitutional changes; others joined the boards of state companies and corporations. Access to these new sources of state power helped dilute economic nationalism and keep it at bay.

The close proximity of the business class to the politicians was one reason for the uneasy relationship between state officials and Nigerian businesspeople. Businessmen were generally regarded as corrupt and seen as supplicants for favours from the state. They were not taken into confidence over state policy. They had no firm institutional presence for putting collective pressure on the government. Periodic pressures from groups of businesspeople and prominent individuals did prompt the formation of various committees to discuss measures to restrict foreign capital and promote local businesspeople, but very little action was taken.[35] It was only in the late 1960s that Nigerian businesspeople began to exercise more influence through the Small Businessmen's Committee of the Lagos Chamber of Commerce.

The political and economic weakness of private Nigerian capital engaged in production affected the general character of the dominant classes and the orientation of public policy. It gave prominence to commercial interests that were not strongly aligned and to managerial groups who favoured an active developmental role for the state rather than capitalist-oriented growth policies. Nigerian intellectuals also generally supported government regulation of a national character and believed that planning would promote economic growth and industrialisation. In this, they could find support from the writings of development economists.

Foreign capital, which dominated corporate enterprise, needed the goodwill of the new controllers of state power and politically influential businesspeople. To get protection, foreign companies started to appoint

Nigerian directors and lawyers, hired properties from landlords and businesspeople, and appointed Nigerians as agents and representatives.[36] From a local perspective, prominent individuals who had close associations with foreign companies would claim to have "invited" them to Nigeria, just as, at an earlier date, large merchants, who acted as agents of the trading companies, claimed to have brought the companies to their hometowns.[37] To get goodwill and integrate their companies more securely into Nigeria, foreign companies started to sell shares to the public in 1959. Between 1959 and 1965, nine companies sold shares worth over £600,000 to more than 6,000 shareholders.[38] Banks, too, liberalised the terms on which they gave loans to highly placed individuals.

Among the various hierarchies that developed during the colonial period (legal, educational, military, commercial, and bureaucratic), it was the elite of civil servants in the federal and regional bureaucracies who were most prominent. Generous financial incentives were given to keep up motivation and morale. The senior service became synonymous with highly subsidised housing in the Government Reserved Areas and car loans and allowances. During the First Republic, allowances to federal ministers and permanent secretaries were conservatively estimated to exceed salaries by a factor of four.[39] Education was essential for access to these highly paid, high-status occupations and came to be seen as the key to economic advancement and power for individuals and the communities they represented.

The emergent propertied classes (traditional rulers, businesspeople, and professionals with marketable skills) and those with access to state power (politicians, civil servants, and the military) were fragmented by political division and conflicts of interest (discussed in the following section). The power and coherence of these groups fluctuated. When the military took over power in 1966, the power of the politicians declined abruptly, and the civil service became a formidable political force with a near monopoly of power over policy and the dispensing of state patronage.[40] The power and influence of traditional rulers also declined as they lost their avenues for formal representation in the regional Houses of Chiefs, and power was centralised under military governors in the new states that were created in 1967. The traditional rulers, did, however, retain considerable power at the local level. They were consulted informally and sometimes used by subsequent regimes to mobilise support.

Politics and Patronage

I have already alluded to competition between the regions.[41] After 1945, the nationalist movement in southern Nigeria fragmented, and political parties became increasingly regional in character. Each regional government was controlled by a political party that was built up with the support of the majority ethnic group of the region. In the Eastern Region, the National Convention of Nigerian Citizens (NCNC dominated by Nnamdi Azikiwe and once the main nationalist party, became increasingly identified as an Igbo party. In the north, the Northern People's Congress (NPC), a northern establishment party led by Ahmadu Bello, the Sardauna of Sokoto, had the core of its support from the Hausa-Fulani. The strategy of the NPC was to achieve regional power and then use it to take national power. Federal resources could then be tapped to help the north catch up with the other regions.

After 1963, Ahmadu Bello became increasingly identified as a Muslim leader in additiòn to his role as premier of the Northern Region. He established close international ties with Muslim countries and embarked on a series on controversial conversion campaigns among non-Muslim communities in the north. The NPC was opposed by the Northern Elements Progressive Union (NEPU), led by Aminu Kano. NEPU had a populist appeal among commoners based on its opposition to the emirates and Native Authority system of government.

In the Western Region, politics was dominated by the Action Group (AG), led by Obafemi Awolowo. It had its main basis of support among the Yoruba professional and commercial elites and the traditional intelligentsia. However, there were political divisions in Yorubaland that had their roots in nineteenth-century conflicts that had followed the collapse of the Oyo Empire. Opposition to the Action Group in the west initially allied itself to the NCNC, which had considerable support in Ibadan, Oyo, Ogbomosho, and other centres, like Ilesha.

Leaders of minority groups sought to ally themselves with governing parties outside their own region. They also attempted to have new regions created before independence. In this they failed, partly because of opposition from the British, who did not want to see existing arrangements disturbed before independence, and partly because the major party in each region opposed the idea. The majority parties tried to eliminate independent sources of opposition from their regional bases. Only in the Western Region after 1962 did this pattern change because of serious dissension within the ruling party and outside intervention in the region's politics.

During much of the 1950s, there was equal representation for north and south in the Federal House of Representatives. This favoured the NPC, which gradually came to dominate at the federal level, especially after the 1959 general elections when seats were distributed according to population. The NPC strategy was to ensure that it had compliant allies in the south rather than encouraging opposition within the other regions. It made an alliance with the NCNC in the east. The NCNC had already rejected overtures from the Action Group partly because of resistance by western NCNC elements.

The coalition strategy between the NPC and NCNC drove the west into political isolation. Differences over political strategy and education policy then developed within the Action Group. Chief Awolowo, who had given up the premiership of the west in 1959 to compete for power at the federal level, wanted to confront the NPC and NCNC in their regional strongholds. Chief S. L. Akintola, who had succeeded to the western premiership, on the other hand, wanted to join the coalition at the centre and was willing to collaborate with the northern political leadership. He was also opposed to the socialist leanings of Awolowo who, as leader of the opposition in the House of Representatives, had begun to emphasise "democratic" socialism. In 1962, the Action Group was riven in two and toppled from power. Chief Akintola was removed from the premiership, and disturbances in parliament ensued. The federal government declared an emergency in the west, and Chief Awolowo was tried and imprisoned on treason charges in 1963. Chief Akintola was then restored as regional premier with the active support of the federal government. He later formed the Nigerian National Democratic Party (NNDP) and allied the party with the NPC. This realignment in the west and bitter disputes over the 1962 and 1963 censuses weakened the federal coalition between the north and east.

The 1962 census appeared as the last chance for a built-in northern majority to be challenged. The census result of 45 million, which put the north at a slight disadvantage (47 percent), was highly controversial and was rejected. A second census was conducted in 1963 under much less satisfactory conditions. It gave a total population of 56 million and was greeted with great scepticism.[42] The balance between the north (54 percent) and the rest of the country was restored to roughly what it had been before. The total population of 56.6 million may have been overestimated by as much as 30 percent.[43] This extremely high margin of error in the base population needs to be kept in mind when figures are presented. After 1963, and for the whole period covered by this book, current population figures were based on projections from the 1963 census, and those figures were used for all official purposes. They came to have a life and power of their own. According to the World Bank, Nigeria's population passed 100 million in 1985.[44] Yet if we apply a 2.5 percent growth rate until 1980 to Ojetunji Aboyade's preferred figure of 42 million in 1962 and then 3.3 percent for the period 1980–1985, the 1985 population estimate is 77 million. The World Bank, by using higher growth rates than the official projection, which gave an estimate of 96 million for 1985,[45] was compounding the error in the base population. The 1991 census confirms this (see Table 2.3).

By the time of the 1964 federal elections, a new bipolar alignment had emerged with the NPC in alliance with the NNDP (forming the Nigerian

National Alliance) in opposition to the two major southern parties, the Action Group and NCNC (the United Progressive Grand Alliance). The southern parties protested the limits placed on their freedom to campaign in the north, and there was a widespread boycott of the election. The outcome, which left the NPC in an absolute majority, was bitterly opposed in the east and triggered a severe constitutional crisis. The decline in constitutionalism and increasing disorder accelerated with the Western Regional election of 1965. No state of emergency was declared. Instead, the federal government sent security forces to support the NNDP victory. It was under these conditions that a section of the military finally overthrew the government.

The military coup of January 1966 was conducted by seven majors, six of whom were Igbo, including the leader, Major Chukwuma Nzeogwu. Among those killed were the prime minister of the federation, Alhaji Abubakar Tafawa Balewa; the premier of the Northern Region, Ahmadu Bello, the Sardauna of Sokoto; the premier of the Western Region, Chief Akintola; and a number of senior officers. The plotters failed to secure Lagos, and eventually Major-General Johnson Aguiyi-Ironsi, the most senior officer, an Igbo, took power.

The immediate aim of the coup was to put an end to the army being used by the government to suppress its opponents in the Western Region. The main objective was to rid the country of rule by corrupt politicians and create a more radical, nontribal, unified country, though it was never clear how the majors intended the country to be governed. Moreover, the heavy involvement of Igbo in the coup laid it open to the charge of being ethnically inspired. Ironsi never made clear his position on the January coup and lacked political skills, failing to consult with the regions. He appeared to surround himself with Igbo advisers and in May embarked on a disastrous attempt at unification by abolishing the federal system. This precipitate action abolished the regions at a stroke. There was an immediate reaction in the north, where northern civil servants felt threatened by more highly educated southerners. Igbos in the north were attacked and some hundreds killed. In July, there was a second army coup, staged by junior northern officers, in which many Igbo officers were killed. This redressed the balance of power in favour of the north and brought Lt-Col Yakubu Gowon to power.[46] From this time on, a secessionist stance among Igbo leaders gathered momentum. It was given its final impetus by a second round of massacres of Igbo in September when between 8,000 and 10,000 people were killed. This action destroyed any confidence the Igbo had in the federation, and more than 1 million Igbo from all parts of the country fled back to their homeland. Successive attempts at compromise broke down, and on 30 May 1967, the secession of Biafra, the former Eastern Region, was declared by the military governor Lt-Col Ojukwu.

The secession of Biafra had its origins in the uneven pace of economic development and educational advance in the regions, combined with a competition for power at the centre where federal resources, powers, and institutions had expanded. Here power had shifted decisively northwards away from the southern regions. For the Igbo, the loss of political and economic power and the absence of protection in the wider federation was underlined in dramatic fashion by the massacres in the north. Oil wealth, much of which was located in the Eastern Region, was not a basic cause of secession. Oil did, however, hold out the prospect of a solid economic base. From a federal perspective, the loss of oil production in Biafra was clearly a factor in the determination to prevent secession. Had the secession gone ahead as planned, the Igbo would have increased their share of total Nigerian oil revenues over which they had control from 43 percent under the prewar federal sharing arrangements to 67 percent.[47] Under the new state system, which Gowon introduced just prior to secession on 27 May and which appealed so strongly to minority groups, it was only 14 percent.

Access to oil was not the only issue that became entangled with secession. The creation of Rivers state with its capital at Port Harcourt effectively cut off the Igbo from direct access to the sea. Many Igbo had built up substantial businesses and property holdings in Port Harcourt, and the loss of the city was keenly felt. The creation of Rivers state met the longstanding demands of the Rivers state movement.[48] However, support for the federal position among Rivers people and those of neigbouring South Eastern state was not total, and a minority threw in their lot with the secessionists.

What was the struggle for control and representation at the regional and federal levels about? Since the nationalist politicians had gained control of the regional state apparatus in the 1950s, the exercise of state power was closely linked to the economic advancement of individual, community, sectional, and ethnic interests. Access to the state meant access to state resources and to the growth of state patronage in its various forms. Representation was important to secure a voice in the sharing of state resources and to overcome fear of political and economic domination. As federal power, institutions, and resources increased, so more was at stake at the centre.

In the regions, the growth of state patronage followed the expansion of the public economy, public institutions, and powers of state regulation. Patronage was distributed in the form of employment, contracts, loans, licences, scholarships, and amenities. The benefits of patronage were regarded as legitimate perquisites of office, and individuals who did secure public office came under intense pressure to distribute patronage to party, community, and kin.

At the federal level, the struggle within the numerically tiny political and professional classes for the top administrative posts and appointments in the public sector was intense. And it was here, among the educated elite, that sectional conflicts intensified. This was evident in the bitter dispute between Yoruba and Igbo over jobs in the Nigerian Railway Corporation and the University of Lagos and in competition within the federal civil service. The composition of the army was also in dispute. There was, too, competition over the location of federal projects and the system of revenue allocation.

The fact that ideological differences were not prominent in the competition over the distribution of state resources and that those in power were fissured by sectional and ethnic differences should not obscure the fact that those individuals with access to state power who lacked a firm economic base of their own were busily engaged in amassing personal wealth and advancing their interests. The struggle for state office was also part of a process of class formation. Members of the political class used financial corruption to defend themselves against poverty and the risks of change and to give themselves power over clients. Through their corruption and shallow nationalism, the political class earned the wrath of intellectuals and the educated elite. This corruption was a major reason for the majors' coup that ended the First Republic and the widespread support the coup enjoyed.

State and Economy

Agricultural exports provided the main dynamic for growth in the Nigerian economy in the 1950s and early 1960s. The volume of agricultural exports rose at an annual compound rate of more than 5 percent from 1950 to 1963.[49] Local food production grew at more than 2 percent a year. Agricultural exports were the principal source of foreign exchange, and government revenues were largely dependent on trade taxes, principally import duties and export taxes. These two taxes accounted for 78 percent of total tax revenues during the period 1958–1960.[50] The growth of GDP averaged 4.3 percent per annum in real terms from 1950 to 1964.[51] It then fell to 2.6 percent in 1966, the year when political disruption began seriously to affect the economy. In that year, there was a surge of food-price inflation to 20.5 percent. Prior to that time, food-price inflation had been steady at relatively low levels. At this point, oil began to make an important contribution to government revenue and export earnings.

Following the commodity-price boom in the early 1950s, there was a gradual deterioration in the external terms of trade from 100 in 1954 to 79 in 1963.[52] For a while, this deterioration did not adversely affect the balance of payments and growth. The authorities could run down the financial surpluses that had accumulated from the previous export boom. By 1963, these surpluses were drawn down, and the balance of payments began to weaken. Two further factors helped to stave off a sharp deterioration of the balance of payments until 1966. One was the steady rise of oil revenues, which reached 32 percent of export earnings by 1966 (though the net contribution of oil was less impressive). The second factor was the inflow of capital in the form of private foreign investment, public loans, and foreign aid. By 1966, the contribution of these items was much weaker. Public capital flows (loans and aid) dried up as a rosy picture of Nigeria's future that Western donors had promoted gave way to pessimism and the inflow of private capital was offset by the declared outflow of profits and dividends.

At the time of independence, steps were taken to create a more autonomous financial system. The colonial authorities had followed conservative financial policies with small recurrent budget surpluses being the norm. In 1959, a Central Bank was created, and in the early 1960s, there were important changes in the banking system. The commercial banks acquired treasury bills so that the money supply could grow by acquisition of domestic assets rather than simply by the acquisition of sterling. The government could now become a borrower from the banking system. This opened up the potential for deficit financing. In 1964, budget deficits and falling reserves led to the first attempts at monetary controls and credit restriction.

The ideology of colonial development that emerged from World War II contained a much more active and purposeful role for the state. Yet the government undertook very little direct intervention in food production or marketing.[53] The main thrust of state intervention in agriculture came in the produce export markets through the Marketing Boards.

The Marketing Boards were statutory export monopolies that had their origins in the growing concentration in the import-export trade in the interwar period and in the wartime regulation of the produce trade. The boards later became an important and controversial instrument for taxing peasant farmers. By setting farmer prices well below world market prices, large trading surpluses were built up in the form of sterling assets held abroad. Initially, the boards used some of their funds for agricultural purposes. In 1954, the boards were regionalised, and the regional boards inherited surpluses worth £87 million. There then began a deliberate policy of building up trading surpluses in order to finance regional development programmes and party political expenditures. Between 1960 and 1967, producer prices fell much more than world prices. These policies had an adverse impact on the output of export crops over the long run.

The exploitation of farmers initially met with little resistance.[54] The trading surpluses were well concealed, and most farmers were still better off in real terms. There was also considerable redistribution by government in the form of communal welfare goods, like education, and there were some benefits from the spending by political parties.

Total public expenditure as a percentage of GDP grew from 5.4 percent in 1951/52 to 15.1 percent at the end of the decade, indicating a more active role for the state.[55] Public capital formation accounted for about one-third of total capital formation during the decade.[56] Federal and regional expenditures were roughly equivalent.[57]

Federal activity was important in the provision of transport and communications and utilities. Direct federal investment in agriculture and manufacture was limited to a sugar estate in Bacita, a paper mill at Jebba, the Port Harcourt oil refinery, and a mint. The first statutory corporations were created from government departments in the 1950s. These bodies did not accumulate capital, and in the 1960s only the Nigerian Ports Authority made a significant operating surplus.[58] As the commissions of inquiry that followed the end of the First Republic made clear, the corporations were beset with numerous problems including nepotism and favouritism, ethnic rivalry over board membership and employment, ministerial interference, and poor management and administration.

The regions took primary responsibility for expenditure on education, health, and agriculture. It was at the regional level, too, that marketing board funds were used to promote a variety of state development institutions. Gerald Helleiner estimated that fully 96 percent of the funds for publicly owned development institutions came, directly or indirectly, from the Marketing Boards.[59] The boards allowed a regional concentration of finance capital in the hands of the political class and bureaucracy at a time when Nigerian private capital was very limited in scale. The earliest vehicles for the expansion of state capital were the regional Production Development Boards followed by the Regional Development Corporations, which extended their activities from agriculture to manufacture, banking, insurance, finance, property, and hotels. The most important public investments in agriculture were plantations and pioneer oil mills. They were not successful. Direct investment and management in industry by the corporations also turned out to be unproductive.[60]

Investment companies were established in the east and north in 1959 by the Commonwealth Development Corporation, which was anxious to maintain an institutional presence after independence. The involvement of the Commonwealth Development Corporation was particularly successful in the case of the Northern Nigeria Investments Ltd., whose main interests were in the profitable Kaduna textile industry.

Although there were common patterns in all regions, like the expansion of state activity and patronage and support for foreign investment in manufacture, there were also differences of emphasis. In the west, the greater extent of state investment was related to the fact that more funds were at the disposal of the government, to the existence of a stronger capacity for planning, and to the influence of Fabian socialism within the Action Group. It was also linked to Chief Awolowo's desire to have the west as independent of the federation as possible. In the east, state investment was mainly seen as a means of strengthening the private sector. Shares were held in trust by the regional government for citizens until such time as a class of local shareholders emerged.[61] In the north, there was more concern about using state power to advance northernisation and gain a larger share of federal resources in order to close the economic gap with the other regions. State regulation and institutions were seen as necessary to counter the cumulative advantages of wealth and industrial concentration in the west and the attraction of the southern port locations.

Industrialisation came late to Nigeria relative to other African countries like Kenya or Zimbabwe. In 1940, sizeable private industrial ventures were limited to four cotton ginneries, six sawmills, a soap works (1924), two palm oil bulking plants (1924), a cigarette factory (1937), and a drum-making plant (1939).[62] After World War II, imperialist rivalry in the colonies became increasingly multilateral as British power was eroded. At the same time, barriers to entry in the import trade were much reduced by the expansion of the Nigerian market, which permitted increased specialisation and reduced capital requirements. Indian, Greek, Levantine, and Nigerian merchants, together with companies representing foreign manufacturers, all entered the import and wholesale trade.[63] This activity helped to break down the concentration in the import trade and put the old trading companies under pressure. The foreign trading companies gradually withdrew from general importing, retailing, and the produce trade, and they invested in manufacture in order to protect their markets and respond to pressure for industrialisation from nationalists. With the approach of independence, state subsidies (and later, tariff escalation due to the weakening of the balance of payments) encouraged the expansion of foreign capital from its commercial base and prompted a flow of new investment from abroad. Light consumer-goods industries with limited domestic linkages, assembly plants, and a few intermediate plants—like cement, rubber tires, and glass—were set up to replace imports.

One result of these changing patterns was the erosion of the old bilateral relationship between Nigeria and Britain. The British share of total Nigerian imports and exports declined steadily from 45 percent and 72 percent, respectively, in the mid 1950s (1954–1956 average) to 23 percent and 14 percent in the mid 1970s (1974–1976 average), as did its share of foreign investment. However, from a British perspective, the importance of Nigeria as a market and source of profit was to rise significantly in the

1970s as a result of oil revenues and the rapid expansion of the Nigerian market.

Large-scale industry was dominated by foreign capital and supplemented and supported by state capital. In 1963, the structure of equity in large-scale manufacture was as follows: private Nigerian, 10 percent; private foreign, 68 percent; federal government, 3 percent; and regional governments, 19 percent.[64] The United Kingdom held just over half the stock of foreign investment in 1967 and was dominant in manufacture, trade, banking, and the oil industry.[65] U.S. investment was significant only in the oil industry. Foreign investment in agriculture was negligible.

Import substitution was not part of a planned strategy of industrialisation, though industrialisation as a general goal was prominent. The First Plan (1962–1968), which was a collection of regional plans, was essentially a list of public projects and expenditures. The planning process was caught up in the struggle for regional advantage, and federal authority was weak. The classic case of federal impotence in the face of struggles for regional advantage was the failure to locate the iron and steel project that had first been proposed in 1958. Regional competition and public corruption led to considerable waste. As the First Republic ended, industry suffered from duplication of plants by the regional governments, uneconomic location, and a wave of contractor-financed turnkey projects. Contractor finance and supplier credits were popular with the regional politicians because of the opportunities for kickbacks they provided. For the federal authorities, these methods weakened control over external debt and undermined the attempt to plan.[66]

Although there was considerable growth in trade union membership during the 1950s, most trade unions were weak, of small-average size, with unstable membership and insecure finances. Most union activity was concentrated in Lagos. Attempts to form a central labour organisation failed with depressing regularity.[67] Trade union leadership tended to be incorporated into the elite, thereby undermining its legitimacy. Nevertheless, extensive cooperation and mobilisation among workers did occur in 1945, 1963, and 1964. In 1964, a Joint Action Committee was formed and a general strike called. Substantial concessions were forced from the government, which was ill prepared and put on the defensive. There was a general resentment at those in positions of power and privilege who had high salaries, bloated fringe benefits, and the opportunity for corruption.

Collective bargaining worked to some extent in the large industrial firms and in the joint industrial councils at the industrywide level. In the public corporations and government services, which were larger employers than the private unionised sector, collective bargaining was virtually absent. Governments generally adopted a policy of wage restraint, and awards were given only to public sector employees under pressure from declining real wages at regular intervals. On these occasions, the government acted as wage leader with the private sector following behind. Between 1934 and 1964, there were seven wage commissions for manual employees of the federal government. Both employers and unions sought to influence the government at the time of these commissions, and the pattern of strike activity was clearly concentrated at these periods.

Urban real wages for unskilled workers in Lagos increased by 70 percent between 1949 and 1960 and by even more in the east and west.[68] After 1960, government minimum wages fell behind the rate of inflation despite periodic general wage increases and major strikes. By 1976, a year after a major wage and salary review, the purchasing power of the government wage was back to its 1960 level. The pattern in the northern states, where the minimum daily wage was not harmonised with other states until the early 1970s, was different. Here the 1960 wage level was lower than in the east and west. Government wages rose substantially in real terms in the 1960s, and in 1976 were still some 80 percent above the 1960 level.

Differences in income between urban and rural producers have varied over time and place. The evidence is fragmentary and never takes satisfactory account of differences in rural and urban costs of living or different sources of income. Gavin Williams has argued that the evidence, such as it is, does not support the view often expressed by economists that unskilled urban workers earn several times as much as farmers.[69]

At the start of the 1950s, mean farm earnings in the cocoa belt and some parts of the north were much higher than urban wages for unskilled work. The government minimum was well below farm wages for casual male labour. When cocoa prices declined in the 1960s, average household incomes in the cocoa belt fell to the level of unskilled workers, and wages fell behind urban wages. Elsewhere in the southern states, despite the rise of the real urban wage in the 1950s, urban workers would have earned little more than half the average incomes reported for farm households. In the northern states, where rural earnings were lower and rural households larger, wages would have been less than the mean male household income but perhaps above the mean income per adult male.

The secession of the former Eastern Region in 1967 had direct repercussions for the Nigerian economy through the loss of oil output (which was later made up by the expansion of Mid-West and offshore production), the loss of palm produce exports, and the seizure of railway rolling stock. But the economy proved resilient on the whole. After the military intervention, the formation of a National Economic Advisory Council provided the basis for more centralised decisionmaking. Wartime measures were successful in releasing resources for military expansion and obtaining forced savings from the private sector. The war was financed partly by increased taxation, partly by deferred payments on external account, partly by pegging the government's nondefence expenditure, but mainly by borrowing through the Central Bank.[70]

Agricultural output proved remarkably resilient. Despite large-scale deficit financing and increased demand for food from the armed forces, food-price indices actually declined in 1968.[71] Inflationary pressures were controlled and external deficits held to manageable levels. There were stringent import and foreign exchange controls, but the use of foreign exchange for military hardware was not allowed to be at the expense of imported industrial raw materials. After an initial shock, industrial output recovered by the end of 1968, helped by the curb on imports.

Conclusion

Colonial rule entrenched a regional tripartite system of government and administration. Within each region, a single ethnic group came to political dominance, and other minority groups felt insecure and disadvantaged. At the centre, where there was no centralised authority with indigenous roots, decolonisation left a political vacuum. Nigerian nationalism, which had earlier found common cause against British rule, receded in the face of the political mobilisation of vigorous subnationalisms. Political competition for power at the centre resulted in the gradual supremacy of northern politicians. Underlying this competition was a struggle for economic advancement by individuals and communities and the fear of political and economic domination accentuated by the uneven development of disparate communities. These fears were strikingly evident in the bitter controversy over the census and in the aggressive ethnicity that came to the surface. Despite the operation of a federal system of government that ensured considerable decentralisation of powers, there was too much at stake at the centre for a compromise to be struck.

Regional governments were funded to a significant extent by taxes on small producers, who provided the foundation for economic growth in the 1950s and early 1960s. In the longer term, the taxation of agricultural exports through the marketing board system had adverse consequences, restricting output, savings, and the growth of agro-based industries. The boards and associated institutions received strong political support from politicians, leading businesspeople, and civil servants. They provided resources for the regional parties and opportunities for private accumulation. They were also instrumental in shifting state policy from limited intervention in support of trade to a more active developmental role. The expansion of state activity was particularly evident in the promotion of industry and in the large resources devoted to education.

For a number of reasons, public policies and the general direction of development were not sharply defined or contested. Ideas about welfare, public ownership, and redistribution of income and wealth did not find strong ideological or political expression. The prominence of commercial and urban propertied interests and the weak development of agrarian or industrial class divisions was one factor. In addition, the public domain was widely perceived as an area for the advancement of individual and community interests. Finally, there was the political context. The nature of the political parties and the pattern of regional party competition that was generated in the contest for federal power gave priority to distributive concerns.

As the regional and individual struggle for power and wealth intensified, so the basis for federal government and national policies was weakened. The steady expansion of state patronage in which political considerations rather than economic criteria were paramount adversely affected the allocation of resources. Politicians and their business allies engaged in the political forms of accumulation, and the corruption of this class made it deeply unpopular, creating the conditions for widespread support for military intervention. Yet the military could not ride above sectionalism, and its intervention compounded fears of Igbo domination, leading to a countercoup, civilian massacre, and eventually, secession of the Eastern Region in 1967.

Notes

1. J. S. Coleman, *Nigeria: Background to Nationalism* (Berkeley: University of California Press, 1958), pp. 50–51.
2. O. Nnoli, *Ethnic Politics in Nigeria* (Enugu: Fourth Dimension, 1978), p. 113.
3. S. Berry, *Fathers Work for Their Sons: Accumulation, Mobility and Class Formation in an Extended Yoruba Community* (Berkeley: University of California Press, 1985), pp. 23, 26.
4. J. N. Paden, *Ahmadu Bello, Sardauna of Sokoto* (London: Hodder and Stoughton, 1986), p. 56.
5. J. I. Tseayo, *Conflict and Incorporation in Nigeria: The Integration of the Tiv* (Zaria: Gaskiya Corporation, 1975).
6. A. E. Afigbo, *The Warrant Chiefs: Indirect Rule in Southern Nigeria* (London: Longman, 1972), chap. 8.
7. *Report of the Committee on Chieftancy Matters in the East-Central State of Nigeria*, Official Document No. 5 of 1976, Enugu.
8. J.D.Y. Peel, "The Cultural Work of Yoruba Ethnogenesis," in E. Tonkin, M. McDonald, and M. Chapman, eds., *History and Ethnicity* (London: Routledge, 1989), p. 200.
9. A. M. Hay and R.H.T. Smith, *Interregional Trade and Money Flows in Nigeria, 1964* (Ibadan: Oxford University Press, 1970), p. 148.
10. R. K. Udo, *Migrant Tenant Farmers of Nigeria* (Lagos: African Universities Press, 1975), pp. 58–59.

11. Lagos was excised from the Western Region in 1954 and became the federal capital, a move that was strongly opposed by Chief Awolowo and the Action Group.

12. According to the derivation principle, an area from which a revenue is derived should benefit from the revenue over and above the general share. In the 1970s, the main beneficiaries of derivation were the oil producing states of Bendel and Rivers. In 1979, the principle was dropped in favour of sharing through the Federation Account.

13. G. K. Helleiner, *Peasant Agriculture, Government and Economic Growth in Nigeria* (Homewood, Ill.: Irwin, 1966), p. 435.

14. D. B. Abernethy, *The Political Dilemma of Popular Education* (Stanford: Stanford University Press, 1969), pp. 265–268.

15. J. N. Paden, *Religion and Political Culture in Kano* (Berkeley: University of California Press, 1973), p. 317. Sabon Gari was a residentially segregated area set aside for Africans from other areas.

16. Polly Hill, *Dry Grain Farming Families: Hausaland (Nigeria) and Karnataka (India) Compared* (Cambridge: Cambridge University Press, 1982), chap. 16.

17. G. Williams, "Why Is There No Agrarian Capitalism in Nigeria?" *Journal of Historical Sociology* 1/4, 1988, p. 360.

18. Berry, *Fathers Work for Their Sons*, p. 30.

19. J.D.Y Peel, *Ijeshas and Nigerians: The Incorporation of a Yoruba Kingdom, 1890s–1970s* (Cambridge: Cambridge University Press, 1983), p. 128.

20. S. M. Martin, *Palm Oil and Protest: An Economic History of the Ngwa Region of South-Eastern Nigeria, 1800–1980* (Cambridge: Cambridge University Press, 1988), pp. 86–89.

21. T. Falola, "Lebanese Traders in Southwestern Nigeria, 1900–1960," *African Affairs* 89/357, 1990, pp. 538–549.

22. P. Kilby, "Manufacturing in Colonial Africa," in P. Duignan and L. H. Gann, eds., *Colonialism in Africa, 1870–1960*, vol. 4, *The Economics of Colonialism* (Cambridge: Cambridge University Press, 1975), p. 494.

23. Kilby, "Manufacturing in Colonial Africa," p. 494.

24. Isiyaku Rabiu, today one of the largest industrialists in Kano, was one of the first textile factors.

25. Among the most well known were Chief Michael Ibru and Chief 'Bode Akindele.

26. P. T. Bauer, *West African Trade: A Study of Competition, Oligopoly and Monopoly in a Changing Economy* (Cambridge: Cambridge University Press, 1954), p. 69.

27. Bauer, *West African Trade*, p. 220.

28. W. M. Freund, *The Making of Contemporary Africa: The Development of African Society Since 1800* (London: Macmillan, 1984), p. 243.

29. R. W. Shenton, *The Development of Capitalism in Northern Nigeria* (London: James Currey, 1986), pp. xiii, 124–125.

30. E. O. Akeredolu-Ale, "Private Foreign Investment and the Underdevelopment of Indigenous Entrepreneurship in Nigeria," in G. Williams, ed., *Nigeria: Economy and Society* (London: Rex Collings, 1976), pp. 108–109.

31. Kilby, "Manufacturing in Colonial Africa," pp. 516–519.

32. Berry, *Fathers Work for Their Sons*, pp. 34–35, 40.

33. Peel, *Ijeshas and Nigerians,* p. 203.
34. S. Osoba, "The Nigerian Power Elite, 1952–65," reprinted in P.C.W. Gutkind and P. Waterman, eds., *African Social Studies: A Radical Reader* (London: Heinemannn, 1977), pp. 370–372, from a paper given at the Tenth Annual Conference of the Historical Society of Nigeria, Ibadan, 1970.
35. O. Olakanpo, "Indigenous Enterprises in Distributive Trades in Nigeria," Nigerian Institute for Social and Economic Research, Ibadan, 1968.
36. Osoba, "The Nigerian Power Elite," p. 373.
37. Peel, *Ijeshas and Nigerians,* p. 133.
38. Unpublished paper by A. C. Callaway.
39. Richard Burghart, "Ministerial Emoluments in Nigeria," *Nigerian Opinion,* no. 8, pp. 10–11, reprinted in *Nigeria 1965, Crisis and Criticism* (Ibadan: Ibadan University Press, 1966).
40. A. D. Yahaya, "Nigerian Public Administration Under Military Rule: The Experience of the Northern States," in L. Adamolekun, ed., *Nigerian Public Administration, 1960–1980* (Ibadan: Heinemann, 1985).
41. The following sketch of the political history draws heavily on R. Luckham, *The Nigerian Military: A Sociological Analysis of Authority and Revolt, 1960–67* (Cambridge: Cambridge University Press, 1971); J. O'Connell, "Political Integration: The Nigerian Case," in A. Hazlewood, ed., *African Integration and Disintegration* (London: Oxford University Press, 1967).
42. O. Aboyade, "The Economy of Nigeria," in P. Robson and D. A. Lury, eds., *The Economies of Africa* (London: Allen and Unwin, 1969), p. 130.
43. Aboyade preferred a figure of 42 million for 1962 based on a total population of 33 million in 1952-1953 and a 2.5 percent annual growth rate. Aboyade, "The Economy of Nigeria," p. 131.
44. World Bank, *World Development Report* (New York: Oxford University Press, 1987), p. 202.
45. *Annual Abstract of Statistics,* 1986 ed., Federal Office of Statistics, p. 14.
46. Gowon's family originated from the Angas people (Plateau), but he was brought up at Wusasa, a small Hausa-speaking Christian mission community near Zaria. He attended Barewa College, Zaria.
47. S. R. Pearson, *Petroleum and the Nigerian Economy* (Stanford: Stanford University Press, 1970), pp. 144–145.
48. T. N. Tamuno, "Patriotism and Statism in the Rivers State, Nigeria, *African Affairs* 71/284 (1972), pp. 264–281.
49. G. K. Helleiner, *Peasant Agriculture, Government and Economic Growth in Nigeria* (Homewood, Ill.: Irwin, 1966), p. 29.
50. Aboyade, "The Economy of Nigeria," p. 157.
51. P. Kilby, *Industrialization in an Open Economy: Nigeria, 1945–1966* (London: Cambridge University Press, 1969), p. 9.
52. Helleiner, *Peasant Agriculture* p. 499.
53. See T. G. Forrest, "Agricultural Policies in Nigeria, 1900–78," in J. Heyer, P. Roberts, and G. Williams, eds., *Rural Development in Tropical Africa* (London: Macmillan, 1981), pp. 222–258.
54. J.D.Y. Peel, "Social and Cultural Change," in M. Crowder, ed., *The Cambridge History of Africa,* vol. 8, c. 1940–c. 1975 (Cambridge: Cambridge University Press, 1984), p. 169.

55. Helleiner, *Peasant Agriculture*, p. 204.

56. Helleiner, *Peasant Agriculture*, p. 205.

57. Helleiner, *Peasant Agriculture*, p. 238.

58. World Bank, *Nigeria: Options for Long Term Development* (Baltimore, Md.: Johns Hopkins University Press, 1974), pp. 167–168.

59. Helleiner, *Peasant Agriculture*, p. 248.

60. O. Teriba, "Development Strategy, Investment Decision and Expenditure Patterns of a Public Development Institution: The case of the Western Nigerian Development Corporation, 1949–1962," *Nigerian Journal of Economic and Social Studies* 8/2 (1966), pp. 256–258.

61. *Report of the 4th Conference of Leading Personalities of Eastern Nigerian Origin*, Enugu, 13–14 December 1963. Official Document No. 28 of 1964.

62. Kilby, "Manufacturing in Colonial Africa," p. 490.

63. Kilby, "Manufacturing in Colonial Africa," pp. 493–494.

64. *Industrial Survey, 1963*, Federal Office of Statistics.

65. Stock of Private Direct Investment by DAC Countries in Developing Countries, End 1967, Organisation for Economic Cooperation and Development, Paris, 1972.

66. A. A. Ayida, "Contractor Finance and Supplier Credit in Economic Growth," *Nigerian Journal of Economic and Social Studies* 7/2 (1965), pp. 183–184.

67. Kilby, *Industrialization in an Open Economy*, pp. 284–289.

68. G. Williams, "Inequalities in Rural Nigeria," Development Studies Occasional Paper no. 16, University of East Anglia, 1981, p. 20.

69. Williams, "Inequalities in Rural Nigeria," p. 19.

70. O. Aboyade and A. A. Ayida, "The War Economy in Perspective," *Nigerian Journal of Economic and Social Studies* 13/1 (1971), p. 27.

71. O. Aboyade, "The Development Process," in A. A. Ayida and H.M.A. Onitiri, eds., *Reconstruction and Development in Nigeria* (Ibadan: Oxford University Press, 1971), p. 54.

PART TWO

Political Development

3

Military Government and Politics, 1970–1979

The Gowon Regime, 1970–1975

The Military/Bureaucratic Alliance

The coming to power of the military in 1966 increased the power of senior federal civil servants. With military cover and protection, they assumed political as well as administrative control of the civil service. During and after the civil war, they played an important role in initiating and implementing state policy. Federal civil servants were, for example, influential in shaping the federal position in negotiations with secessionist Biafra. A condition of their power was the existence of centralised decision-making, which became a reality during the war for the first time after more than a decade of virtual regional autonomy. Their influence was apparent in constitutional policy, in the conduct of economic policy, and in the formulation of national policies in areas like education. After the civil war, the military, who had no plans of their own, relied heavily on civil servants to formulate and execute policy. Bureaucratic power was popularly referred to as the rule of the super-permanent secretaries.

A further consequence of military rule was the increased power of minority groups in the country.[1] The minorities—those who did not belong to the three major ethno-linguistic groups—were generally committed to a stronger federal centre and supported federal initiatives. They gained prominence with the creation of new states and the breakdown of the old regional hegemony. They were also well represented in the army and civil service. For example, indigenes of Plateau and Benue states were prominent in the army, and the highly educated elites of Bendel state had a strong presence in the federal civil service.

With the successful prosecution of the war and a stronger nationalism borne out of that experience, there were hopes that federal leadership with centralised policymaking would be carried over into peacetime. Civil servants saw it as an opportunity to strengthen the federation and enhance national integration. Abdul Aziz Attah, the permanent secretary and secretary to the Federal Military Government who was involved in defence matters, finance, oil company legislation, and the indigenisation decree, exemplified the nationalist impulse among senior civil servants.

The power of the bureaucracy was reflected in its role in propagating ideas and the spread of bureaucratic developmentalism over much of intellectual life. Civil servants participated fully in an important series of conferences and seminars held at Ahmadu Bello University when the war ended, and they wrote many newspaper articles that moulded intellectual opinion. They came to play a prominent role in the influential Nigerian Economics Society. Among the constant themes in the 1970s were the notions of shortage of executive capacity; manpower planning; and instrumental, policy-relevant research. The notion that there were two possible constraints on development, financial and executive, became very popular and influential in 1973 when Philip Asiodu, Permanent Secretary, Ministry of Mines and Power, declared that a shortage of executive capacity (trained manpower) was the main constraint on Nigeria's development.[2] Later, the principle was elevated to new heights of respectability in the Third Plan (1975–1980) when it was held to be the binding constraint, and balance of payments projections were based on it.[3] Unfortunately, there is no evidence that a shortage of executive capacity had any effect on what the government could, as distinct from should, spend.

Areas in which bureaucratic power was exercised included the Second National Development Plan (1970–1974), revenue allocation, and the introduction of the Nigerian Enterprises Promotion Decree in 1972. The objective of the Indigenisation Decree was to increase national control of the economy by restricting foreign ownership, an aim that was also pursued through an increase in state participation in the oil industry and banking. Nigerian businesspeople had long agitated for restrictions on foreign capital but it was only towards the end of the civil war that these views found concerted expression in demands for greater share ownership, greater access to credit, and more opportunities in the distributive sector. Indigenisation was not favoured by civil commissioners because it was thought that it would promote sectional advantage. Igbo businesspeople and professionals were widely felt to be at a disadvantage as a result of the civil war. Many in the northern states thought that the decree would favour Lagos and the Western states. However, the measure was supported by senior civil servants who joined forces with indigenous businesspeople to overcome opposition from foreign companies and civil commissioners.

Another area of national policy that was marked out for federal initiatives was education. Education issues dominated discussion of the Second Plan in the Supreme Military Council and the Federal Executive Council.[4] As the key to social mobility and the advancement of communities, education was a matter of intense public concern. Throughout the 1970s, education was to be the most consistent and widespread topic for public debate.

Among the state actions that triggered debate was the state takeover of primary and secondary schools from private and voluntary agencies (mainly churches) that began in the East Central state in 1970 and then spread to other states. The problem of educational imbalance and the related question of university admission quotas and the role of the Joint Admission and Matriculation Board (JAMB), a central admissions board with the delicate task of balancing the claims of merit and the national interest, also generated controversy and student unrest.

Other issues included the problems associated with the decision to undertake a massive programme of Universal Primary Education (UPE), the widely recognised decline in education standards, the loss of status by teachers, and the free education controversy that erupted at the end of the decade when it was taken up by party politicians.[5] Finally, there was student unrest at all levels, which received most publicity in the universities where student mobilisation led to confrontations with the security agencies and loss of life at Ibadan in 1971 and at Zaria and Lagos in 1978.

State Creation and Revenue Allocation

One of the first acts of the military government under General Gowon was the creation of twelve new states in 1967 from the existing four regions (see Table 3.1). This was a major step that strengthened the hand of the federal government and effectively broke down the powers of the regions. Taken together with the increase in oil revenues, which increased federal resources at the centre, it meant that the old pattern of virtually autonomous regions with considerable financial resources of their own was destroyed.

The idea was to balance north and south with six states each.[6] Lagos state was created from the former federal territory of Lagos, which was expanded to include the industrial centre of Ikeja, thus reducing the threat from the west should it wish to secede.[7] State creation redistributed power away from the regional blocs towards the federal centre and satisfied minority groups who had influence within the army. It also had the effect of giving greater equality of access to federal funds. It reduced the potential for intense social antagonism among representatives of the old regional elites by creating lower levels of rivalry among the states and by diminishing the opportunity for regional gain from the exercise of federal power. In 1976, a further seven states were created, bringing the total to nineteen (see Table 3.1).

Following the creation of states in 1967, a commission under Chief Isaac Dina was set up to review the system of revenue allocation in the federa-

TABLE 3.1 Political Divisions from 1963 to 1991

1963	*1967*	*1976*	*1987*	*1991*
Northern Region	North Western	Niger	Niger	Niger
		Sokoto	Sokoto	Sokoto
				Kebbi
	North Eastern	Bauchi	Bauchi	Bauchi
		Borno	Borno	Borno
				Yobe
		Gongola	Gongola	Adamawa
				Taraba
	North Central	Kaduna	Kaduna	Kaduna
			Katsina	Katsina
	Benue Plateau	Benue	Benue	Benue
		Plateau	Plateau	Plateau
	West Central	Kwara	Kwara	Kwara
				Kogi[a]
	Kano	Kano	Kano	Kano
				Jigawa
Eastern Region	East Central	Anambra	Anambra	Anambra
				Enugu
		Imo	Imo	Imo
				Abia
	South Eastern	Cross River	Cross River	Cross River
			Akwa Ibom	Akwa Ibom
	Rivers	Rivers	Rivers	Rivers
Western Region	Western	Ogun	Ogun	Ogun
		Ondo	Ondo	Ondo
		Oyo	Oyo	Oyo
				Osun
Lagos[b]	Lagos	Lagos	Lagos	Lagos
Mid-West Region	Mid Western	Bendel	Bendel	Edo
				Delta
Federal Capital Territory		Abuja	Abuja	Abuja[c]

[a]Kogi state was created by combining parts of Benue and Kwara states.
[b]Lagos was excised from the Western region in 1954 and became the federal capital. In 1967, it also became capital of the new Lagos State, which included Badagry, Ikeja, and Epe districts from the Western Region.
[c]Abuja replaced Lagos as the federal capital in December 1991.

tion.[8] The report was never published, but most of the ideas in the report were later adopted. The report recommended greater financial responsibilities for the federal government in the areas of higher education, roads, health, and industry. There was to be an enlarged Distributable Pool Account at the centre through which the states shared their revenues and a downgrading of the derivation principle in revenue allocation, which, it was argued, had accentuated uneven development and regional conflict in the past.

Between 1966 and 1979, the revenue allocation scheme was altered six times (1966/67, 1968/69, 1969/70, 1971/72, 1975/76, 1979/80), affecting the division of revenues between the centre and the states and the distribution among the states. These changes occurred at a time when oil revenues increased in importance relative to other sources of revenue. The major alterations and their consequences are considered in the discussion that follows.

In the 1970s, federal expenditures came to dominate expenditure by the states, and the share of federal revenues that was allocated to the states declined. Whereas in the First Republic, federal expenditure was about equal to regional expenditures, by 1975/76 the federal share of combined expenditures had risen to about 70 percent. Federal capital expenditures in the states outweighed capital expenditures by the states by a large margin. In addition, the states became more dependent on federal transfers for their revenue. These transfers included nonstatutory grants, which were a new departure.

Table 3.2 shows the decline in the share of federal revenues that went to the states. In the first half of the 1970s, when oil revenues surged, the share allocated to the states fell as low as 18 percent. Despite changes in the system of revenue allocation that worked in favour of the states, their share generally remained low because the fastest-growing revenues (petroleum profits tax and company income tax) accrued directly to the federal government and were outside the allocation system. Under the 1979 constitution, all important sources of revenue with the exception of personal income tax, which accrued directly to the state of origin, were placed in a central Federation Account. This change, together with an increase in the statutory share of the states, then raised the share of federal revenues that went to the states.

The dependence of the states on federal financial transfers increased. At the start of the 1960s, the regional governments relied on federal transfers for about 55 percent of their revenues (1961/1963 av.). Towards the end of the 1970s, the state governments budgeted for over 80 percent of their revenues from federal sources, an act that had a number of consequences. The combination of a federal structure in which the states had considerable political autonomy and a fiscal structure in which they raised little money of their own, gave the states every incentive to try to get more funds from the centre. It encouraged financial irresponsibility and set up strong pressures for new states. Budgetary control was extremely weak in most states and the publication and auditing of accounts either subject to long delay or nonexistent. In general, the potential for federal control and direction over the states, which the transfers provided, was not exercised. Federal loans to the states were written off on two occasions.

Nonstatutory grants to the states grew in importance through the 1970s as oil revenues increased (see Table 3.2). The intention behind these transfers, which were made at the discretion of the federal government, was to

TABLE 3.2 Statutory and Nonstatutory Revenue Allocation, 1948–1988 (N million)

	Statutory	*Nonstatutory*	*Total*	*Total as Percentage of Federal Recurrent Revenues*
1948/49	9.0		9.0	20.4
1954/55	54.8		54.8	43.8
1959/60	76.8		76.8	43.2
1966/67	139.4		139.4	41.1
1970/71[a]	245.6		245.6	32.5
1971/72	326.8	16.6	343.4	24.3
1972/73	322.7	15.5	338.2	24.4
1973/74	361.9	34.0	395.9	18.2
1974/75	833.7	135.3	969.0	18.7
1975/76[a]	1220.9	496.9	1717.8	29.3
1976	1142.8	502.2	1645.0	24.3
1977	1572.5	424.4	1996.9	24.8
1978	1240.0	532.6	1772.6	23.7
1979	2044.0	827.5	2871.5	26.3
1980	3095.3	599.3	3694.6	24.2
1981	4670.4	240.2	4910.6	38
1982	4264.4		4264.4	36.2
1983	4274.6		4274.6	40.6
1984	4195.2		4195.2	37.6
1985	4965.8		4965.8	34
1986	4332.6		4332.6	30.5
1987	8970.2		8970.2	35.7
1988	11722.2		11722.2	42.9

Note: There is reason to think that the figures for 1970/71–1975/76 may underestimate nonstatutory transfers to the states. *The Report of the Presidential Commission on Revenue Allocation* (1980), vol. 1, p. 42, gives figures of N279 million for 1970/71–1973/74. *The First Progress Report of the Third Plan* gives N605 million for 1975. The 1988 figure is provisional.

Sources: For 1948/49–1975/76: A. Phillips, "Three Decades of Inter-Governmental Financial Relationships in the Federation of Nigeria," paper presented at the Conference on Intergovernmental Relations in Nigeria, University of Ife, February 1979, Table 7. For 1976–1988: Central Bank of Nigeria, *Economic and Financial Review* (various years), and Central Bank of Nigeria, *Annual Report* (various years).

allow federal initiatives to promote development in the states and to increase the share of the states. Most of the grants were for education, health, agriculture, roads, and housing. They were not tightly controlled from the centre. When oil revenues fell, the federal government found itself overcommitted to programmes of universal primary education, housing, and health, and it tried to shift the financial burden down to the states. As a result, the states later criticised the grants for the uncertainty and political difficulties they created. There was, too, the argument that a large nonstatutory element would be open to political manipulation under civil rule and was therefore undesirable. Nonstatutory grants were discontinued after 1981.

Other measures that tended to increase the dependence of the states on federal transfers and restrict their fiscal options were introduced. These measures included the abolition of export duties and sales tax on agricultural produce, the reduction of poll taxes to a uniform level throughout the country, standardised personal income tax rates throughout the country, and the introduction of a uniform fuel price that removed the power of state governments to impose petroleum sales taxes.[9]

How did the distribution of federal funds among the states change over time? The changes in the system of revenue allocation generally worked towards more equal revenue sharing among the states and towards an increased share for less-advantaged states. After 1969, half the Distributable Pool Account (DPA) was shared among the states equally, and half was distributed on the basis of population.[10] In addition, the Distributable Pool increased in importance as more federally collected revenues were switched into it and as the significance of the derivation principle diminished. Revenue shared through the DPA as a percentage of total statutory allocated revenue rose from 61 percent in 1970/71 to 90 percent in 1978/79.[11]

In the early 1970s, both Bendel and Rivers states, as oil producers, gained handsomely from the operation of the derivation principle that was applied from 1971 to 45 percent of onshore oil rents and royalties. In 1974/75, the shares of Bendel and Rivers in statutory revenue allocation were 23.7 percent and 17.1 percent, respectively.[12] After 1975, the principle was applied to only 20 percent of onshore oil production. By 1978/79, the shares of the two states had fallen to 8.9 percent and 8.4 percent. The principle was then dropped in favour of a Special Account for mineral-producing areas.

Table 2.3 gives the share of statutory allocated revenue among the regions and states. It shows that the effect of state creation in 1967 and 1976 and the changes in the system of revenue allocation were to increase the northern states' share to a considerable extent. Thus the share of the northern states in statutory allocated revenue rose steadily from 35 percent in 1966/67 to 52 percent by 1985. This sustained shift brought the share of the northern states roughly into line with their share of the total population.

The distribution of other federal expenditures among the states is much more difficult to assess. Little work has been done on this politically sensitive matter, though everyone has an opinion about it.[13] Casual observation suggests that in the 1970s the less economically advanced northern states did well from the allocation of federal expenditures for agriculture (large-scale irrigation projects and agricultural development projects), industry (vehicle assembly plants, fertilisers, oil refining, steel rolling mills), and road construction. For many years after the civil war ended, Igbo opinion was that the eastern states were starved of federal funds, especially for road building.[14] This feeling of relative deprivation was no doubt buttressed by other factors like the loss of commercial dominance, employment opportunities, and property in Port Harcourt and the fact that in 1976 only one new state was created in the Igbo heartland whereas two new states were created in Yorubaland.

Labour and Wage Policy

After the war, emergency regulations—including a ban on strikes—remained in force. This did not prevent widespread industrial unrest, which peaked in the aftermath of the increases awarded by the Adebo Commission (1970). The Adebo awards adhered to the pattern of periodic public sector pay awards made under pressure of declining real earnings and a widening gap with the private sector. Through these awards and through rent controls and the operations of the Price Control Board, the government hoped to get industrial peace, but the pattern of period awards persisted with the Udoji Commission, which reported in 1974.

In December 1974, the government announced details of large wage and salary awards, together with lump sum payment of arrears backdated nine months to April 1974. Public service pensions were raised substantially. One consequence of this oil bonanza was that the far-reaching reforms of the public service recommended in the report were completely overshadowed by the awards. Another consequence was to accelerate early retirement from the public service because of the generous pension provisions. There was also a sharp acceleration of inflation as the enormous increases in purchasing power swallowed up the goods that were available.

The awards were widely interpreted as an attempt to buy middle-class support for a regime that had lost much of its support.[15] If this was the intention, it was not the result. There was a great deal of industrial action as workers struggled to get their "Udoji." Dissatisfaction over regrading and relativities led to widespread protests and strikes involving practically all the professional and public sector groups. By 24 February 1975, there were 202 trade disputes relating to the Udoji awards.[16]

Loss of Political and Economic Control

The Gowon administration soon lost the sense of strategic urgency that the civil war and the need for reconstruction engendered. One observer noted, as early as 1970, that the states' tail was wagging the federal dog, and that this was potentially dangerous for a corrective military regime.[17]

Unwisely, the government announced on 1 October 1970 a distant terminal date (1976) for the end of military rule. Nine points were to be satisfied before a return to civil rule. These included the reorganisation of the armed forces, national reconstruction (repair of war damage), implementation of the National Development Plan, the elimination of corruption, a decision on the creation of new states, a revision of the revenue allocation system, a new constitution, a national census, the organisation of national political parties, and popular elections. This was an ambitious programme, and there was always a high risk that in the intervening period it would be swept aside by political and economic currents. In the event, only national reconstruction and a revision of the revenue allocation system were achieved before the regime was overthrown in August 1975.

In 1973, university lecturers went on strike over pay and conditions of service. The universities backed down, but capitulation turned them into an alienated group. Academics were already smarting from a relative loss of status and political influence compared to senior civil servants. The administration also suffered a setback with the failure to conduct an accurate census. According to the census, national population had risen to 79.7 million, a staggering 43 percent above the inflated figures of a decade earlier; two states had virtually doubled their population. The figures deflated the returns for the Western and South Eastern states to below the 1963 returns and dramatically inflated the returns of the northern states to 72 percent above the 1963 figures.[18] Claims of fraud and ethnic domination were heard again; and in this troubled atmosphere, the government was forced to abandon the results.

Further undermining of the regime's authority was brought about by the almost complete loss of economic and financial control that accompanied the arrival of massive oil revenues following the Organisation of Petroleum Exporting Countries (OPEC) price rise of 1973. As state expenditure increased, so financial indiscipline and corruption within the public economy was intensified. The leadership, both military and civil, proved quite incapable of resisting the demands that came from all quarters with the oil bonanza. Overwhelmed by the sudden oil wealth, the regime's capacity for decisionmaking was undermined, and paralysis set in.

The loss of financial control over the states was compounded by the absence of any firm political control over state governors by the centre. Most governors, who had been in power since 1967, abused their powers and enriched themselves.[19] As the regime progressed, their offices became more politicised and civilianised, making the regime vulnerable. Lauded by sycophantic government-controlled newspapers and by businesspeople who lavished them with praise in order to secure contracts, some governors ran their states like personal fiefdoms. Lifestyles were ostentatious, and outriders moved citizens off the highways long before a governor's cavalcade appeared.

Despite the growing unpopularity of the governors, General Gowon failed to discipline them effectively or to remove them. Gowon's loyalty and respect for his governors never wavered. His tolerance and his trust in his colleagues allowed them great latitude in the running of their administrations. These qualities of respect and trust were well suited to the need for reconciliation at the end of the civil war. They were not so appropriate to the hard political task of providing effective federal leadership and control in peace time.

Serious charges of corruption had come to the fore with the swearing of affidavits against Governor Gomwalk of Benue Plateau state and Joseph Tarka, the federal commissioner also from the same state.[20] Tarka resigned his position, but Police Commisioner Gomwalk, supported by Gowon, remained as governor. This severely damaged Gowon's reputation as he was identified with Benue Plateau state, and Governor Gomwalk was a personal friend.[21] When the regime fell, the Belgore Commission of Inquiry documented the great extent of corruption emanating from the governor and his entourage. Indeed, only two governors were exonerated by subsequent inquiries from charges that they had illegally enriched themselves. The danger of allowing state governors to stay in power for a long time, so that they could build up their personal powers and patronage, was not lost on later regimes, which changed them regularly.

On 1 October 1974 an indefinite postponement of the return to civil rule was announced. The regime had lost popularity and was on the defensive. This postponement united the government's opponents and contributed to its downfall.

Billy Dudley has suggested that as early as late 1971 the choice of handing over power to an elected government was ruled out by those in power.[22] The alternative that was argued at that time by senior bureaucrats and some military officers was a national movement. The aim was to preserve the impetus of what a leading civil servant, Allison Ayida, called the national revolution.[23] It gave priority to the implementation of the Second Plan and economic transformation. Opposition to this idea came from the intelligentsia and the ex-politicians. According to Dudley, it was the northern intelligentsia, who included what later came to be known as the "Kaduna mafia" and who had close links with northern army officers, who really put an end to the idea of a national movement.[24] The intelligentsia were concerned about southern influence and especially the power of the permanent secretaries that surrounded General Gowon, and they began to mobilise far north elements of the military hierarchy and the local government functionaries against the regime.

The "Kaduna mafia" was a term popularised by a journalist, Mvendaga Jibo, after his dismissal from the *New Nigerian* newspaper in 1976. It became common currency in the late 1970s. It was not meant to convey a criminal mafia in the literal Italian sense of the word. It referred instead to an informal network of younger well-educated technocrats and professionals who acted as a political pressure group that was distinct from the former NPC politicians, their aristocratic supporters, and the most senior northern civil servants. Almost all members of the group had experience of the northern public service, which had become highly politicised with the demise of the politicians.[25] Kaduna, the former colonial and regional capital, was a second home where members chose to live and build residences. Kaduna was symbolic of a northern identity and aspiration that stood above communities of origin or any of the newly created states.[26] Members were linked together through ties of kinship, marriage, religion, and the common experience of schooling and public service.

After the creation of states in 1967, the network identity of the mafia began to take shape. Northern state institutions provided the basis for the exercise of administrative and bureaucratic power. Control of these institutions allowed the operation of an extensive network of patronage, recruitment, and influence. These agencies included the *New Nigerian* newspaper; the Broadcasting Corporation of Northern Nigeria (later the Federal Radio Corporation of Nigeria, Kaduna [FRCN]); Nigeria Television Authority, Kaduna; the Northern Nigeria Development Corporation; and the Bank of the North.

A. D. Yahaya has suggested that the Kaduna mafia was to reach the height of its power under the Obasanjo administration, when it successfully claimed to represent a northern interest at the federal level. Influence was exercised through participation in the affairs of the Constitution Drafting Committee and the Constituent Assembly, through appointments to various panels and boards of parastatal bodies, and through an intellectual input in the formation of the National Party of Nigeria. Among the core members of the group during this period were Adamu Ciroma, Mahmud Tukur, Ibrahim Tahir, Mamman Daura, Turi Mohammadu, Aliko Mohammed, Ango Abdullahi, and Suleiman Kumo. Shehu Musa Yar'adua, chief of staff, Supreme Headquarters, was a strategic military ally.

A scandal over cement supplies and the manner in which the Udoji wage and salary increases were awarded provided further evidence of the incapacity of the regime to govern. In early 1975, the Ministry of Defence ordered 16 million metric tons of cement for a single year for the federal barracks project.[27] To put this in perspective, the total cargo handled by Nigerian ports in 1974/75 was only 4.49 million metric tons. The cement tonnage had been grossly inflated by the rush for lucrative contracts by influential and powerful Nigerian middlemen. Port congestion had begun to build up by mid-1974, reaching a peak between July 1975 and February 1976 when over 200 ships were waiting off Lagos to unload. The distribution of the cement contracts by the Ministry of Defence came under scrutiny and together with the port congestion severely compromised the competence of the regime.

By the middle of 1975, attacks on the administration had become frequent and open. The *New Nigerian* newspaper based in Kaduna, which represented the views of the northern intelligentsia, prepared the ground for a coup. Opposition to the regime took on an increasingly religious tone. As Yusufu Bala Usman put it, General Gowon, "the former 'good northerner' from Barewa College, Zaria, soon came to be the Christian missionary's boy from Pankshin."[28] The former grand kadi of the Northern Region, Alhaji Abubakar Gumi, played a role here. Using the media, he attacked the moral decadence of Nigerian society and portrayed the Gowon regime as anti-Islamic in its nature. In the end, Gowon was isolated even from fellow Plateau officers, and he was removed painlessly on 30 July 1975 while attending an Organisation of African Unity (OAU) meeting in Uganda.

In charting the paralysis that afflicted the regime, the loss of political control over the states, the corruption, and the financial and economic chaos, it is easy to lose sight of other measures that the administration initiated. I have mentioned the early creation of states and the reform of the revenue allocation system. Other measures included a more nationalist oil policy (partially thwarted by comprador bureaucrats), the Nigerian Enterprises Promotion Decree, the start of the National Youth Service Corps, a low-cost housing scheme, preparation for Universal Primary Education, seven new universities and university colleges, and important changes in agricultural policy (see Chapter 7).

It was, too, Nigerian diplomacy, in which General Gowon played a leading part, which was responsible for the creation of the Economic Community of West African States (ECOWAS) in 1975. For many, however, Gowon's close relations with the West represented a subservience that affronted popular nationalism.

The Murtala Mohammed–Obasanjo Regime: The Return to Civil Rule

The new head of state, General Murtala Mohammed, who was commander of the Second Division during the civil war and commissioner for communications under Gowon, was not an active participant in the coup. He was chosen because he was thought by younger officers to have drive and determination.[29]

The new regime immediately embarked on a burst of activity, releasing a more radical brand of nationalism than that experienced in the aftermath of the civil war. Although the regime was to last only six months before Murtala was killed in an abortive coup attempt, it started many important reforms including items left over from Gowon's nine-point programme. The reforms included a second round of the indigenisation exercise, the reorganisation of the trade unions, local government reform, the creation of new states, and a geopolitical decision to move the federal capital from Lagos to Abuja near the centre of the country. Strong leadership and active government galvanised the nation into action and elicited a popular support that had not diminished by the time of Murtala's death. A number of radicals from the universities were co-opted and participated in the inquiries and commissions that the regime set up. This did not mean that the regime had any socialist tendency, nor did it stop the regime from taking a hard line with the trade union movement. It did, however, bring a strong anti-imperialist rhetoric to the conduct of foreign affairs and helped secure the rapid recognition of the Movimento Popular de Liberticão (MPLA) regime in Angola after South African troops had invaded the country.

The regime set out a timetable for a return to civil rule that included a Constitution Drafting Committee to be set up in 1977, followed by a Constituent Assembly in 1978, and culminated in a series of elections in 1979. The former governors of the states were sacked and investigations started into their assets.

The civil service was purged, and altogether some 10,000 persons lost their jobs in the public sector and universities. This was the first time job security in the civil service had been challenged, and it led to a loss of morale within the service. Senior civil servants lost power as outsiders were brought in to advise the government. Executive power shifted away from the permanent secretaries in the ministries towards the cabinet office that was run by Brigadier Olusegun Obasanjo, the chief of staff, Supreme Headquarters, who acted as number two in the regime.

The purge helped to speed up the movement of senior bureaucrats at a relatively young age to more lucrative, higher-status positions in the private sector. Some took directorships, and others entered into business on their own account. They were to be followed later by retired army officers. Technocrats, too, moved to the private sector, disillusioned by geographical apartheid and by the tight control that generalist administrators exercised over them. These movements contributed to a decline in administrative efficiency that had begun with the rapid expansion of the state and its increased responsibilities. In the longer term, these movements to the private sector, together with the loss of security and status attached to public sector employment and the fall in oil revenues that cut away the basis for state expansion were to contribute to a perceptible shift in attitude among the propertied classes in favour of a less prominent role for the state in the economy.

In February 1976, Murtala Mohammed and Governor Ibrahim Taiwo of Kwara state were killed in an unsuccessful coup attempt led by Lt-Colonel Bukar Dimka that implicated Major-General I. B. Bisalla and ex-Governor Joseph Gomwalk. The death of Murtala profoundly shocked and grieved the nation, and subsequently the memory of Nigeria's popular leader acquired a passionate reverence and became a touchstone for patriotic ideals. The coup plotters, who were mainly middle-ranking officers from Plateau and southern Zaria, were executed. General Obasanjo took over as head of state. Lt-Colonel Shehu Yar'adua, an indigene of Katsina, became chief of staff, Supreme Headquarters, a move that involved his accelerated promotion above other senior officers. This secured a powerful position for a representative of the far north. The military remained cohesive and committed to handing over power to a civilian government.

The Obasanjo regime appeared to lack the energy and decisiveness of Murtala's leadership. This image was deceptive. First, most of the reforms initiated under Murtala still had to be carried through. Second, the regime faced a much more serious economic situation than that of 1975–1976. Last, as the process of constitution-making got under way, so did open political discussion and debate that was outside the immediate control of the military.

Radical elements from the universities who had some influence in the brief period of Murtala's rule were now excluded. The loss of radical influence was most clearly seen in foreign policy. Here the self-styled foreign policy elite centred on the Nigerian Institute of International Affairs (NIIA) under the directorship of Bolaji Akinyemi gained influence. It was instrumental in securing good relations with the Carter administration in the United States through the offices of Ambassador Andrew Young. For a brief period, the United States consulted with Nigeria about African policy. For the NIIA, this meant that Nigeria had acquired middle-power status. For the radical left, it constituted a return to subservience.[30] Progressive intellectuals were also very critical of the Festival of Black Arts and Culture (FESTAC) held in Lagos and Kaduna in 1977.[31] Here artistic endeavour collided with an overbearing bureaucracy and was nearly strangled by a voracious elite that gorged itself on cultural displays and struggled to get festival contracts.

Trade Union Reform

The restructuring of the trade union movement had been mooted under the Gowon government, but the government was never in a strong enough position to embark on reforms.[32] Instead, it was the union movement itself that began to move towards a central labour organisation. In December 1975, the leaders of the four competing trade union centres (United Labour Congress, Nigerian Trade Union Congress, Labour Unity Front, Nigerian Workers Council) overcame their differences and founded the Nigerian Labour Congress. The Mohammed government was totally opposed to this development, fearing that a radical trade union leadership would emerge. On the eve of the congress, nearly 200 arrests were made, and in February 1976 a panel was appointed to probe the trade union leadership under Justice S. D. Adebiyi. The government then proceeded to subordinate the labour movement and subject it to a process of restructuring controlled by the state. As Yusuf Bangura has argued, the government was able to do this because of its radical populist support.[33]

When the Adebiyi report came out in 1977, eleven trade unionists were banned from further trade union activity.[34] In February 1977, all existing trade unions were dissolved as a prelude to elections to the restructured unions. In addition, under Decree 27 of 1976, strikes were prohibited in essential services like banking and oil. A Productivity, Prices and Incomes Board was set up (1977), providing a mechanism for smaller, more frequent changes in public sector pay that succeeded in breaking the past pattern of periodic commissions, major awards, and strikes.

The National Executive Council of the Nigerian Labour Congress was launched in February 1978. In 1979, there were 42 affiliated unions, compared with over 1,000 before the reorganisation. The effect of the restructuring on trade union power was ambiguous and uncertain. Some observers saw the change as the start of incorporation of the trade union movement by the state. Others welcomed it as an opportunity for workers to unite and form a radical political force. This latter diagnosis was to prove more accurate.

State Creation, Revenue Allocation, and Local Government Reform

Following the Report of the Panel on State Creation, a further seven new states were created in February 1976: four in the north, two in the west, and one in the east.[35] Two of the panel's recommendations for new states were rejected. Demands for state creation centred on the need for access to government resources in areas that felt relatively deprived or discriminated against. The panel came to the conclusion that political stability could not be guaranteed unless new states were created. As Dudley noted, the breakup of the Western state into three (Ogun, Ondo, Oyo) and the East Central state into two (Anambra, Imo), meant that more state resources would flow to areas that were already advanced economically.[36] But overall, the creation of new states brought a more even spread of state resources and greater participation in government. The problem was that there appeared to be no end to the political demand for more states, underpinned as it was by easy access to federal funds.

The recommendations of the Aboyade Committee on Revenue Allocation were debated in the Constituent Assembly but not acted on.[37] The recommended criteria for the distribution of revenue to the states were, as Pius Okigbo pointed out, too sophisticated and unworkable in practice.[38] Some recommendations from the report were taken up later. The 1979 constitution included a Federation Account and made provision for a statutory share of revenues for local government councils. The system of revenue allocation eventually adopted in 1981 following the report of the Okigbo Commission included a Special Grants Account for the states.[39] Revenue effort was introduced as one of the criteria for allocating revenue to the states as an incentive to raise more revenue locally.

After considerable consultation, local government reforms were introduced. The idea was to create a uniform third tier of government with elected councils. All councils were obliged to have a majority of members elected (directly or indirectly) and to elect their own chairperson. Traditional rulers were assigned a symbolic and advisory role only. The councils would get more autonomy from state governments and get more funds. Initially, the federal government gave the local governments generous grants. Later, 10 percent of the federal statutory allocation was assigned to them, together with funds from the state governments.

The Crisis of 1978

The nadir of the regime's fortunes was reached in April-May 1978 when the full magnitude of the country's balance-of-payments crisis became apparent. Cuts in educational expenditure began in 1977 with the federal government attempting to shift the enormous cost of the UPE programme down to the states. In 1978, university students reacted to increased tuition fees and food and accommodation costs with a boycott of lectures and a campaign to unseat Commissioner for Education Lt-Colonel Ambrose Ali. Protests at Ahmadu Bello University, where tension was already high over the issue of the proposed introduction of a Sharia Court of Appeal at the federal level, led to army intervention and the death of several students. Later there were widespread protests and demonstrations around the country involving university students and secondary school students who had parental support. In Lagos on 29 April, demonstrators were joined by lumpen elements, and there was widespread civil disorder. A customs house in the Ikorodu Road was burnt down and government vehicles destroyed. University lecturers who allegedly instigated or fanned the crisis were summarily retired, and two university vice-chancellors were forced to resign. The National Union of Nigerian Students was proscribed.

To compound the government's problems, these events took place at a time of heightened religious tension over the issue of a Sharia Court of Appeal at the federal level. Muslim members of the Constituent Assembly wanted a Sharia Court of Appeal entrenched in the constitution alongside the Federal Court of Appeal. Members of the Kaduna mafia were prominent in pushing for this provision.[40] Christian members of the assembly, led by representatives of minority groups from Gongola, Benue, and Plateau states, vigorously rejected the proposal. Ninety-two Muslim members of the Constituent Assembly boycotted proceedings from 2 to 24 April over the issue. Eventually the move was defeated, but not before General Obasanjo had taken members of the Supreme Military Council down to the Constituent Assembly and warned that religious divisions posed a threat to the political stability of the nation.[41]

Defeat over the Sharia issue had immediate political implications for the National Party of Nigeria, which was then in its early stages of formation as the Northern Movement.[42] It swung the political advantage within the emerging party away from the young northern politicians of the Kaduna mafia towards the Old Brigade of experienced politicians.

The 1979 Constitution

The new constitution evolved after lengthy discussion in the Constitution Drafting Committee (CDC) and the Constituent Assembly. Later, the military made seventeen last-minute amendments to the draft constitution, inserting the Land Use Decree and the National Security Organisation (NSO) in the constitution. From the start of the CDC, the military indicated its preference for an executive president, for broad-based political parties that would not be confined to any section of the country, and for a cabinet that reflected the "federal character" of the country. The CDC was largely made up of academics and lawyers and was an all-male committee. The Constituent Assembly included more representatives of the commercial and business class and former politicians and commissioners.

Two leading radicals, Bala Usman and Segun Osoba from the history departments of Ahmadu Bello University and the University of Ife, respectively, had been co-opted into the CDC. Predictably, the two academics did not agree with the draft constitutional proposals put forward by the majority of members of the CDC. They therefore submitted their own proposals that came to be known as the Minority Report. The report made far-reaching suggestions on all aspects of Nigeria's political economy, including a comprehensive attempt to redefine citizenship and indigeneity as a means of depoliticising ethnicity. But when the Constituent Assembly met to debate, amend, and ratify the work of the CDC, only the majority report was presented to it.

Although the constitution was essentially a bourgeois one, it was not a charter for the unfettered accumulation of private capital. It was shaped by the ideas and preoccupations of the dominant classes who made up the legislators. Four features of the constitution will be highlighted here.[43]

First, the constitution embodied the principle of an executive presidency. Support for this principle was widespread and stemmed from the strong attraction of the U.S. model to Nigerians and dissatisfaction with the parliamentary system of government in the First Republic. The experience of political instability associated with the dismissal of the Western Region premier by the regional governor and the refusal of the premier to accept dismissal in 1962 had not been forgotten. There was also the clash between the president and prime minister over the conduct of the 1964 federal elections, which contributed to the demise of the First Republic. It was felt that a presidential system would give a focal point of loyalty and the leadership that the country needed.

Compared to the U.S. constitution, the new Nigerian constitution restrained the powers of the president in a number of ways. Thus the president was obliged to consult over certain matters with other bodies like the National Defence Council and the National Economic Council. The legislature also had certain powers with respect to the president that were not present in the U.S. constitution. Thus the conduct of foreign relations was subject to greater legislative control than in the United States.

Second, though the constitution owed much to the U.S. constitution, the extent to which it guaranteed freedom of private enterprise as a legally enforceable right was much less than in the United States of America. The constitution also omitted a guarantee of the right of individuals to own or hold property. Also omitted was the requirement that private property can be acquired compulsorily only for a public purpose with just compensation. In general, the stress was on the duties of the state towards the individual rather than on the rights of the individual. This emphasis reflected more general views about the state held since the late colonial period. The state was the prime mover of development, and state patronage and regulation were seen to support private business rather than impede it.

Third, under the mixed economy philosophy, the state was to own and manage the major sectors of the economy. This position was basically an acceptance of the current situation. The major sectors were not clearly defined, and there was ambiguity in cases like banking where state ownership ranged from 100 percent to 60 percent and where management was not appointed by the state. In the general provisions of the constitution, the state was required to exercise power to bring about greater social justice through redistribution, a planned and balanced economy, and avoidance of the concentration of wealth.

Fourth, a concern to encourage national integration was seen in the constant reference to the need for federal character in the constitution and in the electoral provisions for the parties. According to the constitution, "the composition of the Government of the Federation or any of its agencies and the conduct of its affairs shall be carried out in such manner as to reflect the federal character of Nigeria and the need to promote national unity, and also to command national loyalty thereby ensuring that there shall be no predominance of persons from a few States or from a few ethnic or other sectional groups in that government or in any of its agencies."[44] In addition, "the President shall appoint at least one Minister from each State, who shall be an indigene of such State."[45] This was an attempt to secure the even, though not necessarily equitable, distribution of federal offices and resources throughout the nation.

With the exception of a quota system introduced in 1961 for the recruitment of the officer corps of the military, the principle had not really been publicly endorsed before. The aim was to moderate the struggle for control at the centre and prevent domination, or fear of domination, by any particular ethnic group, thus promoting political stability. Among the areas to which the principle was to be applied were the election of the president, the formation of the political parties, the composition of the cabinet, the recruitment of the armed forces, and the establishment of federal commissions and councils. As commentators pointed out, the operation of the principle could prove divisive in practice[46] and impede the application of bureaucratic principles.[47]

The Parties and the 1979 Elections

The 1979 elections, which completed the military disengagement from government, were a considerable achievement, though they were marred by controversy over the election of the president, Alhaji Shehu Shagari. Where there was electoral rigging, it was not on a scale sufficient to call into question the overall results. It must be recalled, however, that from the outset organised labour was barred by the military from participating in or funding party politics. This exclusion was made to reassure the propertied classes that their interests were secure. This heavily qualified conception of democracy effectively undermined any prospect of a socialist party with the funds and capacity to organise on a national basis. University lecturers and civil servants were also excluded unless they resigned their appointments.

Five major parties contested the elections. The National Party of Nigeria (NPN), the Unity Party of Nigeria (UPN), the Nigerian People's Party

(NPP), the People's Redemption Party (PRP), and the Great Nigeria People's Party (GNPP). The parties can be placed on a political spectrum from left to right, with the PRP on the left wing, the UPN left of centre, the GNPP in the centre, and the NPP and NPN on the right. Yet with the exception of the PRP, which was rooted in opposition to hereditary power and privilege, ideological differences between the parties were not marked. The elections were not generally fought on the basis of competing manifestos. The only issue that really surfaced strongly in the election debates was education, where the NPN felt compelled to respond to the UPN promise of free education at all levels with its own promise of free and qualitative education.

The NPN won the presidency and also secured most seats in the Senate (36 of 95) and in the House of Representatives (168 of 449), though it had no overall majority. The NPN also won the governorship and controlled the state assembly in seven states (Sokoto, Niger, Bauchi, Benue, Cross River, Kwara, and Rivers). In Kaduna state, control was split, with the NPN controlling the state assembly and the PRP winning the gubernatorial election. The PRP victory by a small margin in Kaduna state was a surprising result. It was helped by the combining of the non-NPN vote behind the PRP gubernatorial candidate and by electoral vigilance that prevented malpractices in the counting of the vote. The victory was never accepted by the NPN.

The nature of the NPN will be examined in much greater detail in the Chapter 4. Here it will suffice to say that though the NPN had its original base of support in the far north of the country, it was not a regional party in the manner of the old NPC. Over one-half its nonpresidential votes were secured outside the northern states. The party had very considerable support from minority groups across the country, and in its heartland it failed to gain Kano state and the governorship of Kaduna state, reflecting the breakdown of the old regional political hegemony that Ahmadu Bello, the Sardauna of Sokoto, had so assiduously promoted as premier of the Northern Region.

The NPN was followed in the Senate and House of Representatives by the UPN with 28 and 111 seats, respectively. The UPN also took five states (Lagos, Oyo, Ogun, Ondo, and Bendel). The UPN under the leadership of Chief Obafemi Awolowo, was generally recognised as the best organised of the parties. Drawing on former Action Group loyalties among the Yoruba, it succeeded in blunting subethnic strategies employed by the NPN in Yorubaland and managed to extend its appeal into areas within the former Western Region that had been held by the NCNC and NNDP.[48] Much of the UPN's support derived from the strong welfare component in its programme, especially the promise of free education at all levels. Strenuous efforts to extend the support for the party in other parts of the country met with very little success.

The NPP took three states (Anambra, Imo, and Plateau) and won 16 and 78 seats in the Senate and House of Representatives, respectively. The NPP had its origins in an attempt to form a coalition between minority politicians from the Mid-West, Middle Belt, and east, former NCNC politicians in Igboland, and a group headed by Alhaji Waziri Ibrahim, a wealthy businessman from Borno. The late decision of Nnamdi Azikiwe, the veteran nationalist politician and former president of the republic, to join the NPP and enter the presidential race undermined these plans. Prior to the entry of Azikiwe, the Igbo vote was largely undecided, and the NPN appeared to be making considerable advances. Now the great majority of the Igbo vote coalesced behind Azikiwe and his clients on the principle that their election was the most effective way of getting adequate Igbo representation at the centre. As in the western states, many prominent individuals who had earlier declared for the NPN remained with that party.

The GNPP headed by Waziri Ibrahim was formed after the NPP had come under the influence of Nnamdi Azikiwe. Waziri Ibrahim, a former minister in the First Republic from a notable Borno family, was able to finance a strong campaign. The party provided a stiff challenge to the NPN in parts of the northern states where it played on local rivalries. The party was especially hard hit by rigging at the polls. Nevertheless, it won two states (Borno and Gongola) and secured 8 seats in the Senate and 43 seats in the House of Representatives.

The PRP won two governorships (Kano and Kaduna) and controlled the legislature in Kano state. In the Senate and House of Representatives elections, it secured 7 and 49 seats, respectively. The leadership of the party was divided from the outset. The presidential candidate, Alhaji Aminu Kano, the former NEPU leader, whose asceticism and populist humanism commanded a wide following, had first attempted to join forces with the NPN. When his aspirations to power within the NPN were thwarted, he joined forces with younger, more socialist-inclined activists who were prominent in the formation of the PRP. The tension between these groups was never resolved, and the PRP governors (Balarabe Musa in Kaduna and Abubakar Rimi in Kano) who wanted to confront the NPN with a common front of progressives split away from the Aminu Kano faction of the PRP.

Right at the end of the electoral process, the military and the judiciary altered the common sense interpretation of the electoral rules to allow Shehu Shagari, the NPN candidate, to take the presidency on the first ballot. Shagari had secured a majority of the votes cast (5.6 million) against his closest rival, Chief Awolowo (4.9 million). Controversy surrounded the second requirement for electoral victory. Had Shagari secured 25 percent of the votes cast in two-thirds of the states? Was "two-thirds of the states" to be interpreted as 13 of the 19 states, or was it 12 states and 25 percent of two-thirds of the votes cast in the 13th state? The latter interpretation prevailed and this allowed Shagari to claim the necessary votes in Kano state. This decision was bitterly contested by Chief Awolowo and his supporters in the UPN. President Shagari was not recognised as president by the UPN, and the five states controlled by the UPN adopted a policy of total noncooperation with the Shagari government.

Conclusion

The greater administrative and financial centralisation of the federal government over more than a decade of military rule did not produce a federal authority with a strong administrative or political capacity. The power of the centre fluctuated.

Once the civil war was over, the military rapidly lost its corrective position. This was most clearly seen in the loss of political authority by the centre over the states, where the rule of the governors became personalised and politicised. It was also apparent in the loss of financial control and discipline in the public economy. Under the Mohammed/Obasanjo regime, central authority was partially restored through stronger military control. In the early days of the regime, a populist nationalism provided the support needed for reform. Yet in the economic sphere, there was no reorganisation of state projects or control over levels of state expenditure. The decline in financial discipline continued. Corruption, too, was widespread, though its extent was not revealed because of a tacit understanding between the military and the incoming politicians that there would be no investigations.

Military rule was not heavily authoritarian. It was leavened by a civilian presence in government. The press was relatively free. The return to civil rule and the demobilisation of the army were considerable achievements. Yet the rule of law was formally suspended and the government ruled by decree.[49] When the judiciary challenged the military in 1970, the Supreme Court was overruled by Decree No. 28 (Supremacy and Enforcement of Powers), that declared null and void any law that challenged a decree or edict. There were arrests and detentions under a decree that gave the army and police powers of detention. This decree was used to harass journalists and critics. There were also many incidents of clashes between military and civilians with loss of life.

One reason for the weakness of the centre was the basic misalignment between political power and financial responsibility, which tended to undermine the federal system. The federal structure gave the states considerable political autonomy from the centre. At the same time, the states raised very little revenue of their own, relying instead on transfers from the federal government. This situation gave the states every incentive to get more funds from the centre, encouraged financial irresponsibility, and set up strong forces for the creation of new states. Only a strong political authority could resist these pressures, and the exercise of this power would immediately bring the centre into conflict with the states.

A further reason for weakness was the strength of the pressures on the centre heightened by the large centralised revenues, involving a struggle for a share in federal resources and representation at the centre by individuals, communities, and regions. These distributive pressures on the centre were very strong. They took many forms, including revenue allocation, state creation, the struggle for federal contracts, and competition over the location of federal projects. These distributive struggles placed constraints on economic management and the productive use of resources with adverse consequences for economic growth.

Another reason for the loss of control at the centre was intrinsic to the character of state revenues. Oil revenues were a windfall that flowed directly to central government. They did not require the taxation of personal incomes, farm incomes, or private property. Indeed, large oil revenues reduced the political and economic significance of taxpayers. Thus political pressures that could check the increases in state expenditure demanded by those with access to state power were largely absent. The pressures both to maximise current oil revenues and to increase state expenditures were compelling and immediate.

It would be misleading if our emphasis on the weakness of the federal government created the impression that there were few federal initiatives in this period. There were many. Richard Joseph in his recent study underestimated the capacity of the military to pursue national policies and reform state institutions and structures in this period.[50] This underestimation stems from his insistence on the centrality of prebendal politics—political competition for state office to get direct material benefits. He argued that these political forces grew steadily stronger during the 1970s with the expansion of the state, fragmenting the state, sharpening ethnic and regional identities, and blunting state initiatives.

Apart from the major reforms of the revenue allocation system, state creation, and local government, there were national policies for education, housing, broadcasting, the development of infrastructure, and the indigenisation of business enterprise. There was, too, the shift of certain fiscal powers from the states to the centre. Some of the most important shifts in policy occurred in agriculture, where the marketing board system was dismantled and pricing of crops brought under central control.

It can also be argued that federal power was used to some extent to counteract uneven development, to equalise opportunities among the states and communities, and to ensure national integration. Among the measures taken were the creation of more states, the changes in the system of revenue allocation, the attempt to rectify the educational imbalance between the northern and southern states through the UPE scheme (see Chapter 6), and the expansion of the Unity schools (Federal Government Colleges), the National Youth Service Corps, and the dispersion of federal industrial projects away from Lagos.

The military shared with the bureaucrats a desire to strengthen the centre and enhance national integration. They also shared a belief in the primacy of the state as the agent of development, though this pervasive idea did not find strong expression in planned national development. It was manifest in a weak form in the ideology of bureaucratic developmentalism and the rhetoric of the mixed economy in which support for private accumulation was mixed with state intervention to promote industrialisation and national control of the economy. There was no strong class alliance rooted in the appropriation of the state apparatus and the control of state enterprises. The strength of the ruling groups was sapped by financial indiscipline; tensions within the public service between administrators, professionals, and technocrats; and the attractions of the private sector. State office was used to build up personal wealth in order to secure a basis for private accumulation in the future.

The fact that a state ideology (capitalist or statist) was not strongly developed owed much to the nature of the dominant classes and the political divisions among them. Those who held state power were well aware of the ideological vacuum. It was, for example, a matter of concern for the senior civil servants, army officers, and academics who met at a Conference on National Development in Zaria in 1972. It led to attempts to fill the vacuum from above by inserting liberal democratic principles into the Second Development Plan. The proposals of the Public Service Review Commission under Chief Jerome Udoji attempted to infuse the whole public service with ideological principles drawn from U.S. corporate management, an exercise that was doomed to failure from the outset.

By the end of the decade, with a party in power that supported private enterprise and foreign capital and the adoption of a U.S.- style presidential constitution, it seemed that a more concerted attempt to create the conditions for the capitalist growth of the economy was in prospect. As we shall see later, this was not to be the case.

Notes

1. R. A. Joseph, *Democracy and Prebendal Politics in Nigeria: The Rise and Fall of the Second Republic* (Cambridge: Cambridge University Press, 1987), p. 67.
2. *Daily Times*, 19 and 20 March, 1973.

3. *The Third National Development Plan, 1975–80,* vol. 1, Central Planning Office, Lagos, 1975.

4. A. Joda, "Education in Nigeria 1971–75," in M. O. Kayode and Y. B. Usman, eds., *The Economic and Social Development of Nigeria,* vol. 2, Proceedings of the National Conference on Nigeria Since Independence, March 1983 (Zaria, 1985), p. 234.

5. A. B. Ahmed, "The Free Education Issue," *New Nigerian,* 23 November 1978.

6. B. J. Dudley, *An Introduction to Nigerian Government and Politics* (London: Macmillan, 1982), p. 321.

7. Dudley, *An Introduction to Nigerian Government,* p. 106.

8. *Report of the Interim Revenue Allocation Review Commission* (the Dina Report), Lagos, 1969.

9. *Report of the Presidential Commission on Revenue Allocation* (the Okigbo Report) (Lagos: Federal Government Press, 1980), p. 22.

10. For the effects of this change on state shares, see S. E. Oyovbaire, "The Politics of Revenue Allocation," in K. Panter-Brick, ed., *Soldiers and Oil* (London: Frank Cass, 1978), pp. 228–229.

11. A. O. Phillips, "Three Decades of Inter-Governmental Financial Relationships in the Federation of Nigeria," paper presented at the Conference on Intergovernmental Relations in Nigeria, University of Ife, February 1979, table 7.

12. Phillips, "Three Decades," table 5.

13. For some discussion, see *Report of the Presidential Commission,* 1980, pp. 48–51 and table 4.7.

14. C. Achebe, "Of Roads and Budgets," An Open Letter to the Federal Military Government, *Nsukkascope* 6 (June 1978), p. 89.

15. O. Oyediran, ed., *Survey of Nigerian Affairs, 1975,* Nigerian Institute of International Affairs (Ibadan: Oxford University Press, 1978), pp. 5, 123.

16. Oyediran, *Survey of Nigerian Affairs, 1975,* p. 130.

17. O. Aboyade, "The Role of the Federal Government in the Development of the States," *Report of the Seminar on the Second National Development Plan,* Federal Ministry of Information, Lagos, 1971.

18. J. I. Elaigwu, *Gowon* (Ibadan: West Books, 1985), p. 204.

19. *Federal Military Government's Views on the Report of the Federal Assets Investigation Panel 1975,* Federal Ministry of Information, 1976.

20. I. Campbell, "Army Reorganisation and Military Withdrawal," in K. Panter-Brick, ed., *Soldiers and Oil* (London: Frank Cass, 1978), pp. 69–70.

21. M. J. Dent, "Corrective Government: Military Rule in Perspective," in K. Panter-Brick, ed., *Soldiers and Oil* (London: Frank Cass, 1978), p. 113.

22. Dudley, *An Introduction to Nigerian Government,* p. 94.

23. A. A. Ayida, "The National Revolution, 1966–76," presidential address to the Nigerian Economic Society, 1973.

24. Dudley, *An Introduction to Nigerian Government,* pp. 97–98.

25. A. D. Yahaya, "Nigerian Public Administration Under Military Rule: The Experience of the Northern States," in L. Adamolekun, ed., *Nigerian Public Administration, 1960–1980* (Ibadan: Heinemann, 1985).

26. See the glorification of Kaduna by Ibrahim Tahir in "Verdict Kaduna's Role," *New Nigerian,* 30 March 1968, quoted in J. N. Paden, *Ahmadu Bello, Sardauna of Sokoto* (London: Hodder and Stoughton, 1986), p. 581.

27. Oyediran, *Survey of Nigerian Affairs, 1975*, pp. 71–78.

28. Y. B. Usman, *The Manipulation of Religion in Nigeria, 1977–1987* (Kaduna: Vanguard, 1987), pp. 71–94.

29. For details of the coup, see Campbell, "Army Reorganisation," pp. 77–80.

30. Y. B. Usman, "The Return to Subservience," in *For the Liberation of Nigeria: Essays and Lectures 1969–1978* (London: New Beacon Books, 1979), p. 185–198.

31. Femi Osofisan has vividly exposed the tensions underlying FESTAC in his "FESTAC and the Heritage of Ambiguity," in O. Oyediran, ed., *Survey of Nigerian Affairs, 1976/77*, (Ibadan: Nigerian Institute of International Affairs and Macmillan, 1981), pp. 32–42.

32. Y. Bangura, "Nationalism, Accumulation and Labour Subordination in Nigeria: 1970–1978," paper presented to the Annual Conference of the Nigerian Political Science Association, Ilorin, May 1985.

33. Bangura, "Nationalism, Accumulation and Labour Subordination," pp. 40–41.

34. *Federal Military Government's Views on the Report of the Tribunal of Inquiry into the Activities of Trade Unions*, Lagos: Federal Ministry of Information, 1977.

35. *Federal Government's Views on the Report of the Panel on Creation of States*, Lagos: Federal Ministry of Information, 1976.

36. Dudley, *An Introduction to Nigerian Government*, p. 110.

37. *Report of the Technical Committee on Revenue Allocation* (the Aboyade Committee), mimeo, Lagos, 1978.

38. P. Okigbo, "The Big Debate on Revenue Allocation," *New Nigerian*, 6 and 7 June, 1978.

39. *Report of the Presidential Commission on Revenue Allocation*, 1980.

40. Joseph, *Democracy*, pp. 135–136.

41. *Guardian* (Lagos), 29 November 1988.

42. Joseph, *Democracy*, pp. 135–136.

43. In the following section, I have drawn on the work of Ben Nwabueze. B. O. Nwabueze, *The Presidential Constitution of Nigeria* (London: Hurst, 1982).

44. *The Constitution of the Federal Republic of Nigeria*, Article 14 (4) (Lagos: Federal Ministry of Information, 1979.

45. *The Constitution*, Article 135 (3).

46. A.H.M. Kirk-Greene, "Ethnic Engineering and the 'Federal Character' of Nigeria: Boon of Contentment or Bone of Contention," *Ethnic and Racial Studies* 6/4 (1983), pp. 457–476.

47. A. Gboyega, "The 'Federal Character' or the Attempt to Create Representative Bureaucracies in Nigeria," *International Review of Administrative Science* 84/1 (1984), p. 23.

48. Here, and in my sketch of the NPP that follows, I have drawn on the work of Richard Joseph. Joseph, *Democracy*, chaps. 7 and 8.

49. For conflicting views on military rule, see O. Obasanjo and Folarin Shyllon, "The Demise of the Rule of Law in Nigeria Under the Military: Two Points of View," Institute of African Studies, Ibadan, 1980.

50. Joseph, *Democracy*, chap. 6.

4

A Hollow Democracy: Civil Rule, 1979–1983

The National Party of Nigeria

The immediate origin of the ruling National Party of Nigeria lay in the National Movement in the Constituent Assembly. It was made up of old politicians linked to the Northern People's Congress, new politicians, and businesspeople. Power within the party lay in the north, and southern elements were co-opted via negotiation into the party.[1] Within the northern group, there was a division between the younger professional intelligentsia and the older feudal and commercial elements that were close to President Shagari. This division was apparent in the struggle for the NPN presidential nomination. The candidate of the intelligentsia, or Kaduna mafia, Adamu Ciroma, a former governor of the Central Bank, was defeated by Shehu Shagari, former minister under the First Republic and federal commissioner for finance under Gowon. The division within the NPN was to resurface in 1983 when the frustration of the mafia at the incompetence of the regime led them to try to make an alliance with Chief Awolowo.

Richard Joseph has described the period of civil rule as a return to tripartism, a reference to the three major parties of the First Republic that mobilised support on an ethnic basis from the three regional blocks.[2] This formulation exaggerates the extent to which the NPN drew support from a northern block and the extent to which the party acted as a vehicle for the political dominance of northern interests during the Second Republic. Although elements of the tripartite pattern remained, the creation of states and the size of the federal resources at the centre altered the structural conditions under which power was mobilised. The NPN was not a regional party like the NPC, which was completely identified with northern interests. It was much more a national party in which power was dispersed and fragmented, and in which northern elements exercised rather weak control.

The breakdown of regional hegemony in the north affected the capacity of the party to wield power at the centre. The political fragmentation of the north is demonstrated by the fact that after the elections of 1979, four states and the governorship of Kaduna state were in opposition hands. The party managed to secure the votes of important minority groups in Benue, Rivers, and Cross River states and elsewhere. The party also had a foothold in Yorubaland and Igboland. The policy of distributing offices to these areas ensured that powerful individuals from these areas obtained important posts. Moreover, as we shall see, throughout the country people in big business supported the NPN. The Unity Party of Nigeria and Nigerian People's Party, on the other hand, relied much more closely on the old regional ethnic bases of support among the Yoruba and Igbo, respectively. The main exceptions to this pattern were the NPP victory in Plateau state and the UPN control of Bendel state.

The NPN emerged from the elections without an overall majority in the House of Representatives (165 seats of 443) or the Senate (36 seats of 95). This, together with the bitterness and political uncertainty that surrounded the controversial decision of the Federal Electoral Commission to allow Shehu Shagari's presidential election on the first ballot, brought the NPN into an accord with the NPP.[3] This agreement had echoes of the old NPC-NCNC alliance, but it proved temporary and of little significance. Much of the accord was never implemented. Igbo politicians had hoped for a larger share of federal appointments, more federal resources for Imo and Anambra states, and a just solution to the issue of properties left abandoned by Igbo during the civil war. In the event, all they gained were some ministerial appointments (eight ministerial appointments out of forty-two, five of cabinet rank) and some offices in the Senate and House of Representatives. The accord had an uneasy life of mutual recrimination with tension over ministerial appointments, ambassadorial nominations, and the role of the Presidential Liaison Officers (PLOs) who represented the president in each state. It broke up in July 1981.

The "Party of National Patronage" (PNP)

The NPN was not held together by a clear and distinct ideology but by a careful distribution of office and rewards to regions, groups, and individuals. It was formed on the building blocks of the nineteen states with the express purpose of acquiring power to share state patronage on a national basis. A more appropriate name for the party would have been the "Party of National Patronage" (PNP). The principle of zoning, which the party adopted, promised the equitable distribution of offices among the various constituencies in return for the mobilisation of support for the party. It was understood that the presidency would rotate among four zones, being held by a zone for one term only (though this was not adhered to). The Northern Zone was to supply the presidential candidate. The Western

Zone would supply the national chair of the party, the Eastern Zone the vice-presidential candidate, and the Central Zone (Bendel, Rivers, and Cross River states), the president of the Senate. The first three zones were dominated by the three major ethno-linguistic groups and the last by minority groups.

Zoning had its counterpart in the constitutional principle of federal character, which was an important addition to the political vocabulary. As we saw in Chapter 3, the aim was to secure an even distribution of federal offices and resources and prevent domination by any ethnic or sectional interest, thus promoting political stability. Not surprisingly, the application of the principle fell short of the ideal. Writing in 1983, one commentator saw the application of the federal character principle as marked by infidelity and distortion. Benjamin Nwabueze argued that the strategic departments and functions of the government were concentrated among individuals from the northern part of the country.[4] One aspect of the principle was a strong tendency to link it to representation by states and to the geographical spread of federal institutions among the states. Thus the principle tended to reinforce state centredness and state consciousness.

National patronage as a form of representation and a means of distribution had important consequences. First, as we have seen, it gave the party greater national support than any of the old regional parties of the First Republic received. Second, it meant that distributive issues dominated over policy issues and ensured that the party never developed any distinctive programmes. Voters responded to private and group inducements rather than policies. Politics was to a large extent issueless and nonideological. Long-term policies could not be effectively undertaken, as the political system was flooded with a mass of personal or sectional demands. When difficulties did arise for the executive, the use of patronage was effectively deployed to subordinate the legislature, the bureaucracy, and even the judiciary.

Third, the existence of a widespread government patronage and spoils system meant that those individuals who held public office were subjected to a great deal of political pressure and flattery. According to one minister, "the electorate torment you with demands because they voted for you. … They wanted their share of the national cake." He saw an average of 700 people a day in his office as well as at his residence.[5] Before a contract was signed, the electorate was already aware of it and would approach the minister with demands that posed all kinds of dilemmas.

Fourth, the presence of powerful political patrons supported by sectional interests and wealthy individuals had serious consequences for party discipline, political unity, and presidential power. The president was severely constrained by the requirements of party patronage in making his appointments. It took three months before the final approval of presidential appointments. To meet the various requirements for the sharing of political office and the pressures of those who had helped elect him to office, the president inflated the number of ministers to forty-two. Alex Gboyega has shown how ministerial appointments were constrained by the application of federal character with at least two ministers from each state, by the zoning principle, by the relative strength of the political parties, by the NPN-NPP accord, and by the hurdle of senate confirmation.[6] Many poor appointments were made. Many of the ministers were politicians who had lost elections. Other failed politicians were appointed to the boards of federal parastatals. Most of the people who found themselves as ministers for the various zones did it through a process of lobbying.[7] Donations to the party, old school and classmate networks, and marriage ties were all relevant. Such lobbying enhanced mediocrity rather than merit. At midterm, only two ministers were replaced, and the cabinet was enlarged from forty-two to forty-five ministers. No minister was ever dismissed for corruption, though one was forced to leave office after a press campaign and another was transferred to a less lucrative post.

Finally, the system spawned powerful individuals who began to monopolise areas of state patronage and who were difficult to discipline and call to order. The NPN was an unwieldy party by virtue of its size and the presence of these Big Men. The power of Big Men in the party to wield personal patronage rather than operate a system of party machine patronage weakened the capacity of the party to discriminate against non-NPN states. It also meant that there was the potential for serious friction between Lagos-based members of the party and state-based members including governors. NPN funds were not centralised in one place and were subject to control by powerful figures within the party.

The NPN, Businesspeople, and the Economy

An important feature of the NPN was the support it received from many of the most wealthy businesspeople in the country. Some were active as members of the national executive of the party, as trustees, as officers of the state councils and as financiers. What was the character of this business class? To what extent was it involved in politics, and what were the consequences for the party?

It is hazardous to generalise about a group with such diverse origins, sources of capital, and identities. These people tended to be involved in commerce, finance, real estate, and construction rather than in production, though a shift to industry had become apparent by the end of the 1970s. Some were dependent on state patronage and favours for accumulation and lacked independent sources of wealth. Others had more independent trajectories of accumulation. Enterprises were often diversified, in sole ownership, and employed kin or clients with little corporate structure or management. This was an acquisitive class struggling for wealth and status through the maintenance of large personal networks, consumption, the taking of chieftaincy titles, and educational and religious philanthropy.

The degree of involvement by businesspeople in politics varied widely from simple party donations to entry on a full-time basis and was dependent on the political ambitions of individuals, the amount of pressure from home communities, and the extent to which they depended on state patronage. Some businesspeople spent time and energy building up personal networks and promoting their interests within the state and party apparatus. This activity was partly explained by a drive to secure state contracts and administrative favours. It was also a defensive operation to guard property and business interests against rival predators and the whims of those who exercise state power in an economy where private property was not legally secure, state intervention was rife, and a state governor could ruin a business overnight.

The widespread support given by businesspeople to the NPN is partly explained by the pattern of state patronage that evolved in the 1970s. First, there was an enormous increase in federal resources to be dispensed from the centre and an expansion of federal activities within each state. Second, the scale of many business operations had expanded beyond the confines of the old regions. Businesspeople could not therefore afford to rely solely on local patronage. They often gave support to more than one party in order to minimise the risk to their operations. Among the prominent businesspeople who supported NPN and who were resident in opposition states were Sir Joseph Nwankwo and Mathias Ugochukwu in Anambra state, Nnana Kalu in Imo state, E. O. Ashamu and M.K.O. Abiola in Ogun state and Isiyaku Rabiu and Garba Inuwa in Kano state.

Such national support did not mean that local capital was somehow organisationally aggregated at the national level so that collective pressure could be put on the government. Nor did it mean that the party represented a national bourgeois class. The latter term suggests a coherent, productive class of capital and a continuity in property ownership that did not exist. It was the close link between commercial and political interests that characterised much of the participation by businesspeople in politics. The impact of individual businesspeople was felt in the struggle for import licence and contract, and it was mediated through local bases of support and party structures. Such activity did not support a specifically capitalist ideology for the party. Nor did it enhance the interests of corporate capital.

As Dudley noted, the distinctive feature of the NPN manifesto was the party's promise of more of the same.[8] When pressed on the absence of an explicit ideology, party spokespersons would turn to the constitution where there was provision for a mixed economy. This meant, in effect, support for the status quo. Although the party supported private foreign investment in its manifesto, a concerted policy to attract it was beyond its capacities. So, too, was any consistent line with respect to state involvement in the economy.

No well-defined economic programme or philosophy emerged. The party had a business orientation that stopped well short of being a market oriented, free enterprise strategy. This orientation was not surprising in a society where the limits to individual business success were commonly seen to depend not on the forces of market competition and entrepreneurial drive but on political connections and state patronage.

The NPN and the Opposition States

The main axis of conflict during the Second Republic was between the federal government and the twelve opposition states. Meetings of the twelve opposition governors provided the major forum for the opposition. Attempts to bring the opposition parties together under the umbrella of a Progressive Parties Alliance were not successful. They were thwarted by personal rivalries between Chief Awolowo (UPN) and Nnamdi Azikiwe (NPP), by factionalism within the parties, and by the machinations of the Federal Electoral Commission over party registration.

Differences between the centre and the states were not generally over policy but over questions of political control and the division of responsibilities. Areas of conflict included the role of the Presidential Liaison Officers, control of TV and radio stations, the provision of federal service and projects, and revenue allocation. Thus opposition control of the twelve states did not fundamentally challenge the pattern of patronage and distributive politics outlined earlier. The main exceptions were in Kano and Kaduna states, held by the PRP, and in Lagos state, controlled by the UPN. Here class politics brought a number of issues into the open.

The PRP had mass support from traders, artisans, and small farmers. But as the successor to the Northern Elements Progressive Union, it had a geographically limited appeal. Ideologically, the PRP stressed the fight against feudalism and domination by the northern oligarchy of the NPN. Within the party, there were various tendencies ranging from the socialist intellectuals surrounding Governor Balarabe Musa in Kaduna to the reactionary populist demogoguery of Sabo Bakin Zuwo in Kano that appealed to urban and rural lumpen elements.[9] As the Second Republic progressed, the various factions of the PRP polarised, leaving the party hopelessly divided. A split developed between those who favoured a more conciliatory approach to the NPN and governors Abubakar Rimi of Kano and Balarabe Musa of

Kaduna, who were eventually expelled from the party. The Rimi faction eventually declared for the NPP to contest the 1983 election. The Bakin Zuwo faction became a virtual extension of the NPN, and the Balarabe faction gave electoral support to the UPN and later returned to the PRP.

If Governor Balarabe Musa had not been stymied by a hostile legislature that finally succeeded in impeaching him, a more radical redistributive programme would have been attempted in Kaduna state. Kaduna state led the early moves to abolish the poll and cattle taxes, a move that was later followed by NPN-controlled states. The allocation of urban plots in Kaduna was revoked and a host of VIPs affected. Similar moves to right abuses in the allocation of rural land were blocked by the House of Assembly and by local government councils controlled by the opposition. Coeducational secondary day schools were introduced to expand educational opportunities.

In Lagos state, the UPN governor, Lateef Jakande, was widely acknowledged as a successful governor who had popular support. His capacity to deliver goods, together with improved financial management, was no doubt related to the fact that Lagos state was the only state able to generate more than half its revenue internally. The state housing scheme was superior to the federal one and less costly. A determined drive to extend state schooling among the poorer sections of the population succeeded. Under the Free Education Programme of the UPN, which was designed to provide equal education opportunities to all children, the Lagos state government decided that all schools in the state should be taken over by the government. The abolition of private ownership was contested in the courts by school proprietors, including the Catholic archbishop of Lagos, Anthony Olubunmi Okogie. The right to private schooling was eventually upheld in the courts.[10]

In the provision of services and federal projects, there were a number of conflicts. In Oyo state, houses under construction for the federal government were demolished. In Anambra and Bendel states, the governments refused to make land available to the federal authorities. Federal plans to finance road construction in Anambra and Imo states were thwarted by governors who feared that this action would increase the popularity of the president and NPN. Total lack of coordination was evident in education. Opposition states went ahead and established universities and polytechnics without federal approval. Attempts by the federal authorities to block new TV and radio stations and limit the powers of the old regional broadcasting centres were a constant source of tension with governors of opposition states.

Soon after the NPN came to power, controversy erupted over the appointment of PLOs to each state. As the chief purveyor of federal patronage in a state, a PLO could attempt to gather support locally and posed a potential threat to the authority of the executive in non-NPN states. Most of the people appointed were unsuccessful politicians.

The issue of the PLOs opens up more general questions about discrimination between NPN and non-NPN states and about discipline within the NPN. How far did the NPN use its control of federal and party patronage to discriminate against the non-NPN states? Examples of discrimination can be found, but on the whole the NPN did not use its power in this manner. One reason was the constraint placed by the federal system and the system of revenue allocation that ensured that each state would receive a share of federal resources. There was, too, the fact that the NPN simply did not have the power or coherence to discriminate systematically against whole states in the allocation of resources. Moreover, there were within each opposition state a number of powerful NPN figures, some of whom held important party positions, whose interests could not be ignored. Many of them received contracts. The party also hoped to win over opposition states in the 1983 elections and for this reason could not afford to neglect them. There were a number of instances of opposition governors turning down federal resources for fear that acceptance might jeopardise their position.

Even within the NPN states, the character and organisation of the party meant that serious intraparty squabbles could develop between NPN leaders based in Lagos and state-based parties and governors. Unlike the UPN-controlled states, where the governor of each state was chairman of the state party, the NPN had national vice-chairmen for each state, which opened up the potential for conflict between them and the state governors over the control of state parties.[11] An example of this was the power struggle between the governor of Kwara state and Sola Saraki, the Senate majority leader. The absence of Saraki's support eventually cost the NPN control of Kwara state in the 1983 elections. In time, most governors came to control state party delegates and reduced the influence of the "Lagos NPN." But in the case of Cross River state, opposition from Joseph Wayas, the Senate president, cost the governor of the state, Clement Isong (a former governor of the Central Bank), the NPN nomination.

Party, Police, and State Violence

Law and order was a priority for the civilian regime, and the regime gave priority to the police while the army suffered relative neglect. Early on, the president removed a number of senior military officers who had not either retired voluntarily or been obliged to retire because they wished to enter politics. Later, the president also took over the defence portfolio. The police force was expanded, and new equipment and training were introduced. Close links between the police and the ruling party developed, and the party was later to rely on the police for information and help in the rigging of the 1983 elections. The priority given to the police was resented in the army, and the political role of the police made it unpopular with the population at large.

It was not simply the role of the police in the elections that provoked controversy. This was the culmination of a politicisation that had been stepped up once Sunday Adewusi became inspector general of police in April 1981. Particular controversy centred on the role of the Police Commands in opposition states where they were regarded as federal agents.[12] The unity of the police, and more especially the high degree of centralisation that had evolved, opened up the possibility that they would be used as an instrument of coercion by the ruling party. This fear was well founded. Relations between Police Commands and governors were particularly bad in Kano, Borno, and Anambra states. In Kano, the police appeared to collude with the political thugs who destroyed property and killed Bala Mohammed, a political adviser to the governor, in July 1981.[13]

More generally, public confidence in the police was drained by the oppressive activities of the mobile anticrime patrols who harrassed the public. Often the police appeared to be protecting organised crime and using their powers to extort money from the public. Two incidents in particular demonstrated the oppressive use and incapacity of the police. At the Bakalori irrigation scheme in Sokoto state, thousands of farmers had either been permanently deprived of land or prevented from cultivating it for two or three seasons. They rebelled and the paramilitary mobile police suppressed them, burning villages and killing and wounding hundreds of men, women, and children. The incompetence of the police was demonstrated in their failure to control a series of insurrections by a religious sect, the 'Yan Tatsine, at Kano (1980), Kaduna (1982), and Bulum-Ketu in Maiduguri (1982).

The chorus of protest at police activities could be extended. Yet it would be misleading to abstract the police from the social context in which they worked. As one policeman was heard to remark, after he had been called to the National Assembly to cool passions over the Revenue Allocation Bill, "Dem de chop money finish. Na when trouble come dem go call us."[14]

The Centre and the States

The period of civil rule saw a loss of federal power in relation to the states. Well before military rule ended, there had been political pressures to loosen the power of the centre. The new constitution strengthened the power of the states, and the new revenue allocation formula reduced the share of the federal government in total revenues. There were other reasons for the slackening of federal authority. The NPN lacked political authority and a sense of direction at the centre. What political leverage the federal government possessed in its relations with the states was not used or was exercised very sparingly. This lack of leverage was especially true of its responsibilities for financial discipline and control.

A corollary of the shift in power from the centre and the operation of the "federal character" principle was statism. Each state became more self-centred, less federal, and more discriminating in its employment of nonindigenes and in its control of access to facilities like schools.

State governors were in a strong position, and some behaved as if they owned their states. There were many cases in which they exceeded their powers. The power of the governors was enhanced by the fact that state legislatures displayed minimal independence of the executive. Except in Kaduna state, the executive and the legislature were controlled by the same party. Governors, as leaders of their respective parties in the states, were able to exploit their dominant position in the state wing of the parties to assume control over Assembly members through the use of patronage. In some states, too, the civil service was heavily politicised, with appointments and promotions being made outside statutory rules and regulation.

Revenue Allocation

Differences over revenue allocation constituted the most serious division between the federal government and the opposition states.[15] The formula in operation in 1979 was favourable to the federal government and gave the federal centre 76 percent of shared revenues, the states 21 percent, and local governments 3 percent. In the debates that followed, the main issue was the division of the Federation Account between the federal government and the states. In their submissions to the Okigbo Commission on Revenue Allocation, appointed by President Shagari, no state argued for a federal share higher than 50 percent.[16] NPN-controlled states favoured the highest federal share (50 percent in the case of Sokoto, Benue, Cross River, and Kwara). States controlled by the Unity Party of Nigeria argued for the lowest federal share (30 percent in the case of Bendel, Ondo, and Oyo). The oil-producing states of Bendel and Rivers both argued for a larger share for themselves on the basis of derivation and on the grounds of compensation due to oil pollution and environmental damage.[17]

The Revenue Allocation Bill subsequently passed by the House of Assembly gave the federal government 55 percent, the states 26.5 percent, local governments 10 percent, and a Special Fund 8.5 percent and closely followed the Senate recommendation. However, the bill was subsequently challenged in the courts by Bendel state and declared illegal, with the result that revenue allocation reverted to the 1979 formula. A new bill was then put forward by the president, which compromised by raising the share of the states to 30.5 percent, with the federal share at 55 percent, local governments 10 percent, and 4.5 percent to be split three ways (1 percent for ecological problems, 2 percent for the mineral-producing states, and 1.5 percent for the development of mineral-producing areas). This formula, which came into force in January 1982, was generally accepted, and the controversy was settled for the remaining period of civil rule. With respect to the division of revenues among the states, the formula was modified, with 40 percent for each state (minimum responsibilities of government), 40 percent on the basis of population, 15 percent on the basis of primary school enrollment (social development factor), and 5 percent for Internal Revenue Effort.

Financial Indiscipline

Under President Shagari, there was a further decline in financial discipline and budgeting at the state level, a trend that had been encouraged in the 1970s by easy access to federal funds. The states consistently budgeted for large deficits, and as their economic plight deepened, so the deficits increased in size. Current expenditures quickly accelerated out of control as governors inflated state employment and legislatures increased their salaries and perks. Some states budgeted for free medical services and free education at all levels, as well as for the proliferation of universities and polytechnics. Financial abuses were common. In a number of states, governors set aside security votes for their personal use outside the scrutiny of state legislatures. In Kwara state, Governor Attah made payments of N100,000 each to forty-two legislators and N2 million to himself.[18]

Like their predecessors in the old regions, state-owned banks were particularly vulnerable to political pressure and party political control. Some played a role in the initial funding of the parties. At the end of civil rule, the Rivers state-owned bank, the Pan African Bank, had bad and doubtful debts of N172.9 million that had to be written off, out of a total of N248.8 million loans and overdrafts outstanding.[19] NPN supporters collected overdrafts from the bank without security or any repayment schedules. In Rivers state, too, a census after civil rule ended found over 3,000 persons on fictitious payrolls.[20] The Bank of the North was found to have bad and doubtful debts worth N131 million.[21]

From mid-1981, large arrears in the payment of state employees had built up. By the end of 1981, seven states could not pay teachers.[22] The result was strikes, absenteeism, and the closure of entire teaching services for prolonged periods. Civil services were severely affected, and public services were disrupted or completely paralysed. In some states, salaries payable from consolidated funds were stopped.

The result of all this was bankruptcy and debt. Large internal and external debts were built up. After the regime fell, figures for state government debt totalling N13.3 billion were announced: international loans, N4.7 billion; contractional obligations, N6.6 billion; and external debt, N2.0 billion.[23] These figures were later revised upwards as individual governments announced their debt. No doubt the figures were grossly inflated by fraudulent claims by contractors. Although under the constitution the federal government had a responsibility to monitor and control the level and structure of public debt, it did not do so. Indeed, by guaranteeing part of the external debt of the states, it had encouraged reckless expenditure.

State and Local Government Creation

As I argued in Chapter 2, the fiscal structure and system of revenue allocation were an excellent recipe for strong state creation movements. Until the first months of 1983, the president and the ruling party openly encouraged state creation movements to gain support for the NPN in the forthcoming elections. The leading contenders were Katsina (from Kaduna state), New Anambra (from Anambra state, where there was constant friction between the richer, more educated southwestern part of the state and the "Wawa" area to the northeast), Kogi (excised from Benue and Kwara states), New Cross River (whose case had already been recommended by the Panel on Creation of States in 1976), and Oshun (based on the old Oyo province).

The clamour for new states helped to divert attention from pressing national policy issues. The Senate authorised forty-six requests for new states as valid, and the House of Representatives approved thirty-eight requests.[24] Some of these states overlapped and were mutually exclusive. Perhaps as many as thirty states might have been created. It was only an impossible timetable prior to the elections and the total bankruptcy of the nation that put an end to the movements and prevented further capitulation to distributive politics and economic disaster.

At the local government level, councils remained firmly under the political and financial control of the state governments. No new elections were held, and elected bodies were replaced by appointed ones. Some states withheld funds that were due from the Federation Account and from their own revenues. There was a dramatic increase in the number of local government authorities under civil rule, and this increase in employment absorbed any revenues that were received. For example, the number of local government authorities in Imo state increased from twenty-one to fifty-nine, and in Gongola state from seventeen to forty.[25] This multiplication is explained by the pressure of political patronage, the demands for sharing on the basis of "federal character," and the fact that local governments, like states, were funded directly from federal statutory sources.

Corruption

Bureaucratic corruption and the large-scale privatisation of public funds intensified under civil rule. Corruption was an important aspect of political life and came to dominate discussion of public affairs. It was not a new phenomenon, and it was widely held that the military taught the politicians how to do it. There was an unbroken line of opportunities for corruption that extended from the wartime army contracts, through the cement scandal, FESTAC, the UPE contracts, to the Abuja contracts. A relatively free press and official inquiries ensured that much corruption was documented and publicised. Inquiries did not, however, extend to the accumulation of assets overseas, where a significant proportion of the fruits of corruption were held.

The behaviour of the venal legislators set the moral tone for the regime. Their priorities of taking office were to move their accomodation from Badagry Road to expensive, more central apartments on Victoria Island and to increase their salaries and perquisites of office. Later, senators were involved in a scandal over the allocation of licences to import rice.

Though the constitution made the declaration of assets by officers mandatory, the enabling bill was never passed through the legislature. Moral exhortation and admonition by the president had no effect; neither did the National Reorientation Committee set up in 1982. If the president managed to give the appearance of standing above corruption, he also seemed to condone it by his inaction and the appointments he made.

It was at the federal level that the scale of corruption was largest. For it was at this level that access could be had to the largest contracts and to import licences. The inflation of contracts was the most important source of funds for the party and for individual gain. When contracts began to dry up, attention switched to the struggle for import licences. The legislature could share the spoils only by threatening to obstruct, probe, or impeach the executive, so that they would be paid off. In a number of cases, incumbent governors literally bought off legislatures.

One federal institution generally regarded as very corrupt was the Customs Department.[26] During the First Republic, the chairman of the Board of Customs wielded considerable influence. Customs were then the largest revenue source for the government. Subsequently, there was an erosion of the power of the Customs Department and a decline in morale and confidence in the service. There were a number of contributory factors. The merger of the Department of Customs and Excise with the Immigration Department of the Ministry of Internal Affairs eroded the division of responsibilities between customs and immigration and the checks and balances at ports of entry. There was also a tendency to install military and police personnel above customs personnel, causing interference and confusion. The merger of the Preventative and Technical Divisions of the Customs Department led to the arbitrary promotion of preventative personnel who had direct access to Dodan Barracks.

Within federal agencies, corruption was rife. The following list is far from complete. An audit examination at Nigerian External Telecommunications traced financial abuses back to 1978 with N53 million unaccounted for.[27] Maladministration of the federal Housing Scheme grew into a major scandal with N43 million missing.[28] According to the chairmen of the investigating panels, the board members of the Federal Mortgage Bank "acted in concert to render the bank impotent by systematic plundering and looting of its treasury," and at the Delta Steel Company there was "stupendous fraud."[29] Officials of the National Youth Service Corps were found to have syphoned off over N16 million.[30] Widespread corruption was discovered at the Federal Capital Territory Administration. Those responsible were detained but not prosecuted. A Central Bank foreign exchange manager unlawfully transferred $24.1 million out of Nigeria in 1983.[31] The London manager of the Nigerian National Supply Company stole £1.9 million between April 1979 and December 1980.[32] Finally, renegotiation of the Jaguar jet contract with British Aerospace saved N30 million in kickbacks.[33]

The adverse impact of corruption and the lack of public accountability on budget deficits and the balance of payments cannot be measured. But there can be no doubt that it was substantial. The timing of the second mini oil boom to coincide with return of civilian government served to inflate corruption to a grand scale. Other things being equal, such levels of corruption under a civilian government would not have been tolerated had state revenue been derived from internal sources rather than from an "external" source like the taxation of oil rents.

Karin Barber's study of popular Yoruba theatre provides some clues to the impact of oil revenues on ideas about wealth.[34] She found an essentially reactionary popular ideology in which the drive for self aggrandisement overwhelmed criticism of how wealth was obtained or concern about the condition of the poor. Criticism of wealth that was not the product of productive work was displaced sideways into the common themes of armed robbery and magical money that were by-products of the oil boom.

The 1983 Elections and Their Aftermath

Two cardinal points stand out about the conduct of the 1983 elections.[35] First, the independence of the Federal Electoral Commission (FEDECO) was subverted by politicians and the ruling party. Second, there was rigging on a massive scale at all stages of the electoral process sufficient to throw the results of the election into doubt. Many election results were contested in the courts. But the manner of the elections and the heavy politicisation of the judiciary ensured that many controversial results were not overturned or satisfactorily explained.

A crucial difference from the 1979 elections, which contained rigging that did not affect the overall result, was that the ruling party was seeking a renewed mandate. There was no military government, intent on carrying through its commitment to handing over power to an elected government, to check the excesses of the politicians.

The loss of independent authority by FEDECO was demonstrated in a number of ways. FEDECO acquiesced in the federal government's ordering and taking delivery of ballot boxes and ballot papers. It showed itself to be guided by the federal attorney general in questions involving the application of provisions of the constitution to the parties. It refused to allow the NPP to change its name to the PPP so as to accommodate splinter groups from the PRP and GNPP. Finally, its decision to change the order of the elections by putting the presidential election first instead of last, as in the 1979 election, induced a bandwagon effect for the NPN in the subsequent elections.

The election results gave the NPN dominant party status in many states and at the federal level. NPN state governorships increased from seven to twelve, and the number of states in which President Shagari secured 25 percent or more of the vote increased from twelve to sixteen. In the Senate, the NPN became the majority party with 61 of 95 seats, and in the House of Representatives the party held 307 of 450 seats.

What were the reasons for the desperation of the NPN to retain power? Where a party lacks a programme or ideology, its members depend primarily on access to power for status and livelihood and hence will use all possible means to keep themselves in power. There was the need to end the situation in which twelve state executives controlled by other parties ganged up to confront the federal executive. In particular, there was a determination to win Kano, Kaduna, Oyo, and Anambra states at all costs. Kano and Kaduna were the core, wealthy northern states that were essential to any bid to restore political unity to the north. Oyo and Anambra states, which were won only after bitterly contested results in the courts, were crucial to Yoruba and Igbo claims to the presidency the next time round (the claims of Party Chairman A.M.A. Akinloye and Vice-President Alex Ekueme).

A feature of the elections was the very strong competition for governorships both within and between the parties. Incumbent NPN governors (with one exception) retained their positions because they were able to mobilise state resources and use the money weapon to defeat the opposition. Governorships were considerable prizes in their own right. Victory at the state level could be used to stage a claim to offices and patronage in the federal government for having "delivered" states. Most governors, far from being party political hacks controlled by a party machine, were men of considerable independence. One result of these struggles for control of states was that the tension and violence of the elections was diffused over a wide geographical area and did not follow lines of ethnic division. In the First Republic, the drive for hegemony by the NPC was associated with intense conflict and breakdown of law and order in the Western Region and with increased polarisation among the major ethnic groups in the country.

Did the results of the elections, which gave the NPN a dominant position, herald a stronger presidency, a stronger party, a change in policies, or a stronger institutional or administrative capacity? None of these consequences are self-evident. The nature of the party had not changed. It was still a party of patronage and spoils, with Big Men jostling for positions. The president was not necessarily in a stronger position to exercise executive authority. He was not firmly in control of the Senate or party finances. The new ministerial appointments inspired no confidence. The struggle for the succession in 1987, which began in earnest after the elections, threatened to divide the party. Certainly, there is no reason to suppose that corruption would have been curtailed or that institutional and administrative capacity for economic management and decisionmaking would have improved radically. The creation of a Ministry of National Guidance to carry out an "Ethical Revolution" carried no conviction.

The drive for party hegemony that brought massive rigging in the elections was certainly a contributory factor to the military intervention. By January 1984, all support for the politicians had drained away. Why did the regime last so long, if public disillusionment with the regime had become widespread much earlier? One reason must surely be that many military officers supported the NPN and that any intervention before the 1983 elections would have been judged to be an interference in the democratic process. Another reason lay in the structural circumstances engendered by centralised oil wealth. Oil revenues encouraged a top-down system of redistribution. This moderated the need for a system that relied on the extraction of resources from below. The latter would have demanded a stronger system of political domination from above and been met by more determined opposition from below.

If economic mismanagement and the travesty of the elections provided the conditions for a coup, the actual political dynamic came from the Kaduna mafia and its allies in the army.[36] With the failure of its candidate to secure the NPN presidential nomination and the political fragmentation of the north, the mafia had already lost power under President Shagari. In desperation, the mafia sought an alliance with Chief Awolowo, the leader of the UPN.[37] This alliance was an electoral failure, even in

Kaduna state where it was overwhelmed by the power of NPN patronage. Appalled at the conduct of the elections and the management of the economy, the mafia wanted a more powerful northern presence in Nigerian politics and also wanted to restore order and discipline to the economy. With their professional backgrounds and close managerial ties with corporate enterprise, their perspectives on the economy were distinct from the businesspeople whose commercial interests were linked to party and state patronage.

Conclusion

Under military rule, a high degree of administrative and financial centralisation had emerged within the federal framework. The state had also taken on new responsibilities for economic management. One result of the centralisation was the growth of distributive pressures on the centre. These pressures were accentuated by large oil revenues. The rental nature of the oil income also gave those who held state power a new freedom that tended to undermine public accountability. Under these structural conditions, a strong and purposeful government was required to exercise political control and maintain economic stability. Under civil rule, this was not to be. From open political competition and universal suffrage, there emerged a weak executive presidency, a weak political party, and a form of clientelist politics that sapped the authority of the state.

The NPN came to power through a loose coalition of patrons and political brokers who mobilised political support through vertical political alliances that built on existing clientilist networks. It was a weak and undisciplined party incapable of providing leadership or giving a sense of direction to national policies. The weak organisation of the party meant that it was unable to effectively institutionalise patronage in ways that did not undermine the national economy. Its major concern was the distribution of state patronage on a national basis. This political preoccupation was built into the very structure of the party. Zoning at the level of party representation and the principle of federal character both served to distribute state patronage and secure a measure of national integration. Political dispute centred on the distribution of federal patronage and on federal-state relations where power shifted away from the centre to the states. These political concerns, together with political weight of commercial interests intent on pursuing the accumulation of wealth through personal connection with those who held state power, helped to ensure that no clear issues or policies emerged from the process of political competition. Economic management, policymaking and implementation were exposed to the political pressures of distributive demands, competition for rents, and party patronage.

These forces were also pervasive under military rule, but the military did generally manage to insulate executive authority more effectively against the distributive pressures and the intense drive for individual power and wealth that were directed at the state. The military had the advantage of a unitary organisation, centralised power, and the threat of coercion. Since they were not elected, the channels for patronage-seeking were much more confined, and the sheer volume of demands much less. It is military government that has generally been associated with the capacity to undertake economic and political reform. We should be wary, however, of drawing too sharp a distinction between military and civil governments. As the latter years of the Gowon regime demonstrated, a sharp loss of political and economic control could occur under military rule.

The support of local businesspeople was significant for the financial muscle it gave the ruling party and for the general influence of this group upon the conduct of state and party affairs. Far from representing a bourgeois economic liberalism that might operate to check state interventions and contain the corrupt use of state resources, the political and economic influence of this group worked in other directions. In return for supporting the party, some businesspeople gained access to contracts, import licences, and other fruits of state economic regulation. These commercial and political pressures tended to favour state regulation and licensing at the same time as they tended to undermine the capacity for national economic control and prevent consideration of alternative policies.

Keen electoral competition, the more representative character of the ruling party that largely removed the threat of sectional dominance that had plagued the politics of the First Republic, the constitutional provisions, and a free press did not protect the citizen against economic ruin, corruption on a grand scale, and the abuse of police and judicial powers. The conclusion seems inescapable that democracy, or "the rule of the politician" as Joseph Schumpeter aptly put it, contributed to a loss of political and economic control and hence retarded economic progress.

Notes

1. S. Othman, "Classes, Crises and Coup: The Demise of Shagari's Regime," *African Affairs* 83/333 (1984), p. 446.

2. R. A. Joseph, *Democracy and Prebendal Politics in Nigeria: The Rise and Fall of the Second Republic* (Cambridge: Cambridge University Press, 1987), p. 91.

3. *West Africa*, 19 March 1981. See also B. O. Nwabueze, *Nigeria's Presidential Constitution, 1979–83* (London: Longman, 1985), pp. 126–138.

4. Nwabueze, *Nigeria's Presidential Constitution*, p. 306.

5. *West Africa*, 21 April 1986.

6. A. Gboyega, "Choosing a New Cabinet," in O. Oyediran, ed., *The Nigerian 1979 Elections* (London: Macmillan, 1981), pp. 153–165.
7. *New Nigerian*, 31 May, 1 June, 3 June 1985.
8. B. J. Dudley, *An Introduction to Nigerian Government and Politics* (London: Macmillan, 1982), p. 190.
9. T. Abdulraheem and A. Olukoshi, "The Left in Nigerian Politics and the Struggle for Socialism, 1945–1985," *Review of African Political Economy* 37 (1986), pp. 76–77.
10. See discussion in Nwabueze, *Nigeria's Presidential Constitution*, pp. 210–219.
11. I owe this point to Tajuddeen Abdulraheem.
12. Nwabueze, *Nigeria's Presidential Constitution*, pp. 84–88.
13. Y. B. Usman, *Political Repression in Nigeria*, vol. 1 (Zaria: Gaskiya Corporation, 1982).
14. *West Africa*, 9 February 1981.
15. The twists and turns of the revenue allocation debate can be followed in *West Africa*, 8 December 1980, 15 December 1980, 23 February 1981, 12 October 1981, 2 April 1984.
16. See *Report of the Presidential Commission on Revenue Allocation*, vol. 1, *Main Report*, (Lagos: Federal Government Press, 1980), app. 3.
17. On environmental pollution, see E. Hutchful, "Oil Companies and Environmental Pollution in Nigeria," in C. Ake, ed., *Political Economy of Nigeria* (London: Longman, 1986), chap. 7, pp. 113–140.
18. *Nigerian Newsletter*, no. 144, 28 July 1984.
19. *Concord Weekly*, 27 June 1985.
20. *Nigerian Newsletter*, no. 186, 5 April 1986.
21. *Nigerian Newsletter*, no. 155, 12 January 1985.
22. N. Van Hear, "Recession, Retrenchment, and Military Rule: Prospects for Nigerian Labour in the 1980s," in R. Southall, ed., *Trade Unions and the New Industrialization of the Third World* (London: Zed Books, 1988).
23. *West Africa*, 9 April 1984.
24. *Nigerian Newsletter*, no. 103, 20 December 1982–16 January 1983.
25. *Nigerian Newsletter*, no. 132, 11 February 1984.
26. Pini Jason, "The Endless Woes of Customs," *Concord Weekly*, 27 June 1985, pp. 13–15.
27. *Nigerian Newsletter*, no. 95, 16–30 August 1982.
28. *African Business*, 14 October 1983
29. *Nigerian Newsletter*, no. 111, 11–24 April 1983.
30. *Nigerian Newsletter*, no. 151, 3 November 1984, and no. 155, 12 January 1985.
31. *Nigerian Newsletter*, no. 188, 3 May 1986.
32. *Nigerian Newsletter*, no. 188, 3 May 1986.
33. *West Africa*, 19 November 1984.
34. Karin Barber, "Popular Reactions to the Petro-Naira," *Journal of Modern African Studies* 20/3 (1982), pp. 431–450.
35. My account of the 1983 elections draws freely on Nwabueze's excellent work. Nwabueze, *Nigeria's Presidential Constitution*, chap. 17.
36. Othman, "Classes, Crises and Coup," pp. 453–456.
37. Rufai Ibrahim, "Of the Mafia, Awo and the Race," *Triumph*, 3 August, 1983.

5

The Return of the Military: The Buhari Regime

Order and Discipline

The military elite that took power, and their allies in the Kaduna mafia, were supporters of the National Party of Nigeria for most of its life. The stated aims of the regime were identical with those of the second Shagari administration.[1] The quarrel with the politicians was not with their policies but with their failure to control the economy and the absence of public accountability.

The coup itself was poorly organised and coordinated, but as it had general support within the army and populace at large, this did not affect the outcome. One feature of the coup was the inability of the new regime to detain top party officials and ministers of the NPN, even though they were wanted persons. Among those who left the country were Umaru Dikko, Richard Akinjide (attorney general), Chief A.M.A. Akinloye (NPN chairman), Joseph Wayas (Senate president), Uba Ahmed (NPN national secretary), Isiyaku Ibrahim (NPN patron), and several ministers. The nonarrest of these politicians, who were able to scatter to various Western capitals, raised the suspicion that the regime was content to see them go. Yet it may be more accurate to say that the slack organisation of the coup was responsible for their not being arrested.

The prime aim of the regime was to improve the economy and win the confidence of trading partners, so that international credit could be restored. Until that time, political discussion and debate would have to wait, and the emphasis would be on domestic austerity and bringing order and discipline to Nigerian society. Structurally, the leadership adhered to the institutional setup of the Obasanjo period with a Supreme Military Council, a National Council of States, a Federal Executive Council and a chief of staff, Supreme Headquarters. The head of state, Major-General Muhammadu Buhari, a Katsinawa, had been director of supply and transport in the 1970s. He was appointed military governor of North Eastern state to supervise its division into three separate states and was then recalled to Lagos where he was co-opted onto the SMC and appointed federal commissioner for petroleum and energy (1976–1978). Prior to the coup, he was commander of the Third Division based in Jos.

The military introduced an authoritarian style of government with numerous decrees and military tribunals to bring politicians and other corrupt individuals to trial. A War Against Indiscipline (WAI) was announced. There was intimidation of the press and a purge of the civil service. The military did not develop any ideological weapons of their own to mobilise support. Discipline was their watchword. The WAI began in April 1984, just four months after the regime took power. It went through five phases in fifteen months—queuing, work ethics, patriotism and nationalism, anticorruption, and environmental sanitation.[2] One observer saw it as an attempt to turn Nigeria into a vast military parade ground. Despite the fact that the various phases came too fast and contained more rhetoric than action, the campaigns generally had public support. One advantage was that unlike many other government initiatives before and since, WAI involved little government funding. This meant that it was less open to abuse and detractors could not pin corruption charges on it. On occasion, though, WAI brigades, acting as vigilante groups, used excessive force and took the law into their own hands.

The last campaign, for environmental sanitation, had a visible impact upon the cleanliness of the state capitals. Before the regime fell, it had initiated a competition among the capitals for the cleanest city with cash prizes of N2 million.[3] Here, too, there were conflicts of interest. The drive to clean up the capitals was directed largely at petty commodity producers and low income groups. Spasmodic efforts to clear urban areas of petty traders and producers had been a feature of military rule in the 1970s, but this campaign was more concerted and effective. In some towns, "illegal structures" were torn down without adequate alternative provision.[4] Market women, street traders and roadside mechanics were forcibly removed. In Enugu, over 800 motor mechanics were affected.[5] Official recognition of chief of touts was withdrawn at motor parks in Kano in a bid to stamp out touting.[6] A ban on hawking by children under 14 years of age was announced in Bauchi state.[7] In Port Harcourt, some 150,000 traders were affected by legislation on environmental sanitation.[8] In Kano, it was estimated that at least 50,000 self-employed enterprises disappeared from the streets.[9] These actions swelled the ranks of the petit bourgeois opposition to the regime. The legislation also provided the police with further opportunities to harass the public.

The regime soon ran into opposition that went beyond the usual antagonism of elites to a military that indulges in promotions and salary awards soon after it takes office. A number of measures were taken to reduce the overall level of dissent, but this repression did not ensure stability. Indeed, it contributed to divisions and tensions within the Supreme Military Council that ultimately contributed to the regime's downfall.

Under Decree No. 2, State Security (Detention of Persons), persons could be arrested and detained for an indefinite period without trial. Under this umbrella, the National Security Organisation expanded its activities. Later the NSO came to be seen as an arm of the military, more specifically a pro-Buhari faction headed by the powerful Chief of Staff, Supreme Headquarters, Major-General Tunde Idiagbon. Military officers were themselves put under surveillance by the NSO, and the army chief of staff, Ibrahim Babangida, had his phone tapped. The NSO was widely held to be behind the bungled kidnapping of Umaru Dikko from London. The NSO itself appears to have been divided, with one element pursuing an unprecedented campaign of investigation to bring to justice those responsible for some of the worst corruption of the Second Republic.

Among those held without trial were Haroun Adamu and Rufai Ibrahim, journalists associated with the Kano-based *Sunday Triumph,* which had been in the forefront of the opposition to the NPN under President Shagari. The *Triumph* was the first to expose corruption at the Federal Capital Authority in Abuja, and it uncovered the systematic distribution of import licences among NPN notables. The attack on the former *Triumph* journalists demonstrated how close the military were politically and ideologically to the NPN. Others detained and arrested without trial included the former governor of Kaduna state, Balarabe Musa, and the social critic, Tai Solarin. The musician, Fela Anikulapo-Kuti, a long-time critic of military rule, was also held on a trifling foreign currency offence and sentenced to five years imprisonment.

The detention of politicians under Decree No. 3 (Recovery of Public Property), which provided for prison sentences of a minimum of twenty-one years for those found guilty of abuse of office, had general support. Sam Ikoku, the former PRP politician, has graphically described his reception on arrival at the maximum security jail, Kiri-Kiri.[10] "As we stepped into the courtyard of the block, we were greeted with vociferous shouts and hand clapping. It was a grand ovation from armed robbers to 'fellow robbers.' For among the loud-throated shouts could be clearly heard, 'welcome, oh fellow armed robbers.'" No doubt this sentiment was widely shared across the country. Yet the manner in which the regime handled the detention of politicians did provoke hostility. Sentences were widely perceived to discriminate in favour of the northern states and against the former opposition parties. Many resented the fact that former President Shagari was not tried and sentenced. The regime also took a great length of time to start investigations at the federal level and at the level of the NPN executive. It was only well into 1985 that inquiries began into government ministries and FEDECO. These inconsistencies helped over time to shift public opinion from calls for punishment to a defence of "our sons."

Under Special Tribunal Decree No. 20 (Miscellaneous Offences), the death penalty was introduced retroactively for a number of offences, and executions were again made public. These offences included drug smuggling, interference with electricity cables and oil pipelines, trading in petroleum products, arson of public buildings, and counterfeiting currency under the Counterfeit Currency (Special Provisions) Decree No. 22, 1984.[11] Long terms of imprisonment were prescribed for tampering with postal matters, exporting produce unlawfully, destroying public property, and cheating at examinations.

A number of persons were executed for trafficking in cocaine. Government concern over drug trafficking was the result of an upsurge in hard drug activity that had begun to spill over into Nigerian society. Dealers had started to use Nigeria as a staging post to Europe and the United States after a crackdown on other international routes.

Professional groups were alienated by the regime. The Nigerian Bar Association boycotted the Military Tribunals, protesting that the trials were held in camera and headed by a military officer.[12] Academics were alienated by the threats to universities. Several prominent leftists, including Ola Oni, Festus Iyayi, and 'Biodun Jeyifo were detained without trial for varying lengths of time. The National Association of Nigerian Students declared a boycott of lectures in May 1984 to protest against the planned introduction of tuition fees in universities and the withdrawal of subsidies. This announcement led to the closure of some campuses and the detention of some student union leaders. Church leaders, especially the Catholic bishops, spoke out about the need for civil rule and against detentions and trials.[13] Trade unions were forced into submission by a strike ban, a freeze on wages, and massive retrenchments in the private and public sectors. The traditional rulers, from whom the military mobilised support, were the only group who appeared to flourish. The powers of traditional rulers had been eroded in the past, and it was felt that they would have provided better security and surveillance of unorthodox religious groups like the 'Yan Tatsine and that their role in local government and law and order should be enhanced.

One of the more serious clashes of the military with professionals was with medical doctors.[14] The Nigerian Association of Resident Doctors and the Nigerian Medical Association were both banned in early 1985. Doctors' leaders were detained and military commandants appointed to teaching hospitals. This action followed a strike by doctors protesting against small budget allocations for health and against the suspension of the overseas residency programme, higher fees in government hospitals, and a government directive that doctors and other medical personnel pay for their own treatment. In the 1970s, when the military clashed with the doctors, the latter got little public sympathy. This time, however, the treatment of the doctors gradually became part of a more general struggle for individual rights and liberties.

Nigeria had an inappropriate, high-cost health delivery system biased to curative medicine at the tertiary level, a system which was defended by highly trained professionals. It provided access for a privileged few and closed out poorer sections of the population. A mushrooming of expensive teaching hospitals in the 1970s and under civil rule left the system hopelessly exposed to any cuts in government expenditure.

In some states, private medicine was more important than public medicine and was subsidised by public facilities. Under these conditions, morale and efficiency in government hospitals slumped, and there was a steady decline in the standard of health-care delivery. Under the Private Practice Decree of 1984, public officers were forbidden to engage in the management or running of any private business, profession, or trade. Unable to go private, many doctors left the government service. In Gongola state, twelve of thirty-five Nigerian doctors were reported to have resigned from the service.[15]

Perhaps the measure that was most widely resented and had the most serious consequences in eroding goodwill for the regime, was Decree No. 4, Public Officers (Protection Against False Accusation). This decree made it an offence to make any false report in the press or to bring the federal government or public officers into ridicule or disrepute through the media. Two *Guardian* (Lagos) journalists, Tunde Thompson and Nduka Irabor, were held under this decree. They were accused of false reports about new diplomatic postings and the likely closure of certain diplomatic missions and sentenced to one year's imprisonment. A strong campaign was mounted for the release of the journalists and led by the Nigerian Union of Journalists and the *Guardian.* The federal government also decided to advertise only in the government-owned newspapers, the *Daily Times* and the *New Nigerian,* and it began to interfere with the supply of newsprint and threatened to handle the bulk import of newsprint.[16] Though the press was effectively muzzled, bitter criticisms of the decree continued. The decree heightened the feeling that power had been arrogated by a small group of men who were deaf to currents of public opinion.

The lack of consultation and the apparent bias of the regime to northern interests heightened ethnic, regional, and religious differences. This behaviour led to accusations that federal character was not being respected, and it intensified debate over the merits of confederation and dyarchy in the political future of the country. A number of former army officers were involved in this debate (Benjamin Adekunle, Olusegun Obasanjo, Julius

Akinrinade, James Oluleye, and Hassan Katsina). General Obasanjo's contribution contained a wide-ranging critique of the government's economic policy. Unlike his 1977 address at Jaji that attacked Nigeria's trading-post status, its foreign dependence, and its comprador elements, a role was assigned to the state in the economy that was close to the views of the World Bank and IMF.[17]

The intervention of the former army officers alarmed the regime, and it attempted to clamp down on all political discussion. But the divisions within the Supreme Military Council had intensified, providing the dynamic for a successful coup attempt after only twenty months of the Buhari regime.

Economic Policy

The immediate economic objective of the regime was to further reduce government expenditure, control the budget deficit, and establish control over Nigeria's insatiable demand for imports. The emphasis was on domestic austerity. The idea was that if Nigeria could hold out for three hard years of domestic austerity, its short-term liquidity problem would be solved, leaving it with a medium- and long-term debt profile that was less burdensome than that of the major Latin American debtors.[18] It would then have the confidence of its foreign creditors. Together with the emphasis on domestic austerity went the drive to root out corruption and, in some circles, a misplaced optimism about the amount of money that could be recovered from corrupt politicians and businesspeople.[19]

Current and capital expenditures were reduced and education subsidies cut. A general moratorium on new public capital spending was imposed, and expenditure on most existing projects was delayed pending the results of the Projects Review Committee that was set up to review all projects valued at over N30 million. There were severe cuts in public sector employment. The scale of the retrenchment in the public sector can be judged from the fact that between January and September 1984 ten state governments announced the loss of nearly 53,000 jobs.[20] Government departments took steps to recover the costs of services provided for public sector employees. A wage freeze was imposed, strikes were banned, and trade union influence reduced. In the private sector, the scale of redundancies accelerated as industry shed labour and increased profitability. Real wages plummeted, with inflation officially estimated at 40 percent in 1984, the highest figure on record. Inflation then fell officially to 5.5 percent in 1985.

Many states introduced development levies, and school fees were reintroduced. Poll and cattle taxes were also reintroduced. In Imo state, there were four levies—development, education, sports endowment, and blood bank.[21] Whether "management by levies" led to significant increases in revenue is uncertain.

On Easter Monday, two weeks before the delayed 1984 budget, a currency change was announced. The announcement took practically everyone by surprise. The aim was to stamp out corruption, counterfeit currency, and the black market by neutralising money held outside the country and forcing hoarders to account for their cash. Individuals were allowed to exchange only a maximum of N5,000 in the bank unless they swore an affidavit on how they acquired the excess. The first effect was to cause a miniboom in consumer spending, with prices of consumer durables rising by 30 percent or more. There was also a rush to pay off old debts, and the Nigerian Electric Power Authority suddenly found longstanding bills being settled in old notes. One unintended side effect was the loss of savings in rural areas for those who could not get to the banks in time.

The exercise could never be a very precise one because there was uncertainty as to how much money was in circulation and much economic activity was in the black market. Convinced that large sums were out of the country in illegal hoards and that millions were kept idle by the very rich, the Central Bank underestimated the amount of money in circulation and hence the demand for new notes. The Central Bank also appears to have wanted to use the occasion to reduce the money supply. The official estimate of the cash in circulation was about N5.5 billion, and the Central Bank issued less than N3 billion. The result was a severe cash shortage, and prices fell after the first inflationary burst. By the end of 1984 the total currency in circulation had risen only to levels similar to the end of 1983.

Nine study groups were set up to review policy in various areas. The government delayed action on these reports, and there is little evidence of their influence in the 1985 budget. In fact, the government stuck to its austerity programme and showed little interest in new policy initiatives as it battled with various interest groups. No action was taken to proceed with privatisation or commercialisation, though some tentative steps were taken in this direction. One measure that was not recommended but was none the less pursued was the expansion of River Basin Development Authorities to nineteen bodies.

Priority in the use of foreign exchange was given to servicing the external debt. The allocation of the residual amount of foreign exchange implied priority for industry and a more protective stance towards domestic food production. An attempt was made to rationalise protection with a reduction in nominal import duties and a pledge that the new rates would be maintained for a minimum of three years. All imports were placed under special imports licence if not banned outright. Although the level of imports was reduced, the distribution of import licences remained highly controversial. As part of the regime's effort to rectify civilian mismanagement and combat corruption, the ministries of Commerce and Industry were merged and licence allocation decided by the permanent secretary of the combined ministry.

The move to centralise authority and widen the scope of licensing created enormous problems of bureaucratic allocation inherent in planning when large amounts of information are required and time is scarce. An expanded system of committees considered applications for licences in the light of published criteria, guided by detailed foreign exchange budgets worked out by the Central Bank.[22] The new controls succeeded to some extent in harmonising foreign exchange disbursements with available receipts. The licensing exercise also managed to channel a larger proportion of import licences to genuine importers than had been the case under the civilian government. Yet because all imports were under licence, in absolute terms probably more licences were allocated wrongly than ever before, despite the greater conscientiousness of the authorities.

The government also intervened in trade in other ways. At first, the regime played down the role of the Nigerian National Supply Company (NNSC) and relied upon the major trading houses for direct sales of essential commodities.[23] It also tried to reduce trading margins by government-to-government purchase abroad. Later the regime tried distribution via the NNSC with the appointment of three distributors from each state based on recommendations from the state government.[24] In principle, a public agency could restrain inflation by importing on its own account and then selling to consumers or through agents at controlled prices. In practice, the agency lacked the ability or will to control the prices charged by most of its designated distributors. Only a small segment of consumers had access to goods at official prices. Moreover, the government was inclined to allocate a large proportion of state-purchased commodities to its own employees. Direct sales to the public were only 28 percent of sales, with state governments taking 50 percent; federal and private companies, 20 percent; and the Nigerian Labour Congress (NLC), 2 percent.[25] By 1985, free allocations of essential commodities, or the right to purchase them at official prices, constituted a large component of civil service incomes, otherwise relatively low by the standards of the urban salariat. In fact, the public service tacitly awarded itself numerous pay increases, without any visible claim on government revenues, simply by increasing the scale of commodity allocations and liberalising the official interpretation of what was considered "essential."

The regime adopted a very cautious attitude to new external borrowing and held out against any deal with the IMF. There was considerable domestic support for the government's position. At the United Bank for Africa conference in April 1984, the strength of opposition to the IMF and devaluation by Nigerian bankers and others was clearly demonstrated.[26] The NLC and the Academic Staff Union of Universities (ASUU) called for a complete cancellation or moratorium on the debt. There was some progress on IMF conditionalities but the abolition of the petroleum subsidy remained a sticking point with the IMF. It was over the question of devaluation and trade liberalisation that negotiations really broke down.[27] The IMF wanted a 60 percent devaluation, with an initial move of 25 percent to 30 percent.[28] Nigerian officials favoured a smaller initial move and less adjustment of the exchange rate overall.

In the absence of any agreement with the IMF, Nigerian proposals to reschedule officially insured debt were rejected by official credit agencies led by Britain's Export Credits Guarantee Department (ECGD). Attempts to bypass the official agencies by offering trade creditors direct settlement of debt did not succeed. However, arrangements were made to refinance some short-term trade arrears with uninsured creditors through the issue of promissory notes.

As an alternative strategy to an IMF agreement and further foreign loans and credits, the government promoted a series of countertrade deals designed to increase imports.[29] When the regime fell in August 1985, agreements worth about N2 billion were in the pipeline with Brazil, Austria, France, and Italy. Countertrade was seen as a means of weakening solidarity among creditor nations by introducing special bilateral relationships. The most important and advanced agreement was with Brazil. If the deal with Brazil had been completed according to plan, Brazil would have become Nigeria's main trading partner, marking an important shift away from the pattern of trade links with Europe.

The deals proved difficult to negotiate because the price of oil was falling in a weak world market. The deals were also open to the objection that oil was being bartered at a discount and that large importers were being favoured. In any event, they exerted a downward pressure on the spot oil price and made conventional marketing strategy more difficult for the NNPC, which opposed the countertrade. It is questionable how far the deals involved any net addition to Nigerian oil sales rather than a displacement of sales. It is probable that Nigeria was able to bring in some imports over and above the foreign exchange budget. When the regime fell, only slow progress had been made with the deals.

Opinion on the merits of countertrade was divided.[30] Some felt that it was a way of avoiding more thorough reforms. Others saw it as an opportunity to restructure trade away from Western Europe and encourage South-South links, especially with Brazil.[31] Still others saw it as a way of financing large-scale projects like the Ajaokuta steel works. When the Buhari regime fell, the deals were suspended and a committee of investigation appointed under Ojetunji Aboyade. The committee concluded that

"Nigeria was not yet equipped for countertrade in its present form of policy formation," an admission that Nigeria was bettered by aggressive bargaining.[32] In particular, high margins for sugar and chemicals in the Brazilian deal were criticised. Moreover, it was shown that countertrade had been used to import consumer goods and other nonessentials. Yet the committee saw countertrade as a useful supplement for establishing long-term contracts and agreed that it should continue to help finance large-scale capital projects. It recommended that existing deals should be renegotiated.

Conclusion

The military takeover that ended the Second Republic was greeted with popular approval. Within twenty months the Buhari regime had managed to lose much of this support. How did this happen? Some of the policies and measures that the regime pursued did have the support of a majority of the propertied classes. These policies and measures included the refusal to come to terms with the IMF (though opinion shifted during the course of the regime), countertrade, the War Against Indiscipline, the drive against corruption, and the detention and trial of the politicians, though detention without trial for long periods eroded the regime's legitimacy. It was, as Onwuchekwu Jemie put it, "the only government in Nigeria's history that attempted not only to probe, but also to prosecute and punish fraud in high places."[33]

It has been suggested that the regime fell partly because of its failure to do a deal with the IMF. There is a large measure of truth in this judgement, but it is not the whole story. Pressure for an agreement with the IMF had begun to gain some momentum by 1985. Import licence regulation was not a success, and the problem of financing trade was not solved. In addition, the policy of fulfilling debt service obligations in full began to be questioned. The regime certainly lacked the imagination to rethink economic strategy or shift the economic debate away from the prospect of unremitting austerity.

The unpopularity of the government stemmed from its increasingly authoritarian tendency and a style of government in which there was little or no consultation. Power was arrogated by a small group of conservative individuals. This situation alienated other officers, split the SMC, and threatened to disrupt the army. There was, too, a pronorthern bias in the makeup of the regime and the appointments it made, which increased tension. There was some suppression of individual liberties. It never reached the proportions of some African or Latin American dictatorships, but the signs were there. The treatment of the press also helped to induce a climate of fear and repression.

Authoritarian rule was linked first and foremost to reaction and the corrective call to order in the aftermath of the excesses and economic chaos of the years of civil rule. It was related to the need for a strong centre that would resist the demands of organised labour and professional groups and cut government deficits. It was related, too, to the nature of the ruling group and the suspicion and surveillance that it engendered within the SMC. The growth of authoritarian rule was not linked directly to the political requirements of a programme of economic reform. It is hard to see how a Structural Adjustment Programme could have been on the agenda in the immediate aftermath of civil rule, when the need was to establish basic economic controls and accountability, a condition for any economic strategy. Despite the steady growth of authoritarian rule, the regime never came close to embracing a Structural Adjustment Programme. The regime found itself locked in a downward spiral of criticism and oppression with a tunnel vision of economic austerity that allowed no glimpse of light at the end.

Notes

1. *Objectives, Policies and Programmes of the Federal Military Government*, Lagos, 1984.

2. *Guardian* (London), 13 September 1985; *West Africa*, 25 November 1985.

3. *Guardian* (Lagos), 31 July 1985.

4. *Guardian* (Lagos), 4 July 1985.

5. *Guardian* (Lagos), 4 July 1985.

6. *New Nigerian*, 1 April 1985.

7. *New Nigerian*, 10 June 1985.

8. *Daily Times*, 21 April 1984.

9. M. Mortimore, "Shifting Sands and Human Sorrow: Social Responses to Drought and Desertification," lecture, University of Durham, 1985.

10. S. G. Ikoku, *Nigeria's Fourth Coup d'Etat* (Enugu, Fourth Dimension, 1985), p. 17.

11. *Nigerian Economic Review, 1986* no. 1 (Lagos: John West Publications, n.d.).

12. *New Nigerian*, 19 April 1984

13. *Guardian* (Lagos), 17 April 1985.

14. I have drawn on the account given in A. S. Mohammed, "The Struggle for Democratic Rights and Socialism in Nigeria, 1979–1986," paper presented to the Review of African Political Economy conference, Liverpool, 1986.

15. *Nigerian Newsletter*, no. 157, 9 February 1985.

16. *National Concord*, 21 June 1985.

17. *Daily Times*, 7 August 1985. The Jaji address is found in O. Oyediran, ed., *Survey of Nigerian Affairs, 1976/77*, (Ibadan: Nigerian Institute of International Affairs and Macmillan, 1981), pp. 143–149.

18. *Financial Times*, 28 August 1985.

19. Nzeribe gives an estimate of the funds recovered by various tribunals and investigating panels after one year as only N112 million and £1.6 million. F. A. Nzeribe, *Nigeria: Another Hope Betrayed* (London: Kilimanjaro, 1985), p. 83.

20. A. O. Olukoshi, "World Bank/IMF Structural Adjustment Programmes and the African Working Class: A Nigerian Case Study," paper presented to Institute for African Alternatives Conference on the Impact of IMF and World Bank Policies on the People of Africa, London, September 1987.

21. Nzeribe, *Nigeria: Another Hope Betrayed*, p. 83.

22. I am indebted to Dan Zelikow for access to his unpublished work on import licensing.

23. *National Concord*, 16 July 1985.

24. *New Nigerian*, 1 April 1985.

25. *Daily Times*, 21 April 1984.

26. "Reality Takes a Back Seat," *West Africa*, 2 April 1984; *Daily Times*, 18 September 1985.

27. *Guardian* (Lagos), 27 September 1985.

28. "Presidential Committee on the IMF Loan, Press Statement," *Guardian* (Lagos), 5 October 1985.

29. The government also asked for the balance of a loan from Saudi Arabia ($1.6 billion) to be paid, but this request was declined under pressure from the United States and the IMF. Y. Bangura, "The IMF/World Bank Conditionality and Nigeria's Structural Adjustment Programme," paper presented to seminar on The IMF and the World Bank in Africa, Scandinavian Institute of African Studies, Uppsala, 27–29 January 1987, p. 12.

30. See *Guardian* (Lagos), 23 May 1985; *National Concord*, 31 May 1985; *New Nigerian*, 17 July 1985; *National Concord*, 9 October 1985.

31. I have discussed links between Brazil and Africa, and South-South relations, in my article, "Brazil and Africa: Geopolitics, Trade and Technology in the South Atlantic," *African Affairs* 81/322 (January 1982), pp. 3–20.

32. *Nigerian Newsletter*, no. 178, 30 November 1985.

33. *Guardian* (Lagos), 10 May 1987.

6

The Babangida Regime

The Exercise of Power

General Ibrahim Babangida had considerable knowledge and experience of Nigerian government and a strong following within the army.[1] He was a member of the Supreme Military Council under the Mohammed-Obasanjo and Buhari governments. During the Second Republic, he had been responsible for Operations and Military Planning. He had been involved in the 1975 and 1984 military coups and had personally confronted Lt-Colonel Bukar Dimka after the assassination of Murtala Mohammed. At that time, he was commander of the new Armoured Corps Division and was involved in the modernisation and equipping of the army.

Consultation and Debate

In order to increase the representation of various organisations in the army and include relatively junior officers who had participated in the coup, the size of the SMC was increased from eighteen to twenty-eight members, and it was renamed the Armed Forces Ruling Council (AFRC). In reaction to the concentration of power wielded by the former chief of staff, Supreme Headquarters, the functions of this post were split in two, with the military role transferred to Minister of Defence Lt-General Domkat Bali, who became chairman of the newly created Joint Chiefs of Staff. He remained in this post until the end of 1989, when the president took over the defence portfolio in a controversial reshuffle. A chief of general staff was appointed whose functions were restricted to the political administration of the country. To broaden participation of the military in national affairs an Armed Services Consultative Assembly was set up in 1989.

None of the three major ethno-linguistic groups in the country could claim any kind of dominance in the makeup of the AFRC. The composition of the council shifted power away from the Hausa-Fulani (two members) towards the northern minorities. When account is taken of all three ruling bodies (AFRC, National Council of Ministers, and National Council of States), it is clear that careful attention was paid to balancing and federal character. It was only after the reshuffle in 1989 that public perception on this point changed.

Ministerial appointments brought in critics of the former regime as well as technocrats and some radicals. The appointment of Kuye Ransome-Kuti as minister of health was an astute move. Not only did it place someone of undoubted integrity and radical inclinations in power, it was also a gesture to the Ransome-Kuti family. Under Buhari, Fela Anikulapo-Kuti, the popular musician, had been jailed for a trivial foreign exchange offence, and another brother, Beko, had led the doctors' strike and been detained. Other critics who secured appointments included the president of the bar association, the former editor of the *National Concord,* and retired General Julius Akinrinade. Prominent leftists were co-opted into government positions or committees. In general, the calibre of ministerial appointments was probably higher than under any previous government, military or civilian.

The early actions of the administration demonstrated a more open style of government that encouraged consultation and debate. Decree No. 4 was abrogated. Trials of politicians were suspended, and those held without trial were released conditionally. Judicial tribunals were set up to review the cases of those convicted by military tribunal, those still held in detention, and those released.

An early commitment was made to return the country to civil rule and a Political Bureau was established to conduct a debate about the new form of government and report after one year. This was to be a military government with a constant pretension to guide the nation to a more democratic form of government. Thus the regime could justify its existence partly by its determination to hand over power to a civilian government. Its main justification, however, lay in its commitment to a programme of economic reforms, which was introduced in 1976. Committees were set up to orchestrate a public debate over the issue of an agreement with the IMF and to examine the controversial question of countertrade. It was thought that the benefits of economic reform would be apparent after about two years, and the government would then be free to concentrate its energies on the political transition (see Table 6.1). This assessment was to prove very optimistic. In the face of opposition to the Structural Adjustment Programme, the government clamped down on its critics and curtailed debate. Decree No. 2, which allowed detention without trial, remained in force. Abuses of human rights and the appalling conditions in Nigerian prisons were highlighted by organisations like the Civil Liberties Organisation and the National Association of Democratic Lawyers.

The regime initially cultivated a relaxed and open style with the press. In 1987, however, relations with the press deteriorated sharply following

TABLE 6.1 The Countdown to Civilian Rule

1987
Third quarter:
Establishment of the Directorate for Social Mobilisation
Establishment of a National Electoral Commission
Establishment of a Constitution Drafting Committee
Fourth quarter:
Elections into local governments on non-party basis

1988
First quarter:
Establishment of National Population Commission
Establishment of Code of Conduct Bureau
Establishment of Code of Conduct Tribunal
Establishment of Constituent Assembly
Inauguration of National Revenue Mobilisation Commission
Second quarter:
Termination of Structural Adjustment Programme (SAP)
Third quarter:
Consolidation of gains of Structural Adjustment Programme (SAP)
Fourth quarter:
Consolidation of gains of Structural Adjustment Programme (SAP)

1989
First quarter:
Promulgation of a new constitution
Release of new fiscal arrangements
Second quarter:
Lift of ban on party politics
Third quarter:
Announcement of two recognised and registered political parties
Fourth quarter:
Election into local governments on political party basis

1990
First and second quarters:
Election into state legislatures and state executives
Third quarter:
Convening of state legislatures
Fourth quarter:
Swearing-in of state legislatures

1991
First, second, and third quarters:
National population census
Fourth quarter:
Local government elections

1992
First and second quarters:
Elections into federal legislatures and convening of National Assembly
Third and fourth quarters:
Presidential election
Swearing-in of new president and final disengagement by the armed forces

Source: West Africa (London), 13 July 1987. Reprinted with permission.

the killing of the *Newswatch* editor, Dele Giwa, with a parcel bomb, and harassment of the press increased. The security services had interrogated Giwa shortly before his death, and many people linked them and the government with his death. Later, *Newswatch* was proscribed for six months for leaking the report of the Political Bureau, but the ban was lifted before it was due to expire. Relations with the press became more sensitive and editors were put under pressure to conform.

Institutional Reform

The regime strengthened the Office of the President. It had strong reservations about the competence and efficiency of the civil service. One result of the disillusionment with the civil service was the tendency to set up a parallel bureaucracy with presidential committees, directorates, and executive aides that was expected to move faster than the traditional bureaucracy. In October 1985, an ad hoc Presidential Advisory Committee was established. It was largely composed of academics without private sector representation and was headed by Ojetunji Aboyade, former vice-chancellor of the University of Ife. After the 1986 budget, in an important move, the post of secretary to the Federal Military Government was re-created. It was filled by Olu Falae, a liberal economist who had been a federal permanent secretary and managing director of a merchant bank. The idea behind this move was to increase presidential power over the ministries and other governmental agencies and to increase the capacity to pursue, implement, and monitor policies essential to the tighter fiscal stance that a Structural Adjustment Programme demanded. Early in 1988, economic management was further centralised with the removal of the Budget Department of the Ministry of Finance and Economic Development to the President's Office. The Central Bank was also made directly responsible to the Office of the President.

In the 1988 budget, measures were announced to increase the political commitment of the executive and the efficiency and professionalism of the ministries. In a major reform, ministers were henceforth to be both chief executives and accounting officers for their ministries. This meant a decisive shift away from the old parliamentary system where the advisory function of the permanent secretary was balanced against the executive power of the minister towards a single line of command characteristic of a presidential system. In addition, permanent secretaries, who were already political officeholders, were to retire with the government that appointed them. Each ministry was to appoint its own staff, who would make their careers within the ministry of their choice. The reforms can be seen as a further erosion of the position of senior civil servants, who reached the height of their power under General Gowon, and as a move towards a presidential system of government. The reforms raised questions about the adequacy of checks on the accountability of ministers. To meet this objection, stronger powers for the auditor-general were recommended.[2]

The National Security Organisation was disbanded. Later it was reorganised and split into three: the Defence Intelligence Agency, the Nigerian Intelligence Agency, and the State Security Services. A coordinator of national security was posted to the Office of the President to allow firm control of security by the president. From a rough and ready start in 1976, the NSO had evolved into a quieter, more sophisticated organ of state surveillance. Although the NSO came to be very unpopular under Buhari, a faction within it was seriously engaged in the fight against corruption. Such inquiries would probably have embarrassed the new regime, so they could now be conveniently stopped under the blanket of human rights. As a result, the anticorruption drive that was prominent under Buhari faded under Babangida. Senior members of the administration, including governors, made asset declarations. These disclosures were not made public, though they could be verified by the security agencies.

In a move to further strengthen the power of the president, the creation of a National Guard was proposed in 1989. The idea was to provide a force independent of the police that would act as a buffer between the military and civil population in the event of serious civil disorder.

Treatment of Politicians

The treatment of the former politicians detained under the Buhari regime raised a number of controversial issues about the role of the former president and vice-president, the relations between politicians and the military, and the course of future politics. As noted above, Babangida suspended trials by special military tribunals and released those who had been held without trial, some for as long as twenty months without charges. Judicial tribunals were then set up to review all cases.

Although there was a feeling that the sentences given out by the military tribunals had been discriminatory and detention without trial inexcusable, the decision to suspend the military tribunals was not a popular measure. Retired Lt-General Theophilus Danjuma and Benjamin Nwabueze criticised the decision.[3] Nwabueze argued that embezzlement of public funds was an offence of a peculiarly political nature and that Shagari and Ekueme must be tried by Special Tribunal for contributing to economic adversity.

The judicial tribunals led to lighter terms in some cases, as government white papers set aside the verdicts. Looking at the sentences of the various tribunals under the Buhari and Babangida governments, it is clear that state governors generally fared much worse than did the former NPN ministers and officials at the federal level. Some of the latter had been released early by the Buhari government; others stayed abroad; and others, who returned home, were cleared.

Former President Shagari and Vice-President Ekueme were released by the government, banned from politics for life, and restricted to their local government areas. This appeared to be a compromise decision. But controversy over the decision not to try Shagari rumbled on.

In all, the federal government banned for life forty-nine persons from seeking political office, including twelve former governors.[4] Other politicians were banned from public or elective office for ten years from the time of a formal return to civilian politics. Later in 1987, these decisions were overtaken by a blanket ban for life for all politicians who had held office since Nigeria gained independence in 1960 and had been found guilty of specific offences. Other politicians and military officers who had held high office were banned from politics until the start of the Third Republic. In the event, this latter restriction was lifted early in 1992 prior to the presidential elections, demonstrating the extent of the involvement of the old politicians in the new parties and the power of their lobbies.

Challenges to Authority

After the initial period of relaxation and debate, the government was confronted with opposition to its programme of economic reforms. The main challenge to the regime's authority was provided by the NLC together with students and university teachers. Other challenges included two attempted coup plots in 1985 and 1990. There were also spontaneous urban riots and many incidents of urban violence, usually directed against the police, in which economic hardship played a major role. Religious tensions and conflicts that threatened the unity and secular nature of the state at another level will be treated separately.

Until it was dissolved in early 1988, the NLC remained an independent body consistently opposing the government's economic policies. NLC solidarity with students in the aftermath of the invasion of the Ahmadu Bello campus in May 1986 led to arrest of union leaders. The government was particularly incensed by union opposition to its proposal to increase petroleum prices. When the NLC executive was dissolved in early 1988 and fuel prices were increased by a small amount, there followed riots in Jos in which at least six persons were killed and a series of strikes in major urban centres. Students were again involved in anti-SAP riots in Benin in 1989.

Trade union power was attacked through a decree that severed senior staff associations, including academic staff, from membership of the NLC. Critics of the SAP were singled out as extremist, and radical lecturers were systematically removed from the universities. Outspoken opponents of the regime, like Balarabe Musa, the former governor of Kaduna state, and

Gani Fawehinmi, a radical lawyer who had challenged the government over its handling of Dele Giwa's assassination, were detained and released.

The motives behind the coup attempt of late 1985 remain obscure. It appeared unwarranted and untimely and had practically no public support. Ten persons were executed, including the minister for the Federal Capital Territory, Major-General Mamman Vatsa, and a number of air force officers. Vatsa was a former classmate of the president from Bida Middle School and had been retained by him in the AFRC. Personal rivalry between the two officers was probably at the root of the affair.

The April 1990 coup attempt was organised by junior Middle Belt officers and financed by a 36-year-old businessman from Bendel state. A ferocious attack was launched on Dodan Barracks, but the president escaped, and other strategic centres in Lagos and elsewhere were unaffected. The plotters made a crude appeal for a Middle Belt–Southern alliance and announced the temporary excision of five, predominantly Muslim, far-northern states from the federation. This was a recipe for civil war and alienated much potential support at the outset. The coup attempt was in part a reaction to the 1989 reshuffle in which prominent Middle Belt officers were seen to lose power. It was a stark reminder that the unity of the country could not be taken for granted twenty years after the end of the civil war.

Throughout the period, concern over law and order and the role of the police increased. Extortion at road blocks by police and traffic wardens ("yellow fever") was common. Public concern was fuelled by armed robbery and by a number of killings, including those of Dele Giwa, the editor of *Newswatch*, and the wife of the former head of state, retired General Obasanjo. The saga of Lawrence Anini, "The Law," a robber from Bendel state, which gripped the Nigerian media late in 1986, gave vent to widespread public concern about insecurity and violence.[5] All manner of explanation and solution to the problem was offered. In the Anini case, understandings between criminals and elements in the police broke down. Anini pursued a vendetta against the authorities, killing several policemen. He was widely perceived to transfer wealth from the rich to less fortunate citizens. Thus he gained some public sympathy, which further demoralised the police force.

The incompetence of the police was demonstrated by their role in the suppression of the 'Yan Tatsine riots. Their politicisation was confirmed under the Shagari regime when the mobile paramilitary force, "the kill-and-goes," became extremely unpopular.

Public bitterness against the police led to violent incidents in which the police were attacked. One potent factor here was the increased burden of police depredations upon petty traders, transporters, taxi drivers, and artisans, as the economy deteriorated with loss of opportunities and stiffer competition. In Minna, the capital of Niger state, the death of a popular butcher in police handcuffs led to riots for six hours and an attack on the divisional police headquarters.[6] This incident was the culmination of many complaints by butchers and traders about police harassment. About two months before the riot, butchers had claimed that police levies on trucks carrying cattle to Minna had forced them to sell meat at very high prices. In Bauchi, a mass protest by transport workers was triggered by the shooting of a driver at a police checkpoint and led to the death of several policemen.[7] On Lagos Island, youths engaged the police in a three-day pitched battle in protest against the killing of two brothers by a police constable.[8]

As a result of police inadequacies, vigilante action by communities and associations increased. For example, in Onitsha, the location of the largest market in Nigeria, action against armed robbers led to the burning of hotels and bars on several occasions.[9] These actions were organised by the powerful Onitsha Market Traders Association (OMATA).

Religious Controversy and Conflict

Since 1970, religious controversy and intolerance in Nigeria have increased, and religious identities have become more overtly involved in political divisions. The danger of political polarisation along religious lines posed a threat to Nigerian unity and the secularity of the state.

Religious tensions, especially intrareligious ones, are not new to Nigeria. Within Islam there was competition between the Qadariyya and Tijaniyya brotherhoods in the 1950s and 1960s. Later in the 1970s there was also localised conflict between the reformist Izala movement and the brotherhoods. But open conflict between Christians and Muslims has been very rare in the past, and such divisions have not emerged so forcibly at a national level and threatened to become so overtly part of wider political struggles. Religion has on occasion been manipulated for political purposes.[10] In general, though, religious identities—as distinct from ethnic, sectional, and class ones—have not been harnessed to mobilise political support. Among the Yoruba, where both Islam and Christianity are present in most communities, religious differences have not given rise to conflict or greatly affected political alignments. Because of the pervasiveness of both religions, there has been little incentive to promote religion as a communal good or to see communities in religious terms.[11]

A number of occasions when religious controversy came to prominence are outlined in the following paragraphs, and a number of factors behind the salience of religion are then examined.

In Chapter 3, I treated the controversy over the Sharia Court of Appeal in 1978. The 1979 constitution was deliberately secular in word and spirit.

Yet the Sharia issue rumbled on, and Christians responded with calls for ecclesiastical courts that would apply canon law, should Sharia law be extended.[12] In 1988, ten years after the original intervention, the military government was again forced to intervene in the Constituent Assembly to cut short an increasingly acrimonious debate on the Sharia. This time, it was Christian members of the assembly who wanted to pursue the matter and expunge all reference to the Sharia from the constitution.

Another major controversy occurred in 1986, when Nigeria became a regular member of the Organisation of the Islamic Conference (OIC). Nigeria's membership was concluded without discussion in the AFRC or the Ministry of External Affairs. When news leaked out, Christian leaders protested vigorously and demanded the country's withdrawal. Informal diplomacy between Islamic leaders in Nigeria and Arab states had gone on for many years and was strongly promoted by Ahmadu Bello, the premier of the Northern Region, who took a keen interest in Nigeria's participation in international Islamic organisations and regarded Nigeria as a Muslim country. The Supreme Council for Islamic Affairs in Nigeria was adamant that Nigeria should remain a member of the OIC. The president was trapped by the intensity of the debate and tried to cool passions by setting up a committee under Colonel John Shagaya to examine the implications of Nigerian membership—a clear admission that the government had not done its homework.

The 'Yan Tatsine riots, which caused great loss of life in or near a number of major cities in northern Nigeria, together with numerous incidents that started in 1978 do not fall within the pattern of Islamic-Christian conflict. They were part of a broader pattern of Islamic revival, which in this case involved armed insurrections by an unorthodox sect led by Alhaji Mohammed Marwa Maitatsine in Kano (1980), Kaduna (1982), Bulum-Ketu in Maiduguri (1982), Jimeta near Yola (1984), and Gombe (1985). In the case of the Kano uprising (18–29 December 1980), 4,177 civilians were killed according to official figures.[13] Paul Lubeck has examined the social and material basis for the millenarian ideology that inspired the 'Yan Tatsine in Kano.[14] Peripatetic mallams (Islamic teachers) and wandering Koranic students who formed a floating pool of seasonal labour in Kano and subsisted on Islamic charity had become a large, impoverished lumpen population and a threat to property. The ideology of the 'Yan Tatsine asserted the moral superiority of material deprivation and condemned the corruption of existing secular and religious elites, especially the orgy of consumption during the oil boom.

The Kaduna State Crisis

The religious disturbances in Kaduna state in March 1987 began in the Christian-majority area of southern Zaria and were triggered by events at the Kafanchan College of Education. Muslim students celebrated Uthman Dan Fodio week; this event was followed by a Christian Crusade organised by the Fellowship of Christian Students. There was a dispute over the interpretation of the Koran in a sermon delivered by the crusade leader, who was a convert from Islam. In the ensuing disturbance, which spread to the town, eight Muslim students were killed and four mosques burnt down.[15]

News of the Kafanchan riot spread to the Muslim-majority areas of Kaduna state, and riots followed in Zaria, Kaduna, Funtua, Kankia, and Katsina. Muslim youths systematically burnt churches, hotels, beer parlours, and residences.

In evidence given to inquiries afterwards, it was clear that the police and army failed to take action against rioters for at least twenty-four hours. In fact, divisions opened up between the police and the army, the army generally being held to be pro-Christian.[16] When the army did act, it was accused of indiscriminate arrests and brutality by Muslim leaders who closed ranks. Reporting by the southern press was seen as biased and part of a deliberately orchestrated campaign to malign Muslims. For Christians, the Federal Radio Corporation of Nigeria, Kaduna was held to have whipped up feeling against Christians through its reporting of the Kafanchan riot. The Donli commission of inquiry appointed by the Kaduna state government was attacked as partial by Muslims while it was sitting,[17] and when it reported, it came under fire from the Christian Association of Nigeria (CAN) for being deliberately evasive.[18]

In a bid to reduce tension, the government placed a ban on religious associations in colleges and universities and acted to curb extremist preachers. State governments also put a ban on religious broadcasting and advertisements. The government also tried to pull the state out of its involvement with religious affairs. An Advisory Council on Religious Affairs was set up with a dozen members from CAN and a dozen from the Supreme Council for Islamic Affairs. The council quickly became deadlocked. Responsibility for the registration of religious bodies was transferred away from the Ministry of Internal Affairs to this new body.[19] The government indicated that it would gradually reduce its sponsorship of pilgrimage and other religious activities. The government was concerned, too, about divisions within the Muslim community. A further response was the reactivation of the Jama'atu Nasril Islam (JNI) with a large rally and appeal in Kaduna, the first since its inception in 1962.[20] A conciliation committee under the emir of Kano, Alhaji Ado Bayero, met to try and resolve differences between Izala, Tijaniyya, and Qadiriyya.[21]

The rioting in Kafanchan was sparked off against the background of a long-standing power struggle between the indigenes of Kafanchan and nonindigenous Muslim Hausa rulers who controlled titles, including the district headship of Kafanchan appointed by the emir of Jemaa.[22] The distinction between indigenes and outsiders does not coincide neatly with religious differences, but the political struggle for more local rights in an area that had been disadvantaged within Kaduna state and within the former Northern Region sharpened religious as well as ethnic differences.

On a broader front, the conflict in Kafanchan and the reaction elsewhere in Kaduna state had implications for attempts to mobilise political power on the basis of northern unity. Religious tension made it more difficult for the core Hausa-Fulani areas to achieve political alliances with northern minority elites, as the case of the Sharia controversy in 1978 demonstrated. This tension was one of the main preoccupations of the meeting of the Committee of Northern Elders in Lugard Hall, Kaduna, in June 1987.[23]

Underlying Factors

To understand the prominence that religious issues and organisations have attained in Nigeria, a number of factors are relevant. First, there was the general growth and dynamism of Islam and Christianity and the rise of fundamentalism in both Islam and Christianity. Second, there was the impact of the civil war and the increased influence of international tensions on domestic divisions. Third, there was the growth of state intervention in areas like education that were hitherto the province of religious bodies. Finally, there was the changed position of Christian populations within the northern states.

Without an accurate census, the numerical strength of the two principal religions is unknown. The situation is complicated by the fact that the majority of Nigerians also practise some elements of traditional African religion. At the time of the not very reliable 1963 census, the breakdown was Islam, 49 percent; Christian, 34 percent; and Other, 17 percent (see Table 2.4). Compared with the 1952 census this showed a large increase in the Christian share entirely at the expense of the traditional religion category.

In a recent article, Ali Mazrui has stressed the expansion of Islam, arguing that the spread of Christianity has slowed down since independence.[24] He may conceivably be right, but none of the reasons he advanced to support his position are at all convincing. In particular, his arguments ignored the indigenisation of African Christianity in terms of personnel, liturgy, and doctrinal emphases, the rapid growth of the African Independent Churches, and the expansion of Pentecostal churches since the 1970s. Mazrui made a facile link between the prestige of Western civilisation and Christianity. He argued that the prestige of the former has declined and with it the prospects for Christianity. He saw a decline in Christian missionary influence and schooling. Yet the indigenisation of Christian churches may well have made them more confident in their missionary work. Also, the expansion of primary schools under the Universal Primary Education scheme may have drawn pupils away from the Koranic schools. Mazrui claimed that there has been a shift from the mission of saving souls to the mission of saving lives within Christian missionary work. He produced no evidence to support this assertion. Although he stressed the role of the oil-rich Arab states in promoting Islamic expansion, he failed to recognise the extent of external support from Christian sources.

During the 1970s, there was a growth of Christian and Islamic fundamentalism and a rise of charismatic and prophetic movements. With the oil boom came an upsurge of materialism and a heightening of inequality. The decline in oil revenue brought increased uncertainty, poverty, unemployment, and lawlessness. Such conditions were favourable to religious zealotry.

In the early 1970s, charismatic renewal movements emerged among college students and university graduates in the southern states. These movements arose from existing interdenominational Christian groups like the Student Christian Movement (SCM), the Scripture Union (SU), and the Christian Union (CU).[25] They were heavily influenced by the pentecostal movement, which emphasised the doctrines of the baptism of the Holy Spirit and speaking in tongues. Born-again Christians attacked the established churches. The Scripture Union was proscribed in some Anglican dioceses and banned from schools.[26] These movements were associated with an upsurge of evangelism that included missionary work in the northern states. Some movements also adopted public positions on social and political issues. Thus the Christian Students' Social Movement, a nationwide evangelical-cum-pentecostal movement founded in 1977 by leaders of Christian Union groups in universities and colleges, aimed to awaken Christians to their political and social responsibilities.[27]

The Muslim Students Society, which was originally founded in Lagos in 1954 as a mainly Yoruba grouping of Muslim students, became active in the 1970s in the universities at Zaria, Kano, and Sokoto, where a radical leadership emerged. It first came to prominence with an antialcohol campaign at Bayero University college, Kano.[28] Later it took up the Sharia issue vociferously and was involved in campus disturbances at Zaria and Sokoto.

Islamic revival and reform since the 1970s has also been associated with the 'Yan Izala, a Muslim movement closely connected with Sheikh Abubakar Gumi, an influential Muslim leader in northern Nigeria with contacts among the political establishment. Izala is seen by its adherents as a liberating, reformist force based on the Sharia. Its adherents regard secularism as an immoral trend and press for Islamic ideas on government and education to be put into practice. It has a considerable following among the educated classes and populist appeal among workers, students, and urban youth, and it has considerable influence with the media (FRCN, Kaduna).

A former ambassador to Saudi Arabia, Sheikh Gumi was an adviser to Ahmadu Bello, the Sardauna of Sokoto, helping him to establish the Jama'atu Nasril Islam in 1962. He became grand kadi of Northern Nigeria in 1962. After the Sardauna's death, Gumi became more outspoken, promoting Izala and attacking the Sufi brotherhoods, especially the Tijaniyya with its strong following among the commercial classes in Kano. Corrupt mallams and traditional rulers were condemned. The remnants of traditional African religion still prevalent among Muslim communities were also attacked. In 1987, Sheikh Gumi stated that a Muslim could not accept a non-Muslim to lead the nation and that if a Muslim leader was not acceptable to Christians, the country would have to be divided into two parts.[29]

The traumatic experience of the civil war divided the Nigerian churches and jolted them into taking stronger positions on national issues. The churches were caught up in controversy over relief work in secessionist Biafra. More generally, as Bala Usman has written, the civil war led to the open and direct political use of religion and religious institutions, both Muslim and Christian, to support the cause of Nigerian unity against the very powerful prosecessionist propaganda from many Christian missionary organisations from Western Europe, the United States, and many parts of Africa.[30]

An international dimension to religious divisions within Nigeria was again apparent in the 1970s. Ripples from the confrontation between Israel and the Arab states and from the Iranian revolution reached Nigeria. In concrete terms, this influence meant the penetration of fundamentalist influences within Islam and Christianity and a stronger international interest in Nigeria's political and religious alignment. There was a large flow of funds and literature from Islamic countries and from the Americas, whose Christian sects have been very active in propagating the gospel.

Another contentious issue was the takeover of voluntary agency schools by state governments. This action, which contributed to a decline in educational standards, together with the introduction of Universal Primary Education in 1976 and the takeover of mission hospitals, brought the Christian churches together to face the government. The Christian Association of Nigeria (CAN) was formed in 1976 as an umbrella organisation for all denominations after leaders had been summoned to Dodan Barracks to be informed about the launch of the UPE scheme.[31] CAN acted as a liaison committee and watchdog, and it promoted evangelisation.

Finally, Christians in the northern states became more vigorous in asserting their identity. During the 1960s there was a rapid expansion of church attendances in some areas.[32] After 1963, Ahmadu Bello, the northern regional premier, embarked on conversion campaigns among the non-Muslim populations. He felt that Christian missionaries had for too long had a monopoly of educational and conversion privileges in the north.[33] These campaigns alarmed Christian populations and put them on the defensive.

With the assassination of the Sardauna in 1966 and the breakup of the Northern Region into new states, the old regional political hegemony established by the Northern People's Congress started to break down. With these political changes came a newfound confidence among northern Christians. The withdrawal of the Igbo immigrant population following the massacres of 1966 forced missionaries in the northern states to speed up the indigenisation of their churches. Formerly Christianity in the north had been viewed, at least from the perspective of the south, as the domain of richer, more educated Igbo immigrants who tended to dominate culturally Christian congregations in the major urban centres. The vigorous role of northern Christians in the Sharia debate and their leading role in CAN helped to dispel this view. Subsequently the main areas of religious conflict and tension were located on the southern fringes of emirates where communities with significant Christian populations felt at a political and material disadvantage. The disturbances in Kaduna state in 1987, in Bauchi state in 1991, and at Zangan Kataf in 1992 followed this pattern.

The Return to Civil Rule

The Political Bureau

The Political Bureau was inaugurated in January 1986 and submitted its report on the political future of Nigeria in March 1987.[34] Intellectuals tended to write off the work of the bureau as an irrelevancy, and others criticised its composition for being overloaded with academics. Despite the fact that the government found the bureau's advocacy of socialism unacceptable, the bureau did have some impact on the transition programme, the shape of party politics, and the constitutional arrangements. Essentially the government took what it wanted from the report.

The report was notable for the strongly interventionist role assigned to the state in promoting the development of the economy and in overcoming essentially political problems. According to the report, the state should own the commanding heights of the economy, with private enterprise being limited to agriculture and medium- and small-scale industry.[35] The federal government should also establish an effective industrial presence in each state. All peasant farmers should be organised into farmers' cooperatives to enhance production and disposal of their products, and government should establish mechanised farms.[36] None of these proposals were accepted by the government. Indeed, they ran counter to the thrust of the Structural Adjustment Programme, which was launched while the Bureau was at work.

The report saw the provision of welfare by the state as a long-term panacea for the problems of federal character, ethnicity, statism, and regionalism.[37] Although commending the doctrine of federal character, the bureau thought that the issue would ultimately be dealt with when social justice in the form of unimpeded access to education, basic health care, social insurance, housing, and food was assured for all citizens. Precisely how increases in state welfare were supposed to overcome the distributional struggles over access to state power and resources that underlay sectional conflict was not explained.

Among the recommendations of the bureau that were accepted by the government were a two-party system of government, the rejection of any form of dyarchy, the rejection of zoning and rotation of office, the rejection of any important role for traditional rulers, the use of referendum and recall, the establishment of a permanent National Revenue Mobilisation Commission to review revenue allocation, a more powerful National Electoral Commission, and a Code of Conduct Bureau and Tribunal.

Support for a one- or two-party system was widespread and drew on a number of different currents. In the past, a multiparty liberal democratic system was the preferred form of government. Now, as Jibrin Ibrahim observed, there was a clear shift in the tenor of the debate towards some limitation on the number of parties.[38] The palpable weakness of the Nigerian state during the Second Republic had shocked Nigerian intellectuals. Political scientists and intellectuals, including those on the left, propagated more restrictive, potentially authoritarian, forms of government.

Multiparty politics had come to be associated with instability and ethnic politics. The case for a two- or one-party system generally rested on a desire for more order and stability and the need for a stronger state capable of pursuing national objectives and managing the nation's economy. For retired Lt-General Danjuma and Chuba Okadigbo, former political adviser to President Shagari, a two-party system was seen as a way of sweeping aside the tripartite ethnic basis of party politics and creating national parties with an effective opposition.[39] In any case, it was argued that the experience of civil rule in the First and Second Republics showed that there was a strong tendency for two- or one-party systems to emerge from the plurality of parties and alliances.

The foregoing views also carried weight with members of the Political Bureau. With one exception, members proposed a weak two-party version in which both parties would accept the national philosophy of government and would differ only over the priorities and strategies of implementation.[40] The national philosophy, conceived in reaction to the prevailing dependent capitalist ideology, was broadly social democratic in conception. It emphasised social justice, equity in distribution and exchange, and participation and self-reliance in economic production.

Positions in favour of a one-party system or a zero-party option with some form of corporate representation were also common. For the emirs and chiefs of the ten northern states, party politics contributed nothing but lawlessness, insecurity of lives and property, entrenchment of tribalism and sectionalism, corruption, moral decadence, and retrogression.[41] The evolution of truly national parties was a forlorn hope.

A formal system of dyarchy involving joint military-civilian government had little support. In fact, the military rejected the bureau's proposal for military participation in the National Electoral Commission[42] and the National Population Commission.[43]

The idea of zoning and rotation of offices among the majority and minority ethno-linguistic groups, which had been introduced by the NPN, had much greater support. Among those who advocated some form of zoning were retired Lt-General Danjuma, Chief Abiola, and the emirs and chiefs of the ten northern states. This was rejected by the bureau on the grounds that it "amounts to acceptance of our inability to grow beyond ethnic or state loyalty."[44]

The government also rejected the Bureau's proposal for a single five-year term for officeholders, which had wide support, in favour of two four-year terms.[45] Given the determination of politicians to stay in power, the use of a maximum of two four-year terms of office instead of one five-year term makes the chances of a successful succession after the first term of office less likely. The second part of a first term would be devoted to amassing wealth in order to stay in power.

Although the government accepted the need for closer public control over the remuneration of legislators, it rejected the view that the assets of officeholders should be publicly declared.[46] The thorny question of placing limits on the corrupt private funding of political parties was also aired. The government accepted that it should fund the parties substantially. But it left any question of effective monitoring and enforcement to the National Electoral Commission.

Traditional rulers had pressed strongly for a more powerful role in the Third Republic, attacking the centralisation of power that had occurred under military rule and the educated elite for its role in misgovernment.[47] They argued for a Council of Chiefs in each state, with the chairman of each council having a seat in the Senate, where the other members would be nominated. These radical proposals received an equally strong rejection from the bureau.[48]

On state creation, the Political Bureau was divided.[49] Some members wanted to keep the nineteen-state structure. Others wanted two more states (Akwa Ibom and Katsina), and still others argued for six new states (Akwa Ibom, Delta, Katsina, Kogi, Sardauna, and Wawa). Later the government announced that only two new states would be created, Akwa Ibom from Cross River State and Katsina from Kaduna state. It explicitly rejected neglect and parity of treatment of ethnic groups as criteria for state creation.[50] Probably the group most disappointed at this outcome was the Igbo, who felt at a serious disadvantage with the Yoruba, who had four states. Igbo leaders had called for a confederal solution.[51] Agitation for more states continued. In August 1991 the government dropped its opposition and announced the creation of nine new states, including two new states in Igboland, to bring the total to thirty (see Table 3.1). With the finances of the states heavily dependent on the distribution of centralised oil revenues and representation at the federal level often dependent on state affiliation, it would be rash to predict an end to state creation. However, the economic case for spending more resources on the maintenance of bureaucracies and state infrastructures is very weak. If local government were to prove successful in harnessing local support and effective in the provision of infrastructure and services, the case for more states would be further undermined.

The government accepted the Bureau's proposal to give more responsibility and resources to the third tier of government, making the local government councils the basic unit for development.[52] It was noted earlier that the local government reforms of 1976 were not paralleled by real shifts of power and responsibility from the state governments to the new local government councils. The state governments generally kept political and financial control. No elections were held. Nevertheless, the reforms did transfer formal power away from traditional rulers, establish a more uniform system of local government throughout the country, and introduce federal funding.

The Babangida regime increased the share of local government in the Federation Account from 10 percent to 15 percent and then 20 percent (1992) and gave them responsibility for primary education and health care. Payments were now to be made directly, no longer via the state governments that had often withheld them in the past. State governments were also supposed to give 10 percent of their internally generated revenues to the councils. In 1988, ministries of local government were disbanded and the powers of the chairmen of the local councils increased. But, state governments kept a supervisory role, and local government secretaries, who acted as accounting officers, were still appointed by state governments.

Although the attempt to bring about greater responsibility and participation at the local government level was laudable, it remained to be seen how effectively power could be shifted downwards to check the steady accumulation of powers at the state and federal levels. Part of the problem derives from the present fiscal arrangements. The flow of revenue from the top down systematically removes the incentive to accountability and responsibility at the lower tier. Increased local revenues may well be a prerequisite for a more vigorous, independent system of local government.

The Transition Programme

In line with a minority opinion in the report of the Political Bureau, the government opted for an extra two years for the transition programme, extending the final handover of power to 1992. The postponement was well received partly because the public was less enthusiastic about the return of the politicians than formerly. The programme is outlined in Table 6.1.

Local government elections provided an inauspicious start to the transition programme. *The Guardian* saw them as characterised by inadequate preparation, confusion, frustration, and not a little skullduggery.[53] Before the elections were conducted, 72 million voter cards were issued in the registration exercise.[54] This figure was far above any reasonable estimate of the number of eligible voters. The elections were well contested, but because of malpractices and inadequate preparation elections were nullified in 312 local government wards, over half of them in Lagos.[55]

The role of the Constitution Drafting Committee and the Constituent Assembly in drafting the 1992 constitution was less significant than that of their counterparts in the 1970s. This was because the 1979 constitution was already in place for amendment and because the military had declared certain areas like the executive presidency and the two-party system outside the competence of the Assembly. When the new constitution was promulgated, it retained reference to the Sharia courts but restricted their jurisdiction to Muslims only. The number of senators and special advisers and state commissioners was reduced to cut the cost of government. An attempt by the Assembly to make it justiciable for Nigeria to be a welfare state was rejected.

The attempt by the military to create a new politics through political reform and social engineering had three elements. First, there was the restriction to two national political parties. Second, there was the attempt to create a new political leadership with a wide ban on political participation by former politicans and military and civilian officeholders. This attempt to wipe the slate clean appeared to be motivated by the belief that the malfunctioning of the representative system could be corrected if a set of corrupt, subversive and irresponsible politicians could be purged from the system. In the past, Nigerian politicians and other officeholders have shown a remarkable capacity to bounce back after their conduct has been found wanting. This was changed, if only temporarily.

Third, the government committed itself to an ambitious programme of social mobilisation and political education that was aimed at inculcating democratic values and conduct and changing the political culture. A Directorate for Social Mobilisation was launched in 1987 to execute the programme of Mass Mobilisation for Self-reliance, Social Justice, and Economic Recovery (MAMSER).

The government's determination to intervene was dramatically demonstrated in October 1989 when, in a surprise move, it rejected all of the six political parties that had been short-listed since the lifting of the ban on party politics in May. In their stead, the government announced the registration of two parties of its own creation, the National Republican Convention and the Social Democratic Party. This was an attempt to create two issue-based parties to be built up from the local government level through government sponsorship, funding, and supervision.

State government and National Assembly elections were reasonably well contested with neither party gaining a dominant position. However, the next step, the presidential primaries, conducted without supervision by the National Electoral Commission, was fraudulent. Politicians used their money to factionalise and control party executives. The elections were cancelled, party officials dismissed, and all presidential candidates disqualified. A further postponement of the final handover of power to August 1993 was announced in November 1992.

The attempt to guide the political process entailed a number of contradictions and inherent tensions. First, given the level of popular opposition to SAP, the government was unwilling to allow open debate over economic strategy, the very issue that might have provided the basis for ideological differences between the parties. Second, when the two parties emerged, it was again apparent that their antecedents lay in earlier patterns of political mobilisation. The core of the National Republican Convention lay in the far north, and its use of zoning to allocate party offices was reminiscent of the National Party of Nigeria. The Social Democratic Party had clear affinities with the opposition parties of the Second Republic and included disgruntled sympathisers of the NPN. Finally, once party politics gathered real momentum, the military found it increasingly difficult to control the political and economic agenda. The government was forced to give ground over the creation of states, the ban on politicians and control of public expenditure. With strong pressures for a return to civil rule, which I discuss shortly, the postponement of the handover increased the risks attached to the transition process.

Conclusion

In conclusion, after a brief assessment of the Babangida regime, I look at the forces behind the return to civil rule and the prospects for democracy.

Are there grounds for thinking that the kind of politics that so eroded the authority of the state in the Second Republic might reemerge? How is the return to civil rule related to pressures for economic reform? I leave until Chapter 10 consideration of how the politics of civil rule might be reconciled with the strategy of SAP and the demands of economic management.

The Babangida government demonstrated considerable political skills. The president proved a shrewd strategist and power broker who consulted widely, yet kept his opponents and supporters guessing about his ultimate intentions. Until the reshuffle of senior military officers at the end of 1989, which was widely perceived to shift power away from the Middle Belt to the far north, the government demonstrated a capacity to negotiate and balance different interests. Strong measures like the ban on politicians and the dissolution of the NLC and fledgling political parties were taken, but where political prudence dictated, the government reversed or moderated its stand. Thus the abolition of the national minimum wage and the attempt to introduce the compulsory wage deductions for the lower paid were withdrawn. The government also went back on its attempt to extend its power under the State Security Decree No. 2 after widespread protest.[56] However, unencumbered by a legislature and partisan politics, the president could dissolve and reappoint the AFRC and move to consolidate power by the creation of a National Guard.

The government relented, too, on its ban on *Newswatch* magazine, after a show of contrition by the editors. Under the relatively open form of military government in Nigeria, the press plays a central political role. It is one that differentiates Nigerian military government sharply from more authoritarian regimes elsewhere, both civil and military. Since 1979 the growth of private newspapers and magazines has been explosive. The press sets the tone for much intellectual discussion—hence the power of the press to inform and influence opinion, its vulnerability, and the fragility of relations between press and government. For the military, the press acts as a political barometer and sounding board. For opponents, pressure groups and the politically ambitious, it is a central avenue for protest, influence, and recognition.

The government attempted to defuse religious tension after the major blunder of the OIC membership. It is too early to assess whether the increase in religious tensions will mean that religious identities—as distinct from class, ethnic, and sectional ones—will have more prominence as a basis for political mobilisation than they have in the past. Open political debate and party competition may well reduce religious tension at the national level, as it did during the Second Republic, because of the need to make alliances that cut across religious divisions.

The regime is likely to be judged on the success of its economic programme (see Chapter 10) and the outcome of its attempt to create a more democratic form of government. For the great majority of the population, the SAP had failed to bring any respite from economic hardship. It was, moreover, seen to be very devisive and unequal in its economic impact. To assess the prospects for democracy, we need to look at the pressures behind the return to civil rule.

Where does the pressure to return to civil rule come from? First, there is middle-class resistance to military rule from professionals and intellectuals who uphold the universal ideal of bourgeois democracy. They resent the arbitrary nature of military rule, government by decree, and the periodic clashes between military and civil personnel. The trade unions also oppose the military on the grounds that they block the chance of a more popular democratic opening. The main ground swell of opposition to the military comes from politicians and some businesspeople who see military rule as narrowing the channels of access to state power and wealth. They are anxious to assert their own claims to economic advancement, as well as those of the communities they claim to represent. Above all, they dislike the monopolisation of power by the military and are quick to point out the benefits that military acquire from holding state office. They resent the fact that military officers retire early and then use their wealth and connections to establish themselves in the private sector or secure positions with state bodies. A related pressure arises from the expectations of junior officers who stand to gain from the retirement of the top officer corps which accompanies a military handover. There is here a strong element of elite competition and circulation in the return to civil rule, an element that is lacking in the much longer-term transitions from highly authoritarian regimes in Latin America.

The movement to return to civil rule is not the product of the political strength of bourgeois forces that seek to overturn authoritarian military government and establish favourable legal, political, and ideological conditions for capitalist development. The domestic bourgeois class has political, economic, and ideological weakness. It is in no position to gain power as a class, directly or indirectly. It is not bourgeois in life-style, culture, status, or political orientation.

Superficially, the coexistence in time of the movement to return the country to civil rule and the introduction of extensive economic reforms might suggest that the two trends are the product of common political and social forces. For example, from a neoliberal market perspective, democratisation, which involves the breaking down of concentrations of state power and greater public accountability, would be held to be reinforced by moves to deregulate the economy and "depoliticise" it through the withdrawal of the state. The latter would in turn promote economic growth and release entrepreneurial capacities. Yet the distinction between the state and an autonomous civil society that is underpinned by the market and private property, upon which the analysis rests, already assumes the existence of a bourgeois society. It fails to address the political and social context within which state power is exercised. I would argue that the forces behind these movements are distinct and contradictory.

The pressures to return the country to civil government that are outlined above do not contain within them an impulse to deregulate the economy or to diminish the role of state enterprise. Indeed the experience of civil rule in Nigeria demonstrates that the opportunity to benefit from control of state patronage in its various forms is a major force behind the competition to get access to state office and power. The Structural Adjustment Programme, on the other hand, aimed to promote private enterprise, encourage market forces, and rationalise the public sector. As we will see in the final chapter, it derived from the leverage exercised by the IMF and World Bank and the presence of a military government that could overcome domestic opposition to the reforms and get support from managerial corporate groups. Contrary to the argument of Bjorn Beckman, the reforms did not derive from the strength of a domestic ruling class that was bourgeois in orientation.[57]

In the face of these pressures, the military have only managed to retain their legitimacy through periods of corrective rule and by active preparation for a return to civil rule. In these circumstances, the only viable alternative for a military government intent on retaining power would be a far more authoritarian form of government that confronted existing political forces and imposed a system of state authority. The military would be obliged to extend and entrench their control through the state bureaucracy and establish bases for accumulation within it. The precise political alignment of such a regime could vary from a strongly authoritarian alliance with big business and international capital to a more populist and nationalist position in which interest groups and political organisations were incorporated in institutions under military control.

Despite the experience of almost twenty years of government, a more centralised state, and a wider political role, the Nigerian military has shown little capacity or inclination to embark on this path. All military regimes have been leavened by civilian participation. Limits to more authoritarian rule have been placed by demographic size and cultural diversity and by the constant need to balance and integrate various interests and prevent serious divisions. The vigour of the press and dissent from trade unions, students, professional associations, and civil rights organisations have also constrained the exercise of state powers. The military itself has been prone to division and has been weakened as a corporate body by the tendency of military officers to retire at a relatively young age and establish economic interests in the private sector. Retired military officers, whose ranks have grown enormously, do nevertheless have considerable political influence and retain some following in the military. These patterns may change with time. For one thing, the army has become increasingly professional and officers can match civilians in terms of qualifications. The training of military officers has increased substantially through the Command and Staff College at Jaji, the Nigerian Defence Academy, the National Institute for Policy and Strategic Studies at Kuru, a new university, and overseas courses. Second, the military may develop its own corporate interests. The Defence Industries Corporation of Nigeria at Kaduna has begun in a minor way to expand beyond the manufacture of armaments to other areas of investment.

Would the substance of politics change if there were a return to civil rule? This would depend essentially on how power is mobilised and to what purpose. Would open political competition again usher in a largely issueless politics where the power of the purse is correspondingly large? What difference would more constitutional safeguards, a two-party system, a partial ban on old politicians, and a campaign to inculcate more democratic forms of political behaviour make? All these measures come from above. They do not in themselves indicate any shift in the social basis of political support and alignment that would alter the nature of party politics and the kind of issues that are generated through political competition. Political pressures for greater participation, distributive pressures for a share of centralised oil revenues, and competition for state patronage from private interests will continue to make demands on the state, raising questions about the authority of the state and the political capacity of government to exercise economic control. It is here that pressures to increase the authority of the state will arise most acutely.

Notes

1. Babangida, a Gwari, was an indigene of Niger state.

2. *Presidential Task Force on the Implementation of the Civil Service Reforms* (Lagos: Federal Government Printer, 1988).

3. *Guardian* (Lagos), 10 April 1986; *Guardian* (Lagos), 20 July 1986.

4. *West Africa*, 4 August 1986.

5. O. Marenin, "The Anini Saga: Armed Robbery and the Reproduction of Ideology in Nigeria," *Journal of Modern African Studies* 25/2 (1987), pp. 259–281.

6. *West Africa*, 20 July 1987.

7. *West Africa*, 17 August 1987.

8. *West Africa*, 17 August 1987.

9. "The Rampage in Onitsha," *African Concord*, 14 August 1989.

10. For instances, see J. N. Paden, *Religion and Political Culture in Kano* (Berkeley: University of California Press, 1973), p. 313; Y. B. Usman, *The Manipulation of Religion in Nigeria, 1977–1987* (Kaduna: Vanguard, 1987).

11. J.D.Y. Peel, "The Cultural Work of Yoruba Ethnogenesis," in E. Tonkin, M. McDonald, and M. Chapman, eds., *History and Ethnicity* (London: Routledge, 1989), p. 212.

12. *Sunday Concord,* 28 June 1987.

13. *Report of Tribunal of Inquiry on Kano Disturbances* (Lagos: Federal Government Printer, 1981), p. 69.

14. P. M. Lubeck, "Islamic Protest Under Semi-Industrial Capitalism: 'Yan Tatsine Explained," *Africa* 55/4 (1985), pp. 369–389. His analysis may be less appropriate to locations outside Kano.

15. Statement by National Council of Muslim Youth Organisations of Nigeria, *Sunday Concord,* 5 April 1987.

16. *West Africa,* 27 April 1987, p. 842.

17. *Sunday New Nigerian,* 10 May 1987; *New Nigerian,* 28 April 1987.

18. *Sunday Concord,* 28 June 1987.

19. *New Nigerian,* 30 April 1987.

20. *New Nigerian,* 30 April 1987.

21. *New Nigerian,* 19 January 1988.

22. *Guardian* (Lagos), Supplement, 3 May 1987.

23. Rufai Ibrahim, "Northern Elders Meet: The Politics of Religion?" *West Africa,* 20 July 1987.

24. A. Mazrui, "African Islam and Competitive Religions: Between Revivalism And Expansion," *Third World Quarterly* 10/2 (1988), p. 505.

25. M. A. Ojo, "The Contextual Significance of the Charismatic Movements in Independent Nigeria," *Africa* 58/2 (1988), p. 176.

26. S. U. Erivwo, "The Church in a Changing Nigeria," in M. O. Kayode and Y. B. Usman, eds., *The Economic and Social Development of Nigeria,* vol. 2, Proceedings of the National Conference on Nigeria Since Independence, March 1983 (Zaria, 1985), pp. 388–390.

27. Ojo, "The Contextual Significance," pp. 187–189.

28. J. Ibrahim, "The Politics of Religion in Nigeria: The Parameters of the 1987 Crisis in Kaduna State," *Review of African Political Economy* 45/46 (1989), pp. 38–48.

29. "Gumi's threat to peace," *Guardian* (Lagos), 13 October 1987.

30. Usman, *The Manipulation of Religion,* p. 82.

31. Erivwo, "The Church," p. 391.

32. For Sunday church attendances in the Evangelical Churches of West Africa (ECWA) and TEKAS (formerly Sudan United Mission), see A. Hastings, *A History of African Christianity, 1950–1975* (Cambridge: Cambridge University Press, 1979), pp. 166–167.

33. J. N. Paden, *Ahmadu Bello, Sardauna of Sokoto* (London: Hodder and Stoughton, 1986), p. 720.

34. *Report of the Political Bureau,* (Lagos: Federal Government Printer, 1987).

35. *Report of the Political Bureau,* p. 50.

36. *Report of the Political Bureau,* p. 68.

37. *Report of the Political Bureau,* pp. 200, 201.

38. J. Ibrahim, "The Political Debate and the Struggle for Democracy in Nigeria," *Review of African Political Economy* 37, 1986, p. 38.

39. *Guardian* (Lagos), 20 July 1986; *Concord Weekly*, 20 February 1986, no. 78.

40. *Report of the Political Bureau*, p. 126.

41. "Memorandum of the Emirs and Chiefs of the Ten Northern States of the Federation to the Political Bureau," *West Africa*, 3 November 1986, pp. 2312–2314.

42. *Government's Views and Comments on the Findings and Recommendations of the Poitical Bureau* (Lagos: Government Printer, 1987), p. 45.

43. *Government's Views*, p. 58.

44. *Report of the Political Bureau*, p. 74.

45. *Government's Views*, p. 46.

46. *Government's Views*, p. 46.

47. "Memorandum of the Emirs and Chiefs of the Ten Northern States."

48. *Report of the Political Bureau*, pp. 146, 147.

49. *Report of the Political Bureau*, pp. 176–180.

50. *Guardian* (Lagos), 24 September 1987.

51. *Report of the Political Bureau*, p. 179.

52. *Government's Views*, pp. 40, 41.

53. *Guardian* (Lagos), 16 December 1987.

54. *New Nigerian*, 9 December 1987.

55. *New Nigerian*, 24 December 1987.

56. *West Africa*, 4 August 1986.

57. B. Beckman, "The Post-Colonial State: Crisis and Reconstruction," *Institute of Development Studies Bulletin* (Sussex), 19/4 (1988), p. 30.

PART THREE

Economic Development

7

The State, Oil Dynamics, and the Economy, 1970–1979

Oil Dynamics, Agriculture, and Industry

After the end of the civil war, oil revenues rose steadily to constitute over 80 percent of total federal revenues and over 90 percent of export earnings by 1974 (see Table 7.1). In 1974, following the oil price rise, oil revenue rose three and one-half fold, and the share of oil in revenues rose to over 80 percent. Government expenditures did not lag far behind. Total federal expenditure increased by a massive 100 percent in 1974 (see Table 7.2) and doubled the next year. Oil revenues continued to rise, although modestly in real terms. In 1978, a fall in price and output reduced nominal revenues for the first time and induced cutbacks in government expenditure and a recession. There followed a mini–oil boom in which the share of oil in total revenues again exceeded 80 percent. Dependence on oil for foreign exchange earnings remained acute and in the mid-1980s was almost total.

Large oil revenues had a number of largely unforeseen and unintended consequences. First, the rentier nature of the income that flowed directly to central government meant that there were strong pressures to maximise current oil revenues and increase public expenditure. A windfall revenue meant that the government could bypass taxpayers and begin spending immediately. Political pressures arising from the taxation of personal incomes, farm incomes, or private property, which would check the increases in state expenditure demanded by politicians and bureaucrats, were absent. This situation had negative consequences for the expansion of the public economy, for the use and accountability of public funds, and for attitudes towards the state. In the quickening of expectations set off by the rise of revenues, it appeared that all things were possible and that finance was no longer a constraint on government activities. Non-oil tax revenues were neglected and some taxes abolished. The rapid expansion of state expenditure took place without any sense of priority in the allocation of public expenditure as demands were pressed in on the centre. There was, too, a deterioration in financial discipline and accountability as

TABLE 7.1 Oil Sector Statistics 1970–1993

	Annual Output (million barrels)	*Average Price Index*	*Oil Exports as Percent of Total Exports*	*Government Oil Revenue (N million)*	*Percent of Total Revenue*
1970	396	5.3	58	166	26
1972	643	7.8	82	767	54
1974	823	31.7	93	3,726	82
1976	756	36.3	94	5,365	79
1978	692	39.5	89	4,556	62
1979	840	58.5	93	8,881	81
1980	753	100	96	12,353	81
1981	525	108.4	97	8,563	70
1982	470	99.4	99	7,814	66
1983	451	84.6	96	7,253	69
1984	508	83.3	97	8,268	74
1985	544	79.9	97	10,915	75
1986	534	42.4	94	8,107	66
1987	464	52.1	93	19,027	76
1988	507	41.1	91	20,934	77
1989	614	49.5	95	41,334	82
1990	648	60.8	97	55,216	79
1991	677	54.1	96	60,316	77
1992	691	52.3	98	115,392	83
1993	689	47	98	106,155	76

Sources: Output is from *Petroleum Economist* (1970–1993); price index and exports are from IMF, *International Financial Statistics* (1970–1984) and from Central Bank of Nigeria, *Annual Reports* (1985–1993); revenues are from Central Bank of Nigeria, *Annual Reports* (various years).

the struggle to gain access to state resources intensified. Thus the expansion of state resources went together with a loss of control and discipline.

Second, the increase in public expenditure had manifold consequences for the public sector. There were major changes in the pattern of expenditure and large increases in public employment. Grants and subsidies for parastatals accelerated with a concomitant neglect of tariffs and accounting. The state governments became increasingly dependent on the federal centre, and the federal goverment retained a growing proportion of total revenues. The increase in revenue raised public savings to a high level. The share of capital expenditure in federal government expenditure net of transfers rose from 44 percent in 1973 to 82 percent in 1977.[1] But the conversion of savings into productive public assets was to prove most difficult.

Third, the rapid growth of oil revenue set up levels of government expenditure and imports that could not be sustained. The dominance of oil

TABLE 7.2 Selected Economic Indicators, 1970–1993 (annual percentage change)

	GDP	*Manufacturing*	*Government Expenditure*[a]	*Money Supply*	*CPI Price*[b]	*Food Price*
1970	29.8	11.4	105.6	42.3	13.8	22.9
1972	7.3	6.3	46.5	11.2	2.8	2.5
1974	12.1	– 3.3	100.5	42.4	12.8	16.9
1976	10.9	23.4	28.8	16.1	21.9	26.3
1978	– 7.3	13.9	6.5	– 0.1	16.6	17.7
1979	2.5	48.0	2.7	28.4	11.7	8.0
1980	5.3	5.3	72.7	50.0	9.9	7.6
1981	– 8.4	14.6	– 8.0	5.6	20.8	25.2
1982	0.1	9.6	21.9	3.1	7.7	8.9
1983	– 4.1	– 26.3	– 19.5	12.2	23.2	23.2
1984	– 6.8	– 11.9	0.5	8.2	39.6	42.9
1985	7.9	19.9	23.1	8.7	5.5	3.9
1986	– 3.2	– 3.8	7.9	– 4.1	5.4	0.1
1987	1.8	33.6	46.8	17.1	10.2	8.6
1988	4.0	12.8	29.2	43.6	38.3	52.2
1989	7.4	2.1	38.0	21.5	40.9	39.1
1990	8.2	5.6	46.0	44.8	7.4	3.7
1991	4.7	9.3	12.0	32.5	13.0	11.9
1992	3.6	– 4.8	53.9	52.7	44.6	46.5
1993	2.6	– 4.1	50.3	54.6	57.2	57.9

[a]Government expenditure is federal current and capital expenditure including statutory appropriations to state and local governments.

[b]Price indices are lower-income urban group (1970–1976) and composite covering all income groups in urban and rural areas (1977–1993).

Sources: Manufacturing index, government expenditure, money supply, and prices are from Central Bank of Nigeria, *Annual Reports* (various years); GDP is from IMF, *International Financial Statistics* (various years).

meant that economic expansion became dependent on an increase in real oil earnings. Unless measures were taken to counter the shock of external fluctuations in oil revenue, through a stabilisation fund or other means, oil would be a source of economic instability. This instability was magnified by the fact that after a short period of financial surplus, expenditure tended to outstrip revenue, leading to large internal budget deficits, which were financed in an inflationary manner and which led to a rapid erosion of the foreign reserves position. This led to a buildup of external debt far more quickly than anyone foresaw. Nigeria has experienced one minor (1978 and 1979) and one major oil-induced recession (mid-1981 to 1992).

Fourth, large oil expenditures had an impact on relative prices and hence on resource allocation. Large government expenditures had the effect of raising incomes, especially urban incomes, and large increases in market demand followed. This demand had the effect of raising the price of food and services relative to the price of imports and import substitutes like manufactures. Measured on a 1973 base, food prices had risen by 273 percent by 1981 compared to a 111 percent rise for manufactures.[2] Reliable information on farm incomes is not available over this period. Fragmentary evidence on rural real wages suggests that they rose by about 45 percent (1971–1979) in the northern states, boosted by the strong demand for food and increased production.[3] In the cocoa belt, real wages rose even more strongly, by over 100 percent.[4] Here the rise reflected not prosperity but the attractions of alternative occupations in both urban and rural locations. Cocoa producers were caught in a price-cost squeeze, and many opted to leave their cocoa farms. In contrast to the rise in rural wages, the government minimum for unskilled workers declined in real terms by 32 percent over 1970–1979, falling well below the level of rural wages.[5]

The real exchange rate rose by 87 percent between 1970 and 1981, as the naira appreciated and domestic inflation accelerated, led by food prices.[6] The currency appreciation together with a fall in import duties made imported goods cheaper and put the domestic production of some manufactures and food items under pressure.[7] There was an enormous surge in imports and much wasteful consumption. It was only after 1977, in response to balance of payments difficulties, that there were moves to restrict imports and impose tight foreign exchange controls. Importing and commerce at all levels were generally extremely profitable activities attracting many new entrants and resources. Exports, on the other hand, were discriminated against through the change in the incentive structure. The export of produce was cut back drastically and agroindustrial exports virtually disappeared. Thus the groundnut-crushing industry closed down, and vegetable oil was imported.

Agriculture

With the sharp increase in demand for foodstuffs triggered by the rise in incomes and the influx of migrants, supply lagged behind demand. The growth of agricultural output had slowed down before the onset of the oil boom. The oil boom did not bring stagnation or a decline of agricultural output. Without oil revenues, the pressures to maintain heavy taxation of agricultural producers would have been much stronger. Large state expenditures had the effect of shifting the internal terms of trade in favour of agriculture. Some consumers took advantage of relatively cheap food imports, which were encouraged by the appreciation of the naira, to switch demands away from domestic staples to imported wheat and rice.

The expansion of state expenditures was concentrated in the urban areas, especially in the state capitals where there was a large expansion of construction and commercial activity. The expansion of urban services and the construction industry attracted migrant labour from neighbouring countries. Some labour was also attracted from rural areas, especially from areas where crops like cocoa, rubber, and palm produce faced a cost-price squeeze. As I will argue in Chapter 9, it would be incorrect to extend this argument about the movement of labour from agriculture to food production and the rural economy in general. In some areas, food production expanded rapidly. There was a great deal of rural-rural migration to grow food crops for the internal market. Rural employment in commerce, transport, and other services also expanded. Moreover, the categories "urban" and "rural" are too restrictive and far from watertight in Nigeria. High occupational and geographical mobility, multiple sources and flows of income, and strong identification by urban dwellers with home communities weaken the distinction.

How did agricultural policy change in response to the impact of oil on government revenues and to the perception of a food crisis that was fuelled by the rise in food imports and by food price inflation? Some of these policies and state initiatives will be discussed much more fully in Chapter 9. First, taxation through the old marketing board system was reduced and the system subsequently dismantled and replaced by seven national commodity boards, which included domestic food crops for the first time. These boards offered guaranteed minimum prices and appointed licensed buying agents, and they had exclusive rights to export produce. The problem for the boards lay in the stagnation of exports and the growth of the home market, which offered better prices. Cocoa was the only crop to offer much scope for the generation of trading surpluses.

Second, there were a number of federal initiatives aimed at increasing food production. The World Bank–sponsored Agricultural Development Projects, which began in the mid-1970s with projects at Funtua, Gusau, and Gombe, though initially seen as a means of promoting cotton and groundnuts, soon found a rationale under the promotion of food production. Three large-scale irrigation projects near Sokoto, Kano, and Lake Chad went ahead at great expense and were justified largely in terms of their potential for wheat production and the need to combat drought. Large-scale production schemes included sugar estates, the mechanised food farms of the National Grains Production Company, the cassava plantations of the National Roots Production Company, and the National Beverages Production Company (tea). The provision of subsidised fertiliser, seeds, credit, and other inputs was stepped up.

Other initiatives taken after the acceleration of food-price inflation in 1974 included the launch of Operation Feed the Nation, which was a hurried political initiative in 1976 aimed at mobilising students and urban dwellers, and the Accelerated Food Production Programme, which aimed to deliver packages of inputs for specific crops. This latter programme was overshadowed by the Agricultural Development Projects and lacked support. State supply agencies began the large-scale importation of rice and meat in the second half of 1975, and tariffs on food items were reduced. Efforts were also made without success to attract foreign investment into agriculture through new incentives.

Industry

Industrialisation as a general goal remained very high on the policy agenda, as it had in the 1960s. The priorities of government industrial policy were growth and structural change in the direction of more intermediate and capital goods industries. The public sector was to play a leading role in establishing capital-intensive industries, including steel and petrochemicals. It was also to promote the transfer of technology, which was a constant theme of government spokesmen. Another objective was to spread industry away from its concentration in Lagos and achieve a significant degree of industrialisation in each state. Between 1964 and 1975, the imbalance in favour of Lagos grew with its share of employment in large-scale manufacturing, rising from 35 percent to 45 percent, and its share in value added, rising from 37 percent to 69 percent.[8] As a result of this concern, the federal government regulated the location of new industry, and agencies like the Nigerian Industrial Development Bank increased their lending outside Lagos. A further strand in industrial policy was the indigenisation of industry, which was aimed at securing greater Nigerian control through changes in ownership and management.

Once the large state expenditures started, industry experienced rapid overall growth. Output increased at an average rate of 13 percent over the 1970s. This growth was not steady, and industrial output was affected on occasion by supply constraints in the form of port congestion and power shortages. The erratic and inconsistent nature of government intervention in areas like price control, import regulation, and foreign exchange controls also affected industry adversely. When oil revenues fell in 1977, the government attempted to restrict imports; this led to extensive smuggling fuelled by the overvalued exchange rate.

The general impact of large government expenditures and the appreciation of the exchange rate was to shift the incentive structure confronting industry in a way that encouraged imports and imported raw materials. Foreign exchange intensive patterns of investment and output were favoured but could not be sustained when oil revenues declined and the country faced an acute balance-of-payments crisis. Whereas early import substitution had been effective in saving foreign exchange, manufacturing now became a net user of foreign exchange and a burden on the balance of payments. A further negative contribution was apparent in the fact that the positive flow of net direct foreign investment in industry was now totally eclipsed by the flows of profit and dividends abroad and payments of management, technology, and consultancy fees.

The immediate impact of increased government revenue and foreign exchange earnings was the erosion of tariffs, a large appreciation of the naira, and domestic inflation. This effect was combined with a rapid expansion of the domestic market. Tariff cutting was not restricted to essential items. Importing became extremely profitable in what amounted to a seller's market. Many "manufacturing" operations were set up primarily to increase the flow of imports from parent companies abroad rather than to produce for the Nigerian market. In some cases, companies simply opted to import finished products. It is here that part of the answer may lie for the strong growth of industrial output despite relatively unfavourable prices and import penetration in the economy as a whole. With domestic inflation, profits could be maintained through markups. Transfer pricing ensured the rapid repatriation of profits.

Much of the growth was concentrated in the consumer goods sector service industries and assembly-type operations and was not associated with structural change. The highest industrial incentives were reserved for import-substituting consumer industries with low value added and assembly plants based on imported raw materials. Industries using local raw materials were discriminated against, and there was no incentive to develop exports.

The fastest growth occurred in textiles, vehicle assembly, soap and detergents, soft drinks, pharmaceuticals, beer, paints, and building materials. The service and construction industries also expanded rapidly. By the end of the decade, the textile industry, with some 100,000 persons employed, accounted for some 20 percent of industrial employment in large-scale plants. The growth of this industry was then checked by smuggling, which accounted for at least half of domestic consumption of textiles. The expansion of the industry in the 1950s and 1960s had been based on local supplies of cotton. By 1982, the decline in the domestic supply of cotton had reached the point where it accounted for only 21 percent of all materials in the industry, compared to 55 percent only five years earlier.[9]

Agroindustry had a mixed experience. There was a drastic fall in the output of the vegetable-oil milling sector (groundnut and palm oil) and cotton processing. The fall stemmed from the low prices that the commodity boards, their sole supplier, paid to the farmers and from competition from imported vegetable oils. However, flour milling and livestock-feed milling expanded, based on imported wheat and maize.

Given the high demand and the locational advantages provided by high transport costs, the performance of the cement industry was poor. In

1977 the proportion of domestic production to total supply was only 15 percent. The industry, which was largely state owned, suffered from management and infrastructural problems and difficulties with technical partners.

Direct federal investment in manufacture in the 1970s included the following projects: cement (4); car and truck assembly (6); pulp and paper (2); fertiliser (1); wood and furniture (2); machine tools (1); electric meters (1); transformers (1); distilling, yeast, and alcohol (1); and sugar refining (1). This investment gave the state a monopoly in some areas (fertiliser, salt, pulp, and paper) and a substantial presence in others, but overall the state never came near to constituting a dominant force in manufacture. Many of the projects were joint ventures with the state performing a passive role with the provision of funds and a protected market. For reasons of scale and profitability, most of these projects would not have been attractive to foreign capital.

Plans for oil-related industrial projects with export potential, like petrochemicals and liquified natural gas, were subject to delay and did not materialise. Delays in initiating these projects were perhaps the most important missed industrial opportunity of the decade. They demonstrated the lack of clear priorities and the difficulties of implementing federal projects when conflicting ministerial and geopolitical interests were involved.

T. O. Adeboye has argued forcibly that the record of the federal government in manufacture showed a weak entrepreneur, a negative impact on the transfer of technology, and high costs.[10] The dependence of public sector enterprises on foreign management, consultancy, and technology is borne out by foreign exchange payments for contract and services.[11] In 1978, the management of Nigerian Railways and Nigeria Airways was given over to Rail India and KLM, respectively.

The fate of local initiatives to adapt technology to local conditions and boost local learning processes has, in the case of Nigeria, been determined largely by the impact of external conditions. At one extreme, under conditions of autarky in secessionist Biafra without the presence of multinational companies, adaptive innovation in the oil and weapons industry flourished. The high status and freedom accorded to scientists and engineers in Biafra was unprecedented, and the power of the bureaucrats declined sharply.[12] Some attempt was made to carry over the wartime initiatives through the Products Development Agency (PRODA) at Enugu, but this initiative was on a small scale and most of the scientific personnel involved in the war effort had scattered. The lessons of the wartime experience were recognised, but they could not be learnt. Basically, the oil boom and the flood of imported technology were incompatible with any attempt to monitor the flow of technology to see how it related to local resources and capacities. The National Science and Technology Development Agency and, later, a Ministry of Science and Technology and a National Office of Industrial Property were set up. Despite these initiatives, Nigerian technological capacity, its ability to absorb and use technology and to innovate, remained very limited. Research in isolated institutes was not commercialised. The rush to set up state projects simultaneously allowed no cumulative learning from experience or the unpackaging of the technology involved. Civil servants involved in superintending such projects tended to adopt a least-risk, fully-packaged approach and to select the latest technology. These conditions surrounding the acquisition and organisation of technology resulted in the waste of trained manpower and in the truncation, disorientation, and fragmentation of learning processes.

Macroeconomic Management

The Second Plan, Recovery, and Reconstruction, 1970–1974

The guidelines to the Fourth Plan (1981–1986) open with the statement that "Nigeria is now preparing to enter her third decade of planned development since the country became politically independent in 1960."[13] Such statements, along with the existence of a large literature on plans in Nigeria, give a totally false impression of the importance of planning in the Nigerian economy. There has never been a planning mechanism in Nigeria. Planning implies minimally that there is some central direction and control of the economy and that there are definite targets for output and growth. But planning units have not had any real power in Nigeria. The Ministry of Finance has remained responsible for the capital expenditure estimates in the annual budgets. The centre has never effectively controlled investment in the regions or states. Nor has the federal government developed the means to plan the public sector.

A number of features distinguished the Second Plan from the First Plan. First, it was a national plan, more integrated, and wholly Nigerian in conception. Second, there was a stronger role for state intervention and public investment. Different interpretations were placed on the idea of public sector leadership. Although some planners saw it as a means of promoting industrialisation, structural change, and national control, others wanted to extend public sector ownership and planning throughout the industrial sector. Third, there was the objective of indigenisation, which was directed at the progressive elimination of foreign dominance in the economy by increasing local ownership. Some also put emphasis on increasing the level of local managerial and technological control. Others linked indigenisation to the need to extend state ownership and control. Fourth, there was a social welfare element in the provisions for housing and education, though this was not strongly developed. Fifth, there was the use of specific grants to the states to finance capital expenditure in agriculture, education, and town and country planning. These grants were at the discretion of the centre and were intended to give the federal government the initiative and leverage to direct development within the states.

The fiscal position improved substantially as oil revenues increased sharply. In the early 1970s, state savings exceeded investment, giving rise to overall budget surpluses (see Table 7.3). Revenues were consistently underestimated in this period by a wide margin, and capital expenditures were slow to pick up after the war.

The Oil Boom and the Loss of Control, 1974–1977

The oil price rise of 1973–1974 brought an enormous expansion of state revenues. This increase was quickly translated into massive state expenditures, which maintained their momentum well after state revenues had declined. In general, economic policy was passive and took the line of least resistance. There were cuts in taxes and large salary and wage awards, and the naira was appreciated relative to foreign currencies.

Nigeria did not, like the low-population oil producers of the Middle East, invest its oil wealth in Western economies and thereby secure a flow of investment income for the future. Nor was revenue set aside in a stabilisation, or development, fund. Yet there was some outflow of capital on public account, which peaked in 1975–1976, plus a modest aid programme. Nigeria lent N225 million to the IMF oil facility, $80 million to the African Development Bank, and $52 million to the OPEC special fund.[14] The aid programme included small sums to drought-affected states, grants to some countries in West Africa related to ECOWAS diplomacy, and a cash donation of N13.5 million to Angola in 1976.

The pressure of aggregate demand contributed to inflationary pressures that at their peak gave an official annual rate of inflation of 34 percent in 1975. In 1975 alone, there was a rise of N2.6 billion in aggregate demand attributable to the federal government.[15] GDP over 1974–1977 grew at an annual average rate of 7.0 percent in real terms.

The result of the large increase in government expenditure was an explosion of purchasing power that ignited an enormous consumption boom. Some of this income flowed down no matter how successful the elites were in bringing about a one-sided division of the spoils. The 1974 and 1975 budgets were the great consumption budgets. Both budgets saw substantial falls in import duties and excises and a further relaxation of foreign exchange controls. It was government policy to control inflation by increasing the volume of imports. Import volume increased by 62 percent in 1975 and 38 percent in 1976.[16]

TABLE 7.3 Federal Government Finances, 1970–1993 (N million)

	Total Revenue	*Retained Revenue*	*Current Expenditure*	*Capital Expenditure*	*Surplus Deficit (–)*
1970	633	365	638	201	–474
1972	1,405	1,074	681	296	97
1974	4,537	3,893	873	1,223	1,797
1976	6,766	5,121	2,171	4,041	–1,091
1978	7,469	6,045	2,896	5,092	–1,943
1979	10,912	8,041	2,360	4,219	–1,462
1980	15,234	13,139	6,424	8,092	–1,377
1981	12,180	7,510	5,500	5,700	–3,690
1982	11,764	7,500	7,418	5,522	–5,440
1983	10,509	6,234	5,656	4,034	–3,456
1984	11,134	6,939	6,276	3,278	–2,615
1985	14,606	9,640	7,215	5,465	–3,040
1986	12,302	7,969	7,697	8,526	–8,254
1987	25,100	16,129	15,646	6,373	–5,890
1988	27,311	15,589	19,409	8,340	–12,161
1989	47,798	25,894	25,994	15,034	–15,134
1990	69,788	39,033	36,220	24,929	–22,116
1991	78,641	31,774	38,243	29,286	–35,755
1992	138,617	51,774	70,853	38,453	–57,532
1993[a]	138,874	73,398	132,170	42,354	–101,126

[a]1993 is provisional.

Source: Central Bank of Nigeria, *Economic & Financial Review* (various years); Central Bank of Nigeria, *Annual Reports* (various years).

The expansion of state expenditure in 1975, which marked the beginning of federal budget deficits, merits further attention. Among the factors at work were the Udoji wage and salary awards, federal transfers to the states, inflated project expenditures, and the deficits of public corporations.

The very substantial Udoji wage and salary awards[17] and the payment of arrears early in 1975, which spread to the private sector, added momentum to a monetary expansion already fuelled by the accumulation of foreign exchange. In the first four months of 1975, the money supply rose by 47 percent.

Although the Udoji Commission was primarily concerned with the reform of the public service, by the time the commission reported, public attention and expectations were focussed exclusively on the wage and salary revision. Everyone had a right to their "Udoji" and a share in the oil wealth. One objective of the commission was to bring public sector salaries into line with those of the private sector. This adjustment was achieved at the top end with enormous increases of 90 percent. The authorities vainly tried to forestall private sector demands by arguing that the private sector had benefited from approved pay awards since the introduction of wage restraint in 1969. Soon after the awards, the private sector granted increases to senior staff that went some way to reestablishing the differentials.

At the lower end, the public sector led the private sector with increases of 130 percent for the lowest-paid public employees. Awards were backdated by nine months to April 1974 and paid in a lump sum. This extraordinary decision was not part of the Udoji report, which recommended no arrears and salary increases in two phases. Similar increases were recommended for the Armed Forces.

Dissatisfaction over grading and relativities led to widespread protests and strikes by bureaucratic and professional groups. Doctors and bank, oil, and electricity workers went on strike. The government was forced to make more concessions. In a series of decisions, a minimum increase of 30 percent was granted to all those who would enjoy less than this as a result of regrading. Doctors got a 40 percent increase.

There were large increases in federal discretionary transfers to the states under ad hoc grants in lieu of oil revenues and programme grants (see Table 3.2). The level of grants was well above the planned level and contributed to the breakdown of federal control as well as to the erosion of responsibility for budgeting in the states. In 1977, debt worth N804 million owed by the states to the federal government was written off.

There was enormous capital spending on projects included in the Third Plan (1975–1980). Much of this spending involved construction work (barracks, infrastructure, schools, housing), and the inflexible supply of building materials and port congestion resulted in a further inflationary twist. Port congestion began to build up by mid-1974. It was compounded by the importation of cement by the Ministry of Defence. The payment of compensation for port delay (demurrage) became a racket, with ships arriving at Lagos simply to collect the demurrage fees. The total demurrage charge for 1975 was estimated at N109 million. Additional costs arising from the congestion included surcharges on freight (N60 million), penalty charges imposed by haulage firms (N35 million), extra interest charges (N32 million), plus losses due to the deterioration of cargo estimated at N273 million.

A further source of federal spending was the deficits of the public companies and corporations. Many of these agencies suffered from rigid tariffs and high wage costs. They ran deficits that could only be covered by federal transfers.

By the time of the 1976/77 budget, the rapid rise in imports was causing concern, and the Anti-Inflation Task Force had reported. The task force had no perceptible effect on the budget, partly because it had no clear priorities. The level of government expenditure and budgetary indiscipline were not tackled. There was a net addition to demand from federal sources in 1976 of N1.7 billion that was certainly expansionary. (See note 15.)

Oil Shocks and Recession, 1977–1979

The 1977/78 budget was only slightly restrictive and protective. A number of measures were taken to control imports, including outright bans and increased duties, but these were insufficient to stem the deterioration on the current account (see Table 7.4). The loss of reserves was aggravated by the failure to respond quickly to price cutting among OPEC members as new sources of oil in the North Sea, Alaska, and Mexico came into production. Incentives for fresh exploration and drilling in Nigeria were also inadequate. In 1977, a fresh package of incentives for the oil companies was announced. These incentives were critical to the willingness of international bankers to lend to Nigeria when the balance of payments crisis deepened. In early 1978, Nigerian production had fallen to 1.5 barrels per day from an average of 2.1 barrels per day in 1977. The deficit on trade account that had begun in August 1977 peaked in March 1978, just prior to the budget.

The external position was maintained only by borrowing $1.7 billion in the Eurodollar market. The limits to this form of borrowing for balance-of-payments support were quickly reached, and the target for the second loan was not met. The whole episode revealed serious deficiencies in oil policy and its coordination with macroeconomic management. It was from this point that Nigeria's external debt began to increase sharply (see Table 7.5).

Internally, the main burden of adjustment fell on expenditure cuts. The 1978 budget was severely deflationary. Monetary restraint was tightened. Capital expenditure cuts were particularly severe on manufacturing and included the oil refineries and pipelines. Education and general administration were also hit. Cuts in educational expenditure began in 1977 with the federal government attempting to shift the enormous costs of the UPE programme down to the states. There were also increases in boarding and lodging fees, the loss of federal scholarships, and the transfer of bursaries and loans to the state governments. These cuts prompted student strikes and demonstrations in the universities.

More imports were prohibited or placed on licence. There was a slowdown in foreign exchange approval, and compulsory advance deposits for letters of credit were introduced. In January 1979, a comprehensive import inspection scheme was introduced. This measure brought some savings and had a deterrent effect. The 1979 budget maintained these restrictions

TABLE 7.4 Balance of Payments, 1970–1993 (N million)

	Exports	Imports	Trade Balance	Services and Incomes	Transfers	Current Balance	Long-Term Capital	Short-Term Capital and Errors and Omissions[a]	Reserve Movement[b]
1970	891	-718	173	-268	452	-50	126	-29	-47
1972	1,437	-960	477	-786	35	-323	331	-58	50
1974	6,106	-1,666	4,440	-1,315	-77	3,063	131	-92	3,102
1976	6,343	-5,050	1,293	-1,455	-119	-260	-18	-62	340
1978	6,633	-7,374	-741	-1,475	-234	-2,387	1,016	78	1,293
1979	10,107	-7,139	2,968	-1,724	-315	1,010	807	52	-1,869
1980	14,186	-8,053	6,133	-3,462	-315	2,356	-48	95	-2,403
1981	10,875	-11,287	-412	-2,948	-348	-3,708	599	72	3,037
1982	8,182	-10,017	-1,835	-2,780	-289	-4,904	1,027	2,479	1,398
1983	7,503	-8,284	-781	-2,071	-286	-3,138	1,374	1,463	301
1984	9,088	-6,788	2,300	-1,957	254	89	-39	305	-355
1985	11,721	-6,656	5,065	-2,618	-232	2,215	-3,802	1,936	-349
1986	8,921	-5,477	3,444	-6,203	-240	-2,999	-3,646	5,861	784
1987	30,361	-16,393	13,968	-14,167	-96	-295	-8,274	8,728	-159
1988	31,193	-19,758	11,435	-12,819	-54	-1,438	-11,879	11,023	2,294
1989	57,971	-27,200	30,771	-41,155	1,141	-9,243	-11,967	29,937	-8,727
1990	106,626	-39,771	66,855	-53,847	3,615	16,623	-24,299	26,174	-18,498
1991	116,856	-76,855	40,001	-66,327	7,291	-19,035	-24,358	49,353	-5,960
1992	201,384	-124,613	76,771	-102,016	12,680	-12,565	-46,244	-6,465	65,274
1993	213,778	-146,955	66,823	-106,225	17,925	-21,477	-9,024	44,117	-13,616

[a]Includes exceptional financing.
[b]Minus (–) indicates increase in assets/decrease in liabilities.

Source: Central Bank of Nigeria, *Annual Reports*.

and placed an extra twenty-five items on import licence. The result was that imports fell by 7 percent in 1979. This, together with the oil-price rise, brought about a recovery in the reserve position so that reserves stood at N2.9 billion when military rule ended and President Shagari came to power.

Some other measures were taken as a response to the deterioration of the federal budget position after 1977. An attempt was made to increase contributions to the National Provident Fund from N4 to N10 in January 1978. This measure was withdrawn after a hostile reception from workers. New airline and shipping taxes and a turnover tax on construction companies were announced but not implemented. A potentially important move was the decision to allow state governments to raise funds on the Lagos capital market without federal government guarantee.[18] This measure could force state governments to keep up-to-date accounts and make them compete with each other to establish their credit rating in the capital

TABLE 7.5 The Growth of Indebtedness, 1970–1992 ($ million)

	Debt Outstanding and Disbursed (long-term)	*Disbursements*	*Total Debt Service*	*Net Transfers*[a]	*Debt Service Ratio*	*Short-Term Debt*	*Total Debt*[b]
1970	567	81	96	−14	4.3	n.a.	n.a.
1975	1,143	133	270	−137	2.7	n.a.	n.a.
1980	5,381	1,753	774	979	4.2	3,553	8,934
1982	10,419	3,724	1,714	2,010	16.2	2,535	12,954
1984	12,793	2,023	3,474	−1,450	33.8	5,744	18,537
1986	19,686	1,344	1,765	−421	32.7	3,716	23,402
1987	29,016	1,403	1,074	329	14.2	1,639	30,655
1988	29,595	1,045	2,178	−1,133	30.4	1,651	31,246
1989	31,402	1,638	2,207	−569	26.1	595	31,997
1990	32,977	937	3,343	−2,406	22.8	1,561	34,538
1991	33,527	844	3,347	−2,503	25.2	909	34,436
1992	28,789	706	3,737	−3,031	30.6	2,210	30,999

[a] net transfers = disbursements − total debt service.
[b] total debt = debt outstanding and disbursed + short-term debt.

Source: World Bank, *World Debt Tables, 1990/91, 1993/94,* Washington, D.C., for 1970, 1980 and 1982–1992; *1988/89* for 1975 and 1981.

market. Finally, in 1979 a decree obliged all employers with more than 500 workers to provide housing for a cross section of employees.[19] Employers opposed this attempt to transfer the burden of housing provision to the private sector and the decree was later shelved.

The Growth of Public Expenditure and the Expansion of the Public Sector[20]

Public Expenditure

The growth of oil revenues led to a dramatic increase in federal spending. The share of federal expenditure in GDP (including transfers) rose from 19 percent in 1973 to 54 percent in 1977/78. Public employment approximately tripled from .5 million to 1.5 million from 1973 to 1981.[21] A notable feature was the rapid rise of social categories of expenditure, which was most marked for education and housing. There was also heavy capital expenditure on infrastructure (transport and power) and industrial ventures (oil, steel, mining, and manufacture).

The federal government undertook a large investment in infrastructure. After the end of the civil war, when lack of maintenance and heavy military use reduced roads to a poor condition, priority was given to the development of a national road network. The federal government took over responsibility for additional roads from the states. Missing links in six north-south routes and eight east-west routes were filled. Little investment was made in rail transport. Indeed, federal policies gave overwhelming support to roads and private vehicle ownership. Not only were roads given priority, domestic gasoline prices were kept low, and there were cheap credit and car allowances for all senior members of the public service.

As we saw in Chapter 3, the federal government gave priority to education and specifically promoted national education policies in the 1970s. At its peak in 1975, education absorbed N1,051 million (19 percent) of federal current and capital expenditure (including all transfers). The federal government established the National Universities Commission, took over the funding of thirteen universities, and created seven new ones. The number of university students rose from 14,000 in 1970 to 53,000 by 1978. State governments took over private secondary schools from voluntary agencies (mainly churches) and a Universal Primary Education programme was launched.

The UPE programme was, in part, an attempt to bridge the educational disparity between the northern and southern states.[22] Announced in 1974, it was launched as scheduled in 1976. A number of problems with the free primary education programmes of the 1950s in the southern states were repeated. There was no perceptible learning from experience by educators, social scientists, or politicians. One reason for this was that the politicians involved in the 1950s programme did not appear to have suffered any damage—rather, the reverse.

Among the experiences that were repeated were the gross underestimation of costs and enrollment and a shortage of teachers. The enormous expansion of primary education entailed a serious decline in the quality of education. Unqualified teachers were pressed into service, and the status of teachers plummeted. Financial stringency later forced the federal government to shift the costs of education to the states and local governments. By the end of the decade, the share of the northern states in primary school enrollment had risen from 19 percent in 1970 to 47 percent.[23] Even if qualifications are raised about the quality of education, reliability of data, and the permanence of the shift, this was a dramatic step towards more balanced educational opportunities in the country. At secondary school level, the shift was much less impressive, with the share of northern states rising from 12 percent to 18 percent. Moreover, gender and class differences were marked and persistent at all levels, with limited access to education for women.[24]

Federal housing plans were first announced by General Gowon in 1972. The heart of the programme was the construction of low-cost housing estates. The objective was to redistribute income towards the low income groups by reducing the proportion of their gross income spent on rent to 20 percent. Tony Seymour's work in Kaduna showed how 95 percent of all low-cost housing units were beyond the means of all but the 10–15 percent of Kaduna's population with income in excess of N2,000.[25] State housing subsidies were thus regressive in their distributive impact. The second element in federal policy was the Nigerian Building Society that became the Federal Mortgage Bank in 1977. Its loans policy was directed at middle- and high-income groups. The third strand was the untouched colonial heritage of heavily subsidised housing for all senior public employees.

Federal Corporations and Companies

Large centralised oil revenues set the scene for an expansion of the public sector. A number of large-scale projects were started in the oil, mining, and manufacturing sectors, often under conditions of state monopoly. There was also an extension of federal finance capital in commercial, development, and merchant banking. Another source of expansion lay in those states, which could not rely on private capital to promote industry.

The range of public corporations and companies was extended with the addition of the Nigerian National Oil Corporation (NNOC) (1971), the Nigerian Steel Development Authority (1971), the Nigerian Mining Corporation (1972), the Nigerian National Supply Company (1972), the National Freight Company (1976), the National Cargo Handling Company (1977), the Central Water Transportation Company (1977) and the Nigerian Airports Authority (1978).

On the whole, the expansion of the state sector led to little conflict or debate over the limits and content of the state drive. The expansion was not at the expense of the private sector. There was much more concern over implementation, organisation, location, and timing of projects. The three areas where conflict with local capital did arise were all areas where local trading interests were affected. They included the activities of the Nigerian National Supply Company, the sale of crude oil that excluded local buyers, and the monopoly on export produce held by the Commodity Boards.

The increase in state companies and enterprises did not lead to state capitalism. At the level of the states in particular, the creation of new parastatals was often an effective way of absorbing and containing the additional oil revenue within the bureaucracy and the political class. Usually corporations did not cover their running costs, and there was heavy financial support from the federal government. In the 1970s, only Nigerian External Telecommunications and the Nigerian Electric Power Authority (NEPA) made consistent small operating surpluses. The accounting, budgeting, and audit functions of the state sector were very poorly developed, and statistical services and reporting were extremely deficient. Many state agencies simply had no published accounts. For example, the strategic Nigerian National Oil Corporation issued accounts immediately after it was set up in 1973, but there was then a gap of six years before the next set of accounts appeared.

For public enterprise as a whole, there was no evidence of increased financial planning and control. If the Fourth Plan documents are an accurate guide, progressively less attention was given to planning public sector enterprise in the period from the First Plan to the Third Plan. An irrelevant attempt was made by the Udoji Commission to infuse the public sector with the jargon of U.S. corporate management (management by objectives and programme performance budgeting) at a time when the basic budget and accounting functions of the state were weak or nonexistent.[26] The Ani recommendation that a central unit for financial control of public corporations be set up in the Ministry of Finance was not acted on.[27]

Technocrats did not establish strong bases within public corporations and enterprises. Ministerial control of federal enterprises was jealously guarded and state bodies had little autonomy over policy and conditions of service. There was a constant drain of professional personnel to more lucrative, less frustrating opportunities in the private sector. Federal initiatives were often subject to sectional and communal pressures over location and employment. There were also conflicts between federal and state authorities. These tensions could dilute the federal drive and lead to losses of economic and managerial efficiency.

Until the late 1960s, the state adopted a generally passive role in the oil industry. Then a number of measures were taken to increase the government's share of the oil rent through taxation of the oil companies. Nigerianisation of the oil sector also began to receive attention as civil servants began to link Nigerianisation to national control of the industry in line with developments in OPEC countries like Algeria. In 1971, the state took a 100 percent interest in new concessions, with private operators getting a share of the output. The state also took a 35 percent participation interest in all existing oil-producing companies through the Nigerian National Oil Corporation. This share was later raised to 60 percent. A controlling share in three oil marketing companies was also taken.

The responsibilities of the NNOC were the subject of controversy between nationalist technocrats in the corporation and comprador elements in the controlling Ministry of Mines and Power.[28] The issue about the appropriate organisation of the NNOC did not end when it was merged with the Ministry of Petroleum in 1976 to form the Nigerian National Petroleum Corporation (NNPC). It has been argued by the former permanent secretary of the ministry that the reorganisation was responsible for the lack of coordination between macroeconomic policy and oil pricing and incentive policy that became evident in 1977.[29] The corporation was very slow to build up a cadre of technocrats or get involved in oil production and exploration. In 1979, the NNPC was the subject of a public inquiry following allegations that large sums of oil money (N2.8 billion) were missing. Investigations did not substantiate these claims.[30]

Plans for a steel industry in its present form were put forward in 1970. The location for a Soviet-built blast furnace plant at Ajaokuta in Kwara state in the middle of the country was decided in 1975. Work started on the plant in 1979. Originally the intention was to use low-grade iron deposits at Itakpe and coal from Lafia. But the rail link to Itakpe was abandoned because of the immense cost, and a fuel benefication plant was not built. It was also found that the Lafia deposits were not suitable for coking. The plant was dogged by inadequate prior study of the country's mineral resources and infrastructural requirements. Both ore and fuel had to be imported and transported by bus.

Because of delays to Ajaokuta and optimistic assessments of the domestic market for steel, an agreement for a second plant on the coast at Aladja near Warri was signed in 1977, this time with German and Austrian participation. This direct reduction plant opened in 1982. Like Ajaokuta it was totally dependent on foreign ore and foreign technology and expertise. In addition, three steel rolling mills were set up with German and Japanese assistance at Jos, Oshogbo, and Katsina. These inland locations were dictated by political considerations and added to the costs of Nigerian steel.

By 1987, total expenditure on steel was over N5 billion, and many projects were still to be executed.[31] The high cost of Nigerian steel raised doubts about the long term viability of the projects. The unit cost of Nigerian steel was more than double the world price of steel because of the high import content. The heavy financial burden, lower estimates of market demand, and opposition from the World Bank, which wanted the projects closed down, combined to put the future of Nigerian steel into question. But a strong domestic lobby in favour of steel and direct funding from overseas accounts kept the projects afloat.

State ownership and control in the financial sector was extended in the 1970s through majority Nigerian ownership of commercial and merchant banks, the establishment of new federal banks, and the Nigerianisation of management. State ownership was also extended in the Nigerian Industrial Development Bank (NIDB), the insurance industry, and the Commonwealth Development Corporation, in which the NIDB took a 60 percent share after the Corporation failed to gain exemption from the provisions of the Nigerian Enterprises Promotion Decree.

In 1971, the federal government acquired a 40 percent interest in the three foreign-owned commercial banks that dominated the financial system (Barclays, Standard, and United Bank for Africa [UBA]). The Okigbo Committee on the Financial System (1977) argued against a state majority interest because management would still remain in foreign hands.[32] In the event, the federal government did secure a majority interest (60 percent) in a number of commercial and merchant banks and found itself in the anomalous position of penalising Barclays for its South African connections after it had done so. These changes in ownership were accompanied by a rapid Nigerianisation of management. Towards the end of the 1970s, federal policy shifted, and a number of banks were promoted with majority private Nigerian ownership.

Parastatals in the States

In the states, the proliferation of parastatal bodies built on and extended the earlier regional pattern of state investment. Many of the new states created parastatal bodies in industry, agriculture, banking, insurance, transport, construction, hotels, property, housing, and publishing. A number of the old regional institutions, notably the New Nigeria Development Company (NNDC) in Kaduna and the Odu'a Investment Company in Ibadan still survived.

The record of these state bodies was a mixed one. Commissions of inquiry revealed weaknesses similar to those seen in the federal corporations in the 1960s.[33] In addition, the personal involvement of military governors in the affairs of various parastatals was amply recorded, as were the opportunities for corruption provided by the sale of enterprises under the Nigerian Enterprises Promotion Decree. Board memberships and distributorships were a long-standing means of patronage. As a result, there was a very well-established pattern of investigation, dismissal, and fresh appointments with any change in political regime. Research in Kwara state confirmed the rapid turnover of board members and the general unimportance of experience and knowledge as against ethnic balancing and political influence in the appointments to boards.[34]

In Bendel state, the Odje Commission of inquiry reported on no less than 74 state boards, corporations, and companies.[35] The luxuriant and indiscriminate growth of parastatal bodies in Bendel state was made possible and perhaps explained by the fact that the state received high revenues per capita due to its oil production and the operation of the derivation principle in revenue allocation. In the period 1974/75–1978/79, over half of the recurrent expenditures in Bendel state were classified as grants and subventions to state boards and corporations.[36] Loans outstanding to the private sector at N53m (March 1978) exceeded those to state boards and corporations, indicating that state funds were also being used to support private accumulation on a large scale.[37]

The New Nigeria Development Company, a group holding company owned by the ten northern states, originally provided a regional support role for foreign capital and was involved in most large-scale projects in the north. In 1978, it had interests in 120 companies.[38] This regional role was eroded in the 1970s by the arrival of active state investment companies in Kano, Kaduna, and Jos, together with higher levels of private Nigerian investment and federal investment. From 1976, the company actively sought out and concentrated capital from groups of Nigerian businesspeople. A common pattern was for a group of five or six individuals to take 10–30 percent of the equity or more if the project was privately promoted. Like other state investment companies, the NNDC bought shares in publicly quoted companies. The purchase of shares by state agencies was justified as a way of attempting to offset the bias of share applications towards Lagos and the western states.

Indigenisation: Foreign and Local Capital

Measures to assist indigenous enterprises and restrict the operation of foreign capital were in evidence before independence, but it was only in the early 1970s that concerted efforts were made to diminish foreign ownership and reserve areas of the economy for the state. What were the origins of the Nigerian Enterprises Promotion Decrees of 1972 and 1977?[39] How did they affect the scale and capacities of local capital and its relation with foreign capital? Did they enhance local control at the national or sectoral level? What was their effect on foreign investment? And finally, what part did the decrees play in the general development of capitalist enterprise?

Commercial pressures to indigenise trade emerged strongly at the end of the civil war with a stronger, more coherent group of traders who had prospered from the civil war. The Indigenous Businessmen's Group in the Lagos Chamber of Commerce attacked the credit policies of the commercial banks and the record of the NIDB for favouring foreign enterprise and argued for more Nigerian equity participation.[40] In 1971, commercial banks were instructed to give 35 percent of loans and advances to indigenous businesspeople, who also received more favourable foreign exchange treatment from the Central Bank.[41] Such business lobbies found allies among federal civil servants and military officers, who were pressing for increased national control and Nigerian participation in the economy. It was thought that foreign capital could be pushed into higher technology areas, thereby creating opportunities for Nigerian businesspeople and changing the industrial structure. Local capital accumulation would benefit from the local retention of profits. The decree itself was put through the Federal Executive Council in a classic exercise of bureaucratic power when civil commissioners, who opposed the decree, were not present.[42]

The first phase of the indigenisation exercise distinguished two schedules of businesses that had to comply with the decree. Schedule one (twenty-two categories), where some 357 enterprises were affected, was reserved exclusively for Nigerians. This schedule included retail trade, services, and a range of small industries where Nigerian businesspeople were already active. Lebanese textile dealers were the most important group affected by this part of the decree.

It is notable that the import and wholesale trades were excluded. Even for the retail trade, the big foreign departmental stores and supermarkets were exempted, provided they had capital in excess of N400,000 or had turnover of at least N1 million. Inflationary pressures in the immediate aftermath of the civil war meant that the government could not contemplate any major disruption in the distributive sector. Three enterprises originally included in schedule one were later transferred to schedule two (electronic assembly, clearing and forwarding, and haulage of petroleum products by road). These were all areas that Nigerians had begun to enter, and there were protests about the transfer from the indigenous trade associations in these industries.[43]

Under schedule two, thirty-three categories of business were listed. Here Nigerian participation at 40 percent of the equity was compulsory, provided that the enterprises concerned had capital in excess of N400,000, or a turnover of at least N1 million. Some 595 enterprises were affected under this schedule. The total recorded value of transactions was N13 million for schedule one enterprises and N109 million for schedule two enterprises. Share prices for twenty-four public issues were deliberately set at low levels for fear of undersubscription. This helped the sale of shares, and issues were heavily oversubscribed.

Large private companies that did not offer shares publicly generally invited a few well-known Nigerians to take up 40 percent of the equity.[44] A company would then arrange bank loans for share purchases, the loans to be paid off from future dividends. The monetary guidelines for 1972/73 liberalised loans for those who wanted to buy shares. Smaller companies often sold equity to a single employee who then joined the board. The sale of shares in private companies led to a high concentration of Nigerian share ownership. Ankie Hoogvelt confirmed this picture for Kano in a survey of fifty-four enterprises that had been affected by the decree.[45] Of the N15 million equity received by 291 individuals, 6 individuals obtained 50 percent of the equity. This pattern of very high concentration in share acquisitions was confirmed nationally. A sample of 384 private placings involving schedule 2 companies showed that 30 percent (115 companies) had one shareholder and 47 percent (185 companies) between one and five shareholders.[46]

What is striking about the decree is that it was essentially an exercise in equity transfer. The sale of shares marked a significant step in the level of share ownership among the bureaucratic, professional, and business classes. Few enterprises were sold outright as going concerns to Nigerian buyers. The main exceptions were the acquisitions by the Ibru organisation, a large, indigenous conglomerate owned by Chief Michael Ibru, which acquired control over at least fifteen enterprises. In Kano, the Gashash brothers also acquired a few enterprises.[47] Other instances where Nigerian entrepreneurs took shareholdings that significantly advanced the growth of their own enterprises and their capacity for accumulation can be found, but this was not a central feature of foreign equity divestment.

The second phase of indigenisation, which was not foreseen by the promoters of the first decree, stemmed directly from dissatisfaction with the results of the first phase and the overthrow of the Gowon administration. The Murtala regime, on taking power, set up the Adeosun Panel to investigate the shortcomings of the first phase. Lax implementation of the decree had led to evasion and widespread fronting. The loudest objections to the decree were reserved for the gross inequalities it encouraged. The decree also favoured Lagos and the western states, for it was here that most of those who were in a position to take advantage of the decree resided. Thus sectional and individual advantage combined to undermine the nationalist legitimacy of the first decree. The Adeosun panel provided a chance for state and sectional interests to reassert themselves under the guise of nationalism and push for an unscrambling of the first decree, an extension of state ownership, and stronger control by Nigerian management. This led to anxiety among foreign investors that a creeping nationalisation was under way. In the event, the recommendations of the Adeosun panel were watered down.

Under the decree, all enterprises were included in three schedules covering full, majority (60 percent), and minority (40 percent) Nigerian ownership. In general, areas of higher technology and management were classified under schedule three, permitting foreign capital to hold up to 60 percent of the equity, though there were significant exceptions. For example, tobacco, textiles, and pharmaceuticals remained with a majority foreign interest. The commercial activities of the old trading monopolies were specifically exempted from full Nigerian ownership, provided they had a turnover of at least N25 million and had branches in at least ten states of the federation. A total of 1,078 companies (916 private and 162 public) was affected by the decree by the end of 1981. The total value of the share transactions was N551.2 million, of which about 25 percent (N138 million) was for offers for sale, the remainder being offers for subscription. Foreign capital still protested at the low asset valuation.

In response to the unequal distribution of shares during the first phase, no individual was to hold more than 5 percent of the equity or N50,000 worth of shares whichever was the higher. Ten percent of share purchases were reserved for employees. State institutions were exempted from these provisions and were given priority under the allocation rules. The *New Nigerian* (Kaduna) had argued in an editorial that state agencies should take up 50 percent of the shares issued in order to get a better geographical distribution of share ownership in the country.[48] The second phase of indigenisation did result in some extension of state ownership in the economy. This was a result of political pressures, largely from northern interests that felt they had been discriminated against in the first phase and wanted to increase their share of the equity on offer.

Although no firm judgement can be made, it would seem that the decrees only marginally lowered the rate of investment in industry through a negative effect on foreign investment decisions. There were many other factors at work that made foreign capital generally reluctant to invest rather than sell to the Nigerian market.

There is no reason to suppose, at least in the short run, that the exercise materially affected the control that foreign capital was able to exercise over corporate enterprise in Nigeria. The relatively wide spread of Nigerian shareholdings usually left the control exercised by blocks of foreign shareholding unaffected. Even when the number of senior Nigerian executives and directors increased, key positions were often left in the hands of expatriates. Another means of maintaining control with a minority shareholding was through the use of technical service and management agreements that became more common after the decrees. In the long run, the increase in Nigerian senior management and directors will no doubt shift more decisionmaking to Nigerian staff, continued technological dependence and the multinational nature of many enterprises notwithstanding. This shift has already occurred in the banking sector.

Transfer of ownership did help to resolve antagonism between Nigerian private capital and foreign capital at two levels. By excluding foreign capital (mainly Lebanese) from small-scale enterprises, it reduced conflict with Nigerian competitors. Also through the programme of equity transfer, it satisfied the aspirations of propertied and professional classes, who gained a stronger interest in the fortunes of capitalist corporate enterprise. The introduction of large numbers of Nigerian shareholders reduced the threat to foreign companies on occasions of mass nationalism and accelerated a process that had begun with the public share issues of the early 1960s.

The effects of indigenisation on the growth of indigenous enterprises, on patterns of investment, and local managerial and technical capabilities are difficult to determine, partly because there were other more important, longer-term factors at work that shaped the development of indigenous enterprise. The decrees were not, on the whole, very significant. It is probably correct to say that the decrees reinforced and accelerated trends that were under way, like the consolidation of local capital in commerce and the advances made by Nigerian management. But general trends like the shift from commerce to industry, entry to more technically advanced areas of manufacture, the rise of large conglomerates, and the evolution of family businesses to more corporate and bureaucratic forms of enterprise owed little to the decrees. In particular, the marked increase in private Nigerian industrial investment towards the end of the 1970s cannot be linked directly to the decrees. Nor did the decrees necessarily encourage joint ventures as a form of collaboration. Many local ventures got access to foreign management and technology without foreign equity participation.

Conclusion

In conclusion, I summarise my position on the impact of oil on macroeconomic management, on overall economic strategy, on the productive sectors of the economy, and on acquisition of wealth and local patterns of capital accumulation.

Neither the Gowon regime, nor the Murtala-Obasanjo administration proved successful at the macroeconomic management of the economy. How far was it the state managers who were reckless and disregarded the constraints of the economy? How far was this the result of particular difficulties set off by the exogenous oil shocks? No regime could have withstood entirely the impact of vast oil revenues that arrived so suddenly and the pressures to spend that they engendered. Any national economic strategy required determined management of the economy to face difficulties that were actually much more demanding than those of the civil war period.

The immediate impact was to increase government expenditures very rapidly and to trigger a sustained appreciation of the naira. Internally, budgetary control was lost, with large surpluses rapidly giving way to large deficits. This loss of control needs to be set in the context of a basic weakness in the accounting functions of the state that extended throughout the public sector. The growth of state expenditure and responsibilities tended to undermine these functions, compounding the underlying fiscal weakness of the state and making the task of management more difficult.

Neither regime confronted the appreciation of the naira, which made the level of imports so much more difficult to control, distorted the internal structure of production, and made massive profits available to all varieties of middlemen. The managers of the economy had no experience of exchange rate management, and the exchange rate never became a subject for serious economic debate. The appreciation of the naira was the easiest option. It benefited the urban middle class and the commercial classes who later resisted devaluation. Insofar as the exchange rate was viewed in instrumental terms, it was seen as a means of controlling inflation through cheap imports.

Both the increase in state expenditure and the appreciation contributed to an import boom that could not be sustained, leading to a prolonged period of import compression. By 1978, Nigeria was on the brink of sliding into a debt trap. How did oil increase indebtedness? In principle, an increase in foreign exchange earnings should allow the managers of the economy to maintain or reduce the existing level of external debt. The paradox is resolved by considering some of the forces at work.

First, recall that the sustained rise in real oil earnings brought about acute dependence on a single source of revenue and imparted a very powerful momentum to government spending and imports. When oil revenues dipped, there was a violent switchback effect on the balance of payments that left the authorities scrambling to cover the loss of reserves by foreign borrowing.

Second, there was pressure from international finance capital to advance loans to Nigeria so that part of the expected future stream of foreign exchange earnings from oil could be appropriated and transferred to the centres of finance capital. The important point here is that private bankers were willing to lend, not because Nigeria needed loans but because they wanted, and expected, a high return on their loans. This pressure on Nigeria to borrow proved irresistible and allowed Nigeria to sustain and entrench a pattern of import dependence and expensive, unproductive projects that undermined the economy. Any idea that unregulated access to the international capital "market" would promote the material advancement of Nigeria was completely without foundation.

The main departure in economic strategy in the 1970s compared to the 1960s was the attempt to restructure the industrial economy through public sector leadership. A related attempt was also made to secure greater national control of the economy through the indigenisation of ownership. Yet the scope, seriousness of intent, and capacity for execution in this initiative should not be exaggerated. The underlying political conditions were not favourable. The state generally played an ambiguous role, neither playing a key role in the promotion of economic growth and technological advance nor supporting private enterprise effectively.

The advance of the state sector on all fronts was to prove vulnerable once the fiscal situation deteriorated. Public expenditure should have increased less rapidly and been subject to clear priorities. Many projects proved costly, wasteful, and inefficent and had to be scaled down or temporarily abandoned.

The federal initiatives never had the popular support or reformist zeal of other extensions of state control and ownership like those undertaken by military governments in Egypt or Peru. The military had no concrete strategy of their own, and they did not articulate one. They relied upon senior civil servants who basically supported a strategy of private accumulation, albeit with a strong dose of state intervention and ownership to promote industrialisation. Both bureaucrats and army officers usually saw their professions as a step on the road to establishing substantial bases for private accumulation after their retirement, and state office was used to acquire private wealth. The state sector was not strong enough and the links between the military and the civil servants not secure enough to support the kind of authoritarian development seen in Indonesia, where the state apparatus was totally appropriated by a class of state officials and senior military officers who propounded a strong ideology of state-led development.

What was the impact of oil on the productive sectors of the economy? Writing in the late 1960s, Peter Kilby painted a vivid picture of the promise of large oil revenues that were then around the corner.[49] Oil would, he thought, free Nigeria from domestic and foreign exchange constraints that had begun to set up distortions in the economy, thereby impeding efficiency and growth. This view was probably shared by most economists at that time, and it contributed to the rising expectations that the prospect of oil engendered. With hindsight, the total inadequacy of such views is painfully obvious.

To try to take account of the impact of a booming sector like oil, economists later adopted the term "Dutch disease."[50] This term referred to the adverse effects on Dutch manufacturing of the natural gas discoveries of the 1960s, which operated to raise the real exchange rate. Did the appreciation of the naira undermine sectors of the Nigerian economy? The many-sided impact of oil on the Nigerian economy cannot be neatly captured by a term like "Dutch disease." "Dutch disease" cannot comprehend the loss of macroeconomic control, the increase in external indebtedness, the expansion of the public sector, and the existence of many unproductive state projects. There is, in any case, little evidence that food production or manufacturing were undermined by "Dutch disease" in the period under review. As I will argue in Chapter 9, only the decline in agricultural exports undermined by currency appreciation and rising domestic costs really fits into this logic. In the longer term, a stronger case for the adverse consequences of exchange rate appreciation can be made for manufacturing than for agriculture.

What was the impact of large-scale oil revenues and state expenditures on indigenous patterns of accumulation and the acquisition of wealth? There is no doubt that the massive increase in state expenditures provided the opportunity for the large-scale personal acquisition of wealth by those with access to state power. After the Gowon regime fell, inquiries showed how civil servants, military officers, and state commissioners had enriched themselves, building up assets in housing, shares, and farms. The inquiries demonstrated how closely those in power collaborated with foreign capital to achieve their ends. The inflation of state contracts was a favoured route (involving state officials, middlemen and foreign companies) for the appropriation of state funds. Some of these funds were received in foreign currency abroad or else remitted overseas. The indigenisation decrees provided the opportunity for the bureaucratic, managerial, professional, and business classes to obtain shares cheaply in foreign companies. In the first phase, a few individuals were able to acquire massive share portfolios.

What is less evident is how the wealth that was acquired was used and how indigenous entrepreneurs responded to the changed conditions and new incentives. Some authors emphasise the waste and high consumption of the period, others the comprador nature of activity, the dominance of commercial, intermediary, and rent-seeking forms of activity, and property investment.[51] More generally, unproductive patterns of accumulation[52] and the lack of a capacity to organise capitalist production are stressed.[53] The dependence of private accumulation upon access to the state and its resources is highlighted. This is seen as the central route to wealth and social mobility. There is a heavy emphasis on various forms of political accumulation and dominant class formation via the state.[54] One influential analysis claims, on little evidence, that Nigeria moved from a phase of nurture capitalism to a form of pirate capitalism and that the economy was inert.[55] In another analysis, unproductive accumulation is linked to the arbitrariness and unpredictability of a patrimonial state that adversely affects the conditions for capital accumulation.[56]

Although these perspectives have some merit, they do not give the whole picture. They do not take adequate account of long-run trajectories of private accumulation that are relatively independent of the state. Nor do they recognise the movement of local capital from commerce into medium- and larger-scale manufacture, agriculture, and financial services, the growth in size of enterprises, advances in corporate organisation, and the capacity of entrepreneurs to use foreign management and technology to promote their own enterprises. My own research suggests that there was an increase in industrial investment by Nigerian entrepreneurs in the late 1970s after the initial impact of the oil boom had provided the finance for investment.

Notes

1. Calculated from *Annual Reports*, Central Bank of Nigeria.

2. According to the World Bank (*Nigeria: Macro-Economic Policies for Structural Change* [Washington, D.C.: World Bank, 1983], p. 9), the movement of relative prices between 1973 (=100) and 1981 was as follows:

Agriculture	332.8
Food	(373.3)
Exports	(157.2)
Manufactures	210.8
Commerce	323.3
Government services	291.6
Exchange rate (adjusted for purchasing power parity)	187.0

3. G. Williams, "Inequalities in Rural Nigeria," Development Studies Occasional Paper no. 16, University of East Anglia, 1981, pp. 89–90.

4. Williams, "Inequalities in Rural Nigeria," pp. 89–90.

5. *Nigeria: Macro-Economic Policies* , p. 31.

6. *Nigeria: Macro-Economic Policies*, p. 9.

7. From 1963 to 1979, the percentages of tariff revenue per naira of imports were (*Annual Reports*, Central Bank of Nigeria):

1963-1965 average	30	1975	17
1970	28	1976	14
1971	27	1977	16
1972	31	1978	21
1973	25	1979	19
1974	19		

8. *Industrial Survey*, Federal Office of Statistics, Lagos, various years.

9. G. Andrae and B. Beckman, "Industry Goes Farming: The Nigerian Raw Material Crisis and the Case of Textiles and Cotton," Scandinavian Institute of African Studies, Uppsala, Research Report no. 80, 1987.

10. Adeboye T. O, "Public Sector Participation in Manufacturing," mimeo, paper delivered to 1978 Annual Conference of the Nigerian Economic Society.

11. S. B. Falegan, "Trends in Nigeria's Balance of Payments and Policy Measures Needed for Self-Reliance," *Economic and Financial Review*, 16/2, 1978, p. 10.

12. I owe this point to discussions with Ken Iteke.

13. *Guidelines for the Fourth National Development Plan 1981–85*, Federal Ministry of National Planning, Lagos, p. 7.

14. See *Annual Reports, Development Co-operation*, OECD, Paris.

15. The net effect of federal expenditures on aggregate demand (defined as annual increase in current and capital spending less annual increase in non-oil tax revenue plus annual increase in statutory and non-statutory allocations, in N million) is as follows (*Annual Reports*, Central Bank of Nigeria):

1970	+370	1974	+996
1971	–364.7	1975	+2,675
1972	+350.9	1976	+1,687
1973	+51.9	1977	+640

16. Nigeria's Principal Economic and Financial Indicators 1970–1978, Central Bank of Nigeria.

17. *Public Service Review Commission, Main Report* (the Udoji Report), Lagos, 1974.

18. Bendel state was the first state to take advantage of the new provisions in 1988.

19. Employees Housing Schemes (Special Provisions), Decree No. 54 of 1979.

20. A fuller account of the public sector can be found in T. G. Forrest, "State Capital, Capitalist Development and Class Formation in Nigeria," in P. M. Lubeck, ed., *The African Bourgeoisie: Capitalist Development in Nigeria, Kenya, and the Ivory Coast* (Boulder: Lynne Rienner, 1987), pp. 307–342.

21. D. Bevan, P. Collier, and J. Gunning, "Poverty, Equity and Growth in Nigeria, 1950–1986," mimeo, Oxford, 1987, p. 85.

22. M. Bray, *Universal Primary Education in Nigeria: A Study of Kano State* (London: Routledge and Kegan Paul, 1981), p. 4.

23. *Annual Abstract of Statistics, 1981*, Federal Office of Statistics, Lagos.

24. R. Pittin, "Selective Education: Issues of Gender, Class and Ideology in Northern Nigeria," *Review of African Political Economy* 48 (1990), pp. 7–25.

25. T. Seymour, "Housing Policy and Income Distribution in Kaduna," *The Nigerian Journal of Public Affairs*, 7, 1977, pp. 81–83.

26. See *A Review of the Federal Budgetary System, Final Report*, Nigerian Institute of Social and Economic Research and Federal Ministry of Finance, 1977.

27. *Report of the Working Party on Statutory Corporations and State-Owned Companies* (the Ani Report), Federal Ministry of Information, Lagos, 1967.

28. T. Turner, "Commercial Capitalism and the 1975 Coup," in K. Panter-Brick, ed., *Soldiers and Oil* (London: Frank Cass, 1978), chap. 6.

29. P. C. Asiodu, *Nigeria and the Oil Question*, Nigerian Economic Society, 1979.

30. *House of Representatives Report of the Special (Investigation) Committee on the Nigerian National Petroleum Corporation (NNPC)* (Lagos: Federal Government Press, 1980); *Report of Tribunal of Inquiry into Crude Oil Sales* (Lagos: Federal Government Press, 1980); *Views of the Government of the Federation on the Report of the Crude Oil Sales Tribunal* (Lagos: Federal Government Press, 1980).

31. *This Week* (Lagos), 6 July 1987.

32. *Report of the Committee on the Financial System*, Federal Ministry of Information, Lagos, 1977.

33. See, for example, *Report of The Panel to Investigate into the Benue-Plateau State Houses and Contract Procedure and Also to Investigate Whether Some Persons Have Made Improper Gains*, Jos, 1975.

34. S. S. Lawal, "The Politics of Board Membership of Public Enterprises in Kwara State," M.P.A. thesis, University of Ife, 1979.

35. *Government Views on Decisions of Odje Commission of Inquiry: Findings and Recommendations on Some Government Owned Companies, Boards and Corporations*, Official Document No. 1 of 1977, Bendel State. See also Official Document No. 4 of 1977.

36. "Prospectus for N20 million 7% First Bendel State of Nigeria Loan Stock 1988," Lagos, 1978.

37. "Prospectus."

38. *Annual Reports and Accounts,* New Nigeria Development Company, Kaduna.

39. For a major study of the indigenisation exercise, see T. Biersteker, *Multinationals, the State, and Control of the Nigerian Economy* (Princeton: Princeton University Press, 1987). I have drawn my figures for the number of enterprises affected and the value of the share transactions from this source.

40. *Commerce in Nigeria* 11 (1969), pp. 20, 65.

41. *Monetary Policy Circular* 3, 1971.

42. Interview with Allison Ayida, Lagos, August 1982.

43. Speech by Chief Henry Fajemirokun, President of the Lagos Chamber of Commerce, *Commerce in Nigeria* 16 (1974–1975).

44. A. Banjo, "The Principal Problems of Indigenisation," *Management in Nigeria,* September 1976, pp. 29–35.

45. A. Hoogvelt, "Indigenisation and Foreign Capital: Industrialisation in Nigeria," *Review of African Political Economy* 14 (1979), p. 62.

46. Adeosun Commission. As reported by Biersteker, *Multinationals,* table 3.1b, p. 145.

47. I owe this information to Adebayo Olukoshi.

48. *New Nigerian* (Kaduna), 1 March 1977.

49. P. Kilby, *Industrialization in an Open Economy: Nigeria, 1954–1966* (London: Cambridge University Press, 1969), pp. 15–16.

50. See W. M. Corden, "Booming Sector and Dutch Disease Economics: Survey and Consolidation," in W. M. Corden, ed., *Protection, Growth and Trade: Essays in International Economics* (Oxford: Basil Blackwell, 1985).

51. W. M. Freund, *The Making of Contemporary Africa: The Development of African Society Since 1800* (London: Macmillan, 1984), pp. 241–243.

52. S. Berry, *Fathers Work for Their Sons: Accumulation, Mobility and Class Formation in an Extended Yoruba Community* (Berkeley: University of California Press, 1985).

53. Fred Cooper, "Africa and the World Economy," *African Studies Review* 24/2–3 (1981), p. 49; Colin Leys, "African Economic Development in Theory and Practice," *Daedalus* 3 (1982), p. 113.

54. L. Diamond, "Nigeria: Pluralism, Statism and the Struggle for Democracy," in L. Diamond, J. L. Linz, and S. M. Lipset, eds., *Democracy in Developing Countries: Africa* (Boulder: Lynne Rienner, 1988), pp. 66, 84–85.

55. S. P. Schatz, "Pirate Capitalism and the Inert Economy of Nigeria," *Journal of Modern African Studies* 22 (1984), pp. 45–57.

56. T. M. Callagy, "The State and the Development of Capitalism in Africa: Theoretical, Historical and Comparative Reflections," in D. Rothchild and N. Chazan, eds., *The Precarious Balance: State and Society in Africa* (Boulder: Westview Press, 1988), pp. 79–88.

8

Civil Rule and Economic Policy, 1979–1983

Economic policy and its dynamic interaction with economic, social, and political forces over the four years of the Second Republic are examined in this chapter. This was a period in which a sharp decline in oil revenues plunged the economy into recession. Stripped of the veneer of much of its foreign exchange earnings, the difficulty of converting oil into productive assets was revealed. This difficulty was aggravated in the period under review by the scale of capital flight that fed foreign interests and a tiny Nigerian elite. Also exposed were large deficits on non-oil trade accounts in industry, services and agriculture. This was a time, too, when a gross materialism that had built up through the long oil boom reached its apogee in the life-style of some politicians and their business associates, who spawned a group of private jet owners.[1] It was also the era of a menial Ghanaian underclass, numbering hundreds of thousands, who found employment in Nigerian cities and were expelled once the recession started to bite.

The rule of the politicians had disastrous economic consequences for Nigeria. Civil politics superimposed its own stamp upon the conduct of economic affairs at the same time as it reinforced certain trends that I have already traced through the period of military rule. These trends included the loss of financial control and discipline in the public economy, the privatisation of public funds, and the continued expansion of the state sector.

The period opened up with oil revenues on a rising trend and a comfortable stock of foreign exchange reserves bequeathed by the outgoing military government. The timing of this increase in oil revenues was important, for it was already under way when the politicians arrived and continued for another eighteen months. This miniboom was sufficient to impart a strong upward momentum to state expenditures and to inflate the scale and costs of projects. It also set in motion other features that find parallels in the earlier oil boom. For example, imports were liberalised and rose swiftly to bring about a rapid reversal in the balance-of-payments position. The real exchange rate continued to rise.

Alan Gelb has made a useful comparison between the use of the oil windfall in the two boom periods (see Table 8.1).[2] This comparison suggests that a higher proportion of resources from the windfall was devoted to consumption, especially private consumption, during the second boom. Even allowing for the unsatisfactory state of the national accounts and problems of interpretation, the allocation is indicative of the priorities of the politicians and the pressures of political patronage.

By mid-1981 oil revenues were in decline. The full impact of the decline was to be partially masked during the remaining two and one-half years of civil rule. One reason was the indulgence of the government in large-scale deficit financing, which was reinforced by the need to get reelected at all costs. The other factor was the buildup of international debt and very large trade arrears that allowed imports to be sustained well above the levels dictated by earnings. No country had previously built up short-term arrears of this magnitude. This was a tribute to the enormous attractions of an open oil economy for international traders and the willingness of international banks to finance trade on credit long after it had become apparent that the Nigerian government had lost control over the level of imports and foreign exchange reserves. It was a corrupt system involving heavy capital flight. When the politicians fell from power, the system ground to a halt, setting in motion the collapse of Johnson Matthey Bankers in London, the secondary banking arm of the Johnson Matthey Group.

Macroeconomic Management

Expansion

By the end of 1980, foreign exchange reserves stood at N5.1 billion. This situation was due in part to the import control measures taken in 1978 and the import inspection scheme. It was also the result of a rise in the price of oil. Revenue collected by the federal government rose from N12.2 billion (1979/80) to N15.2 billion in 1980.

The build up of surpluses in the external and internal accounts set in motion pressures to expand state expenditures and liberalise imports. The slow recovery of domestic demand stemmed from the fact that the new regime wished to make its own contract awards as well as from the protracted discussion of the budget appropriations in the legislature. By the end of 1980, the expansion was well under way. The 1981 budget was expansionary and contributed to large-scale deficit financing (N3.1 billion from the Central Bank). At the very moment when the expenditure expansion gathered momentum, however, oil revenues started to decline. This

TABLE 8.1 Allocation of Oil Windfalls (percent)

	1974–1978	1979–1981
Private consumption	11.3	40.0
Public consumption	28.5	24.4
Investment	60.2	35.6
Total	100.0	100.0

Source: Gelb (1986), tables 2.4 and 2.5, pp. 62–63 and 64.

coincidence quickly turned the surpluses on internal and external accounts into deficits.

President Shagari and his advisers were clearly aware of the earlier oil boom and its disastrous economic consequences. Yet the liberalisation of imports began with the 1980 budget. The external account moved sharply into deficit in 1981, with a record level of imports (N12.9 billion) and a reserve loss of N3.1 billion for that year.

Where did the pressures to expand state expenditures come from? First, there were the general pressures associated with a centralised, rental form of income. Second, political payoffs and rewards contributed to the expansion of state employment at all levels. Third, there were additional costs associated with the presidential system, the legislature, and the police. One of the first actions of the legislators was to vote themselves salary increases and large fringe benefits. As a result, any legitimacy gained from the electoral process was rapidly eroded. Law and order was a priority for the administration. The police force was expanded, and new equipment and paramilitary training introduced. Expenditure figures show that expenditure on the armed services was squeezed in absolute terms, and internal security (the police and NSO) expanded. Between 1980 and 1983, total federal expenditures on administration and internal security rose by 75 percent and 58 percent, respectively.[3] Defence expenditure, on the other hand, fell by 33 percent. The priority given to the police was resented in the army, and its political role made it unpopular with the population at large. Fourth, there were large project expenditures that were often inflated, including the new capital at Abuja to which the government was heavily committed. Finally, there were wage pressures to which I will return.

The 1982 budget was a travesty and totally irresponsible. It effectively masked an extremely serious economic situation that could be foreseen by August 1981 in the loss of reserves and the deficit financing of state expenditure. The complacency of the government is indicated by a remarkable defence of its economic policies given to the press in August 1981 by E. C. Edozien, special adviser to the president on economic affairs.[4] He claimed that the economic foundations were being laid for self-sustaining growth and that the economy was buoyant. He defended the rise in imports in response to economic buoyancy and further attempted to blame the state governments for deficit financing and economic irresponsibility. In the event, there was a foreign reserve loss of $6.3 billion in 1981, and the government borrowed an unprecedented N4.1 billion (net) from the Central Bank in the same year.[5]

The government was apparently hoping that the oil market would improve. However, slack conditions in the international oil market put pressure on the authorities to reduce the price of oil or lose buyers on short-term contracts. A price reduction was resisted in favour of solidarity with OPEC, and there was a rapid fall in oil sales from 1.8 million barrels per day in January 1982 to 0.7 million barrels per day in March. At one point, Saudi Arabia and Kuwait successfully applied pressure on Mobil and Texaco to keep extracting Nigerian oil.[6]

Externally the failure to control the current account led to reserve loss and a buildup of international debt through syndicated loans for specific projects and through trade arrears. External public debt rose steadily from N3.3 billion in 1978 to N14.7 billion at the end of 1982. This latter figure included N2 billion of debt incurred by state governments, which had started to borrow abroad in 1980. Under the constitution, the federal government had a responsibility to monitor and control this debt, but there was no indication that it had done so.

Stabilisation Measures

The loss of reserves prompted emergency stabilisation measures in April 1982. Advance deposits for imports, increases in import duties, and a review of import licences were introduced. There was also a reorganisation of the customs service and closure of private jetties in an attempt to reduce smuggling. Planned cuts in public expenditure amounted to 40 percent. These cuts were across the board without priorities. In addition, there were increases in excise duties, interest rates, and petrol prices.

These measures were not successful in controlling the level of imports or the pressures on foreign exchange reserves, partly because there was a large volume of goods on open general licence under short-term trade credit. The Central Bank resorted to holding foreign exchange reserves constant as the volume of trade arrears rose from N2.2 billion at the end of 1982 to N4.4 billion at the end of 1983.

In April, negotiations were opened with IMF, helping Nigeria secure refinancing agreements that converted a total of about N1.5 billion of arrears on letters of credit into medium-term loans. A small unpublicised loan of $400 million was secured from Saudi Arabia.[7] But political imperatives and prevailing economic opinion ruled out reforms, including devaluation.

Inflation accelerated to over 50 percent in 1983. But for the compulsory advance-deposit scheme for imports (which froze bank assets), monetary expansion would have been very much higher. To counter inflationary pressures, the president set up a preelection task force under Adamu Ciroma to import essential commodities. The task force spent N476 million, but many supplies did not get through by election time, and some goods were still arriving when the government fell.[8]

The basic failure to control imports and relieve pressure on the balance of payments in 1982 was repeated in 1983, despite a further round of stabilisation measures. Tariffs were raised and over 250 goods placed on licence. At the root of the economic incompetence of the Shagari regime was a political failure that made the administration of a tighter economic regime impossible. To quote a Central Bank report, "even in the face of mounting short term trade debts the Central Bank was put under increased pressure throughout the year to open letters of credit at very short notice for such federal government agencies as the Nigeria Police Force, Federal Electoral Commission and the Presidential Task Force on Rice."[9]

As a result of these pressures, the foreign exchange budget for 1983, which was N7.2 billion, was exceeded by 50 percent.[10] Similar pressures made the administration of import licences impossible. Import licences were an important source of funds for party political patronage. On occasion, they were distributed to the states and then sold by governors to wealthy businesspeople who supported the ruling party. The minister of trade and commerce defended the distribution of licences to the states by citing federal character and the need for each state to benefit under civil rule.[11] The total value of import licences issued in 1983 without reference to the licence committee was N682 million.[12]

One result of the political incompetence and economic mismanagement was the hostility of large corporate business interests. Originally big business had favoured civil rule, as it was thought that it would bring easier access to government and more consultation over policy. Now the Manufacturers Association of Nigeria (MAN) became highly critical of the government, campaigning against the Stabilisation Act and attacking the allocation of foreign exchange and the management of import licences, though it did not support devaluation.

Policymaking

Policymaking exhibited a high level of incoherence and lack of coordination between different power centres and interests under President Shagari (ministries of Finance, Industries, and Commerce; Central Bank; Budget Bureau; the economic advisers). When stabilisation became essential, there was some improvement, and an economic stabilisation and implementation committee was set up in the Office of the President, which included the governor of the Central Bank. The economic advisers had no perceptible impact on policymaking other than a defence of the government's record. The Central Bank became bogged down in detailed regulation and control and could not play an effective policy or monitoring role. Illegal transactions flourished, and the energies of state officials were increasingly taken up with policing real or imagined abuses of the trade and payments controls.

The legislature did not initiate any economic legislation, nor did it reform or rationalise existing legislation. Decisions on the budgets and other issues were delayed by the insistence that the two houses consider everything separately before arriving at a consensus. In general, senators appeared to be much more interested in promoting their personal interests and lobbying for them in the ministries than debating national priorities. The various committees of the houses could call for evidence and so promote consultation and debate over economic issues. Thus considerable publicity was given to the views of Allison Ayida on devaluation and Senator David Dafinone on the steel industry.[13] In general, however, committee work was not reflected in subsequent discussion in the House of Representatives and the Senate.

In January 1983, a Committee of Experts was set up by the National Economic Council to advise on economic policy. Like its predecessor, the Anti-Inflation Task Force of 1975, it made a multitude of recommendations with no clear priorities.[14] The key issue of devaluation was avoided, just as the earlier task force had avoided confronting the growth of state expenditures. The picture conveyed by both reports is that they were commissioned to give the impression that something was being done and that it was never intended that they should provide a serious critique of government economic policy.

How far did the second term of President Shagari promise any more effective administration or change of policy now that the NPN had a majority in the National Assembly and controlled twelve states? Belatedly a Projects Review Committee to establish priorities among public sector projects was set up on the advice of the World Bank. The 1984 budget gave priority to the Liquified Natural Gas and Petrochemical projects. If the president's economic advisers, Gamaliel Onosode and Philip Asiodu, were more impressive than their predecessors, the new ministerial appointments inspired no confidence. There is no reason to suppose that the institutional and administrative capacity for economic management would have improved radically, given the nature of the NPN as a party of national patronage and spoils. The 1984 budget, announced just prior to the coup, contained more expenditure cuts and import controls and a commitment to a cut in subsidies and privatisation, measures that were in line with IMF policies. Nothing was said about devaluation.

Capital Flight, Rents, and Smuggling

Official estimates of capital flight from Nigeria over 1979 to 1983 stand at N18 billion (over $14 billion).[15] Capital flight was significant during the oil boom of the 1970s, but it probably reached its peak during the period of civil rule bolstered by the corruption of the civilian regime, the surge in oil revenues at the start of the period, and the subsequent trade restrictions and foreign exchange controls that opened up a widening gap between official and parallel market rates. The most important sources of earnings for capital flight at the beginning were probably inflated contracts and overinvoicing of imports. As oil revenues fell and trade restrictions and foreign exchange controls became more important, so there was a shift in the source of rent from contracts to trade. Food imports, especially the rice and sugar trade, provided a lucrative source of rents that was fully exploited. There were other means of financing capital flight. The smuggling of refined petroleum products and other goods to neighbouring countries to take advantage of price differentials and parallel market exchange rates provided one avenue. The importation and distribution of subsidised fertiliser, cement, and flour was another.

As retired Lt-General Danjuma argued, corruption in the Second Republic was distinguished by its transnational efficiency, maturing from purely local currency deals to exclusively foreign exchange transactions.[16] Commissions could be paid directly into foreign bank accounts. Even when deals were struck in naira, the proceeds were quickly transferred abroad through the Central Bank at the overvalued exchange rate, albeit with "transaction costs" imposed by officials. The appetite for foreign accounts was sharpened by the federal government's approval and guarantee of foreign loans for the states as if they were a kind of statutory allocation. Contracts for all sorts of ill-conceived projects were entered into, and in the process foreign indebtedness was built up.

With import controls, a vastly overvalued exchange rate, and domestic inflation, trading in commodities with Nigeria became extremely profitable. A very large short-term trade debt was built up, much of it through corrupt practices. From 1980, foreign banks began to finance lucrative trade deals attracted by the high interest rates that could be covered by the very high margins. Many Indian businesspeople were involved in the commodity trade, and with their aid Nigerian businesspeople and politicians could move fortunes out of the country at artificially low official rates of exchange. Part of the profit could be recycled back to Nigeria at a much higher black market rate to finance further deals. Some of this trade involved fraud, false documentation, foreign exchange control evasion, and fictitious exports. When the Shagari regime fell, a number of traders and confirming houses found themselves overextended. Some of these deals were exposed in the spectacular collapse of the Johnson Matthey Bank in September 1984.[17] Of the bank's total outstanding loans and other commitments at the time of its rescue by the Bank of England, some £120 million was related to financing trade with Nigeria. A tight-knit group of sugar traders used Johnson Matthey Bank to finance trade. The group included Rajendra Sethia's Esal Commodities, which became the major supplier of sugar to Nigeria.[18] Between early 1980 and the end of 1983, the wholesale price of sugar in Nigeria rose from about £200 to about £1,000 a metric ton while its price actually fell on the world market. Sethia's business practices were unorthodox and relied on close personal relations with government functionaries. *West Africa* reported that

> Sethia used to phone around all the London sugar dealers to get the cheapest quotation for a consignment; once he decided on his supplier he would either ask for credit or borrow the money from one of his tame bankers and then without any supporting documents or import inspection certificates he would load the sugar on a vessel for Nigeria. About two days before the ship was due to reach Lagos, Sethia would fly out to Nigeria and pay off the necessary officials to let the consignment into the country. In about two weeks, the sugar would be on the local market.[19]

If public knowledge of the exploitative sugar trade became widespread only after the collapse of the regime and the troubles of Johnson Matthey Bank, the importation of rice was the subject of much controversy during the Second Republic and came to epitomise in the public mind the corruption of the regime. From 50,000 metric tons in 1976, rice imports had risen to about 600,000 metric tons by 1981. Imports of rice were subject to cycles of expansion and contraction as a result of conflicting political pressures from rice merchants, rice farmers, consumers, and state officials. The result was frequent tariff and quota changes with sharp price movements.

In 1979 the military restricted rice imports. After an unseemly struggle over rice licences among Senate members, President Shagari responded by setting up a Rice Task Force under Umaru Dikko. The distribution of rice licences or access to landed rice granted by the task force proved to be an easy and effective way of granting political patronage and raising money for the party. This led to an increase in rice imports above the level needed to cover the deficit. Whereas the volume of wheat imports peaked in 1981, rice imports continued at a high level, despite a sharp reduction in the overall level of imports. (See Table 9.1.)

The size of the illegal cross-border trade between Nigeria and the neighbouring states of Benin, Niger, and Cameroon depended on the strength of the Nigerian market and on periodic state restrictions that affected the commodity and currency price differentials.

The vast expansion of the Nigerian market in the 1970s fortified the trade and made Nigeria the centre of the regional market. It also periodically strengthened the value of the naira on the parallel market. Thus the naira rose on the parallel market in Benin by 46 percent in terms of CFA francs (Communauté Financière Africaine) over 1978–1981, roughly in line with the movement of the official rate of exchange, where it was priced 80 percent above its parallel market value.[20] The naira in fact became a second currency in all markets and stores in Benin, and it was vigorously recycled back to Nigeria. Price differentials between Nigeria and its neighbours for refined products varied between five and nine to one. This prompted a significant trade and created wealthy communities along the borders. An elaborate marketing hierarchy in Benin is described by John Igue.[21] Tam David-West, minister for petroleum under Buhari, later estimated that Nigeria lost $1 million a day from the smuggling of refined petroleum products.[22] Other unofficial exports from Nigeria included cocoa (official buying prices in Nigeria failed to reflect world market values by a large margin), motor vehicles (especially cars from the Peugeot assembly plant in Kaduna), motorcycles, cosmetics, and construction materials. In the opposite direction, the most prominent smuggled goods were cigarettes (British brands), textiles (wax prints), jewellery, alcoholic drinks, sugar, rice, and dried fish. This flow of goods to Nigeria took place alongside the official transit trade from Togo and Ghana that had sprung to life after Nigeria's ports had become congested. After the austerity measures of April 1982 and the start of the Nigerian recession, the value of the naira on the parallel market fell while continuing to appreciate officially.

Labour and Wage Policy

The Shagari government had much trouble controlling trade unions. Its labour policies were confused, and it procrastinated and refused to take the initiative on wage demands that were outstanding from the time it came to power. Unions managed to exert considerable upward pressure on wages and fringe benefits. These gains, however, were quickly eroded in real terms by inflation and unemployment as the recession mounted.

From the outset, the NLC argued for a N300 a month minimum wage, which was a 300 percent increase for the lower paid. This demand was fuelled by a long period of inflation and wage freeze under the military. Though the government was publicly committed to free collective bargaining, it entered into bilateral talks with union leaders and agreed upon a national minimum wage. This event alarmed employers, who had already restructured employers' organisations on an industry-wide basis to match the new NLC structure. In some industries, agreements on fringe benefits had already been negotiated through collective bargaining. There followed a series of inconclusive tripartite meetings that led eventually to a general strike lasting two days. The strike ended on the understanding that the National Assembly would vote on the issue.[23] Both manufacturers and state governors lobbied strongly against the NLC demand. In the end the Assembly voted for a N125 minimum wage. This was in addition to increases in pensions, rent, and transport allowances that had already been secured. The award comfortably exceeded the government's own guidelines and led it to make payments to the states to cover additional wage costs, as had happened in the aftermath of the Udoji award. Later the NLC managed to resist attempts by the government to establish a rival trade union movement and a move to abolish the automatic checkoff system that provided the NLC with funds.

The major response of the government to the recession was the expulsion of alien workers, a popular move for an election year. The expulsions in January and February 1983 amounted to 2 million persons, perhaps half of them Ghanaians. The government accused them of criminality, currency trafficking, fomenting religious riots, and threatening internal security.[24] The alien workers had been drawn into Nigeria by the oil boom and pushed from their countries of origin by harsh economic conditions and drought. The majority were unregistered, and many were members of a menial underclass in petty trading, domestic labour, transporting, small-scale industry, construction, prostitution, and agricultural labour. This group undercut Nigerian workers, and members were the objects of hostility. The Nigerian owner of a block-making plant reported he had to pay N12 a day to Nigerians on jobs for which he had to pay aliens N7.[25] Alien labour was also used by companies to break strikes and discipline Nigerian labour.[26] The expulsion order was directed at this group rather than the professionals and teachers, who were most likely to be legal immigrants. The expulsion, which was contrary to the spirit, if not the letter, of the ECOWAS protocol on the free movement of goods and persons that had been signed in May 1979, damaged Nigeria's reputation in West Africa. Some migrants were to return soon after the expulsion, and another smaller expulsion took place in 1984 under the Buhari regime.[27]

As noted above, perhaps one million persons, or half of all alien migrant workers in Nigeria, were Ghanaians. Niger nationals affected by the expulsion order were estimated at between 150,000 to 200,000 persons.[28] Ghanaians came to Nigeria out of necessity, seeking employment across a very broad spectrum of occupations, from unskilled labourers and artisans to highly qualified teachers and professionals. With better prospects at home, very few would have chosen to live and work in Nigeria. In reply to Ghanaian protests over the expulsions, Nigerians could cite the precedent of earlier expulsions of Nigerians from Ghana under Kofi Busia's government in 1969.

Ghanaians dominated the construction sites and street hawking in Lagos.[29] They formed communities in slum areas like Ijora. The aim was to make some savings, over a year or two, and then return home with goods that were unobtainable in Ghana, like sewing machines, corn mills, roofing sheets, and the "Agege Certificate" (a big radio-cassette player, named after the place where most Ghanaians lodged on arrival).

The Public Sector

Public sector expenditure as a proportion of GNP continued to rise, and public sector employment rose by 14 percent per annum over 1977–1984. Opposition to the continued expansion of the public economy had begun to develop towards the end of the military period.[30] It was argued that the state should concentrate on the essential functions of providing infrastructure and law and order, functions that it was manifestly failing to perform. This view was fuelled by the inefficiency and waste associated with public bodies, by some conspicuous failures of public entrepreneurship, and by private sector experience of state involvement in joint enterprises. There was also a fear that state participation in some enterprises, like banks, could lead to politicisation, especially after civil rule.

Under President Shagari, no consistent policies on public ownership, state regulation, or public agencies emerged. New public agencies were set up to promote presidential initiatives. They duplicated the activities of existing ministries and agencies (e.g., the Federal Housing Authority, Green Revolution Committee, Federal Capital Territory Administration, Nigerian Office of Industrial Property, Rice Task Force). The fact that the expansion of state investment was checked owed more to a loss of bureaucratic power and a shortage of funds than to any deliberate policy. Commercial and merchant banks were set up without state participation. Price control was abolished, but the Nigerian National Supply Company was retained. Federal holdings in newspapers were not sold off. The federal government took no equity in the proposed light commercial-vehicle assembly plants though it did dictate their location.

The Onosode Commission on Parastatals was a response to dissatisfaction with the performance of public bodies and their lack of autonomy, which had been further eroded by the creation of a unified salary and grading structure for the whole public sector. The report aimed to break the pattern of large state subsidies and tight ministerial control by giving the enterprises more autonomy in their recruitment, pricing, and salary structures and by insisting on commercial operation for some. It also recommended privatisation, starting with the partial sale of Nigeria Airways equity to the public. Privatisation did not go ahead, and a private member's bill in the National Assembly that sought to break up the Nigeria Airways monopoly was defeated.[31] The Onosode report did lead to the revision of salaries and wages to more competitive levels in some corporations and the appointment of non–civil servants as board members.

Most of the problems with public bodies and projects remained, with poor management, low productivity, and a lack of accountability. Corporations were surrounded by webs of patronage involving directors, distributors, landlords, and retainers sufficient to choke off efficiency. Board members were appointed in compensation for the loss of elective political office. A further constraint on the effective operation of federal agencies was the principle of federal character.

In 1987, *Newswatch* magazine made a useful survey of "abandoned" projects that littered the country and were a constant reminder of past profligacy.[32] A number of themes recur. Enthusiasm for projects turned hot and cold with changes in political regime. Each new government wanted to award new contracts and renegotiate old ones. Some projects were ill conceived. Others were literally grounded by corruption. At the federal level, the Aerostat Balloon project, initiated in 1975, managed to absorb N140 million before being abandoned. President Shagari opted to puncture the balloon, and the U.S. company involved received N16 million for breach of contract. In Lagos state, three incinerator plants, costing N40 million, were completed just before the return to civil rule and have lain idle ever since. The Lagos Metroline project, a mass transit system to solve the Lagos transport problem, proved controversial. The project started under the Jakande government in July 1983. It was then abandoned when Buhari came to power, after N75 million was spent. The University of Jos in Plateau state was the site of gross mismanagement and waste; mismanaged funds totalled about N90 million.[33]

Industry and Foreign Investment

The recession brought a severe decline in industrial output and employment. It underlined the high-cost, import-dependent nature of Nigerian industrialisation that had been encouraged by the pattern of incentives prevailing in the 1970s. The decline in the aggregate index for manufacturing began in mid-1982.[34] Some industries, like textiles, where protection had proved inadequate in the face of large-scale smuggling, had already experienced declines with plant closures.[35] In 1983, the aggregate index fell by 26 percent, with declines ranging from 13 percent in paints to 54 percent in electronics assembly. In the construction industry, employment fell from 300,233 in 1980 to 112,579 in April 1984.[36] The inability to effectively control the allocation of import licences and foreign exchange as the volume of imports declined contributed to industrial decline.

The NPN favoured foreign investment, but the net inflow of foreign capital remained at a low level throughout the four-year period.[37] International capital has been reluctant to invest in the Nigerian market rather than sell to it. A joint committee was set up by the Nigerian and U.S. governments in 1978 to encourage U.S. investment in Nigerian agriculture. Six years later, very little investment had materialised from the committee's activities. Repeated relaxation of the indigenisation decree, to allow increased foreign equity participation, also met with little response. Among the reasons for the reluctance of foreign investors were the high infrastructure costs (electricity, water, roads), a heavy bureaucratic presence with a high capacity for obstruction and delay, and the inconsistent and unpredictable nature of goverment policy.[38] These factors certainly operated in the period under review. The main reason was the difficulty of realising profits in foreign currency because of exchange controls. Interpretation of the indigenisation decree was also important in creating uncertainty and delays. Were the companies that had sold equity to Nigerians under the decree to be treated as foreign or Nigerian companies for purposes of fresh investment? To treat them as foreign companies would involve a dilution of the foreign equity. This uncertainty held up a major investment between the United Africa Company and the Matsushita electronics company of Japan. The United Africa Company and other companies campaigned long and hard over this issue.

Conclusion

The rule of the politicians was disastrous for the material advancement of Nigeria and for the living standards of its citizens. The real income of urban households declined by 34 percent between 1980 and 1984.[39] The consequences of this misrule were to remain with the nation for a long time. As we have seen, the regime failed completely to stabilise the economy when oil revenues declined. The fact that oil revenues surged at the start of civil rule was fortuitous, but in retrospect it can be seen to have contributed to the loss of economnic control and the escalation of corruption. State expenditures were not cut back sufficiently to prevent recourse to large-scale deficit financing and the buildup of massive internal debt. Externally, equilibrium was not restored and international indebtedness soared. The large trade arrears were to become a constant source of friction with external creditors.

Policy was remarkably inert and passive, simply responding very late in the day as each constraint became binding. When international credit finally ran out and threatened to undermine all trade, the scene was set for the eventual dominance of the IMF and World Bank in the determination of domestic policies. The measures that were taken, as we have seen, were constantly undermined by political imperatives, demonstrating that civilian rule had indeed let loose forces that could drive the nation to penury. A weak party, preoccupied by the distribution of national patronage, was in no position to resist them. Such pressures were also pervasive under military rule, but the military did generally manage to contain them more effectively.

The extent of corruption and capital flight has been outlined in Chapter 3 and in this chapter. It reached new heights and gained a new dimension in its international efficiency. Corruption in the First Republic was largely to be found at the regional level. Federal agencies were corrupt, but the degree of financial centralisation and the scale of the resources at the centre were far less. In the Second Republic, the consequences of corruption were far more serious, helping to undermine macroeconomic controls and leading in extreme cases to arson attacks on federal institutions, as highly placed embezzlers tried, usually successfully, to cover up the evidence of their crimes.

Civil rule imposed its own extra costs. They included the cost of the presidency, expensive legislatures at the federal and state levels, the cost of FEDECO, and the costly arithmetic of "federal character." I earlier noted the tendency for consumption to rise at the expense of investment. There was also a related tendency for the cost of government to rise. The absorption of current federal revenues by general administration (administration, defence, and internal security) rose from 13 percent during the Murtala-Obasanjo period (1976–1979) to 19.5 percent over 1980–1983.[40] Increased costs of government may be justified if that is the price of good government. This was definitely not the case.

There was also the cost of a politics where large funds had to be mobilised by any serious contender for political office, leading to waste and unproductive forms of expenditure.[41] On the assumption of office, a politician would attempt to recoup his expenses in the shortest possible time in order to show some return on his "investment."

As I argued in Chapter 4, the business orientation of the party was not one that gave it coherence or sense of purpose with respect to the economy. Those businesspeople who were most closely involved with the party were concerned to get political access to the fruits of state economic regulation in the form of contracts and licenses. Despite general support from the business class and the rhetoric of private enterprise, the party was far from being a vehicle for the domination of bourgeois interests.

Notes

1. Eddie Iroh, "The Private Jet Setters," *African Business*, April 1984, p. 14.

2. A. H. Gelb, "Adjustment to Windfall Gains: A Comparative Analysis of Oil Exporting Countries," in P. J. Neary and S. Van Wijnbergen, eds., *Natural Resources and the Macroeconomy* (Oxford: Basil Blackwell, 1986).

3. *Annual Reports*, Central Bank of Nigeria.

4. *New Nigerian*, 18 August 1981.

5. *Nigeria: Macro-Economic Policies for Structural Change*, World Bank, 1983. p. 3.

6. *New York Times*, 27 March 1982.

7. *The Economist* (London), 21 January 1984.

8. *New Nigerian*, 22 June 1983.

9. *Annual Report*, Central Bank of Nigeria, 1983, p. 116.

10. *Annual Report, 1983, p. 118.*

11. *Financial Punch*, 5 July 1982.

12. *Nigeria Newsletter*, no. 132, 11 February 1984.

13. *African Business*, May 1982, p. 38.

14. *National Economic Council Expert Committee Report on the State of the Nigerian Economy*, Federal Ministry of National Planning, Lagos, 1983. See also *West Africa*, 18 July 1983.

15. D. Bevan, P. Collier, and J. Gunning, "Poverty, Equity and Growth in Nigeria, 1950–1986," mimeo, Oxford, 1987, p. 143.

16. *Guardian* (Lagos), 20 July 1986.

17. *Nigerian Newsletter*, no. 179, 15–29 December 1985. *African Concord*, 23 January 1986; *Financial Times*, 3 March 1986.

18. "The Bitter Taste of Sugar," *West Africa*, 19 August 1985.

19. *West Africa*, 19 August 1985.

20. John Igue, "Le Nigeria et ses périphéries frontalière," in D. C. Bach, J. Egg, and J. Philippe, eds., *Le Nigeria: Un pouvoir en puissance* (Paris: Karthala, 1988), p. 226.

21. Igue, "Le Nigeria," p. 233.

22. *New Nigerian*, 24 February, 1984.

23. *West Africa*, 18 May 1981.

24. Statement by the Nigerian Government on Illegal Immigrants, Lagos, 1983.

25. *West Africa*, 7 May 1984.

26. Interview with managing director, multinational company, Lagos.

27. *West Africa*, 7 May 1983.

28. *West Africa*, 7 February 1983.

29. *West Africa*, 24 January 1983. See also *99 Days in Agege: Yaw Brenya's Experience* (Accra, Gapo Publications, 1986).

30. "Memorandum on National Industrial Policy," Nigerian Association of Chambers of Commerce Industry, Mines and Agriculture (NACCIMA), 6 July 1978; "Pre-Budget Memorandum," NACCIMA, 1980.

31. *Business Times* (Lagos), 19 July 1982.

32. *Newswatch*, 7 December 1987.

33. *African Concord*, 12 March 1987.

34. *Annual Report*, Central Bank, 1983.

35. *West Africa*, 6 April 1981, p. 763.

36. *Africa Economic Digest*, 29 June 1984.

37. The net non-oil inflow of foreign capital averaged N180 over 1980–1983, *Annual Reports*, Central Bank of Nigeria.

38. In 1982, a suspension of business permits and expatriate quotas for six months and a tightening of existing quotas were announced.

39. *The Nigerian Structural Adjustment Programme: Policies, Impact and Prospects* (Washington, D.C.: The World Bank, 1988), p. 44.

40. *Annual Reports*, Central Bank of Nigeria.

41. Senator Nzeribe, Chairman of the Fanz Organisation, claimed to have spent over £8 million in his successful senatorial campaign in Imo state in 1983. *African Concord*, 5 March 1987.

9

The State and Agriculture in the 1980s

In this chapter I examine the nature, origins, and impact of various agricultural policies in Nigeria and try to situate them within a broader political and economic context. First, I take issue with a number of writers who attempt to generalise about agricultural policy in Africa. I then examine the macroeconomic context of policy and summarise recent changes in policy before turning to the detail of specific policy interventions.

Contrary to the views of Robert Bates, government policies in Nigeria have not been especially detrimental to the interests of the majority of farmers.[1] Moreover, the agricultural policies that have been pursued cannot be explained in terms of the political weight of urban interests, which impart an urban bias to policy, leaving rural producers exploited and politically isolated. Bates argued that the urban origins of "African food policy" are perhaps most clearly seen in Nigeria.[2] Although some elements of Bates's argument are appropriate to Nigeria, the overall picture is distorted by his vision. In the early 1980s, Bates's views became very influential and were applied indiscriminately. For example, in a review of Chinua Achebe's well known book, *The Trouble with Nigeria,* Roland Oliver swept aside Achebe's own arguments with the claim that antirural, antifarmer policies were to blame for Nigeria's predicament.[3] According to Oliver,

> what is really wrong with Nigeria is that systems of government are so organised as to discourage farmers from farming, at least for the market. The prices paid to producers are still restrained by every kind of buying monopoly imposed by the colonial governments to prevent inflation during the Second World War and its after-math.

Oliver's assertions have little or no validity.

There is no history of widespread and persistent intervention by the government in domestic food production and markets in Nigeria. This important fact tends to be obscured by the voluminous literature about the Marketing Boards and by a pervasive fascination with export crops and foreign exchange. When the state did intervene on behalf of urban consumers to check the rise in food prices in the 1970s, it encouraged the import of food through lower duties, subsidies, and exchange rate appreciation. This response to inflation was preferable to setting up marketing organisations with a monopoly on local grains and roots that could be used to subsidise urban consumers. Overall, Nigeria has pursued, in effect, a high food-price policy through nonintervention. It was precisely because farmers have received relatively high prices through the markets that the aggregate production response has been positive.

I must discount, too, the polemics of Keith Hart.[4] Hart saw a small-farmer strategy as shoring up decrepit village structures with miserable levels of efficiency at the expense of developing a high-productivity agriculture. He argued, on a West Africa–wide basis, for a dynamic capital-intensive sector that would provide a motor for the small-scale rural and urban sectors. Without this we are left, according to Hart, with large-scale government and services financed by an agriculture that can hardly break even. This picture applied to Nigeria of the 1980s is fantastical. For a long time to come, Nigeria will continue to rely on dynamic small farmers both to feed the nation and to export produce. It is to these farmers that efforts to improve technology should be directed.

Goran Hyden saw "the African peasantry" as enveloped in "an economy of affection," which prevents market forces and capitalism from transforming the productive capacity of farmers.[5] The idea of an "uncaptured peasantry" amounts to a misreading of the agrarian history of Nigeria in this century. Hyden's work has been effectively criticised elsewhere.[6]

A point does need to be made about the use of categories. In Nigeria, the multiple economic, political, and social linkages between rural producers and the wider community and the diversity of socioeconomic conditions within the rural economy cannot be reduced to summary statements about "the state," "the peasantry," and "capitalist" agriculture. In addition, large claims about the nature of broad long-term transformations in the rural economy on the basis of short-term, partial, economistic evidence must be treated with caution. There are practically no detailed studies of the rural economy over time. Where close studies have been undertaken, they do not support a picture of rapid transformation with polarisation between large and small farmers or the rise of a class of agricultural labourers. Summarising some local studies, Michael Watts saw unexpected forms of accumulation and decomposition and warned against generalisation about accumulation in agriculture.[7] After looking at the evidence in rural Hausaland, Gavin Williams concluded that there is no clear evidence of growing inequalities in land holdings.[8] However, the growth of inequalities in income among rural households related to differences in access to resources and nonfarm employment opportunities was more marked.

I argue that the agricultural crisis in Nigeria has been exaggerated. Combined with an instrumental view of the state and a preoccupation with policy, the perceived crisis created illusions about agricultural policy and its impact on agricultural performance. For example, David Fieldhouse, in a recent book, claimed that "in Nigeria, as in Ghana, the record of public policy as an instrument of economic development has been very poor. . . . Agriculture experienced virtually no growth."[9] Both the claim that policy was responsible for performance and the claim that there was virtually no growth need to be questioned.

Our purpose is not to replace the picture of bad policy and agrarian crisis with another view in which oil has entirely beneficial effects on agriculture, and agricultural policy creates the conditions for rapid growth. Some policies in Nigeria have been wasteful and corrupt. Some led to rural violence. Others have allowed large rents to be appropriated by varieties of middlemen. Still others have tried to create a class of large-scale capitalist farmers at considerable cost.

Considering that many projects originated from above, it is not surprising that they proved to be bureaucratic, elitist and wasteful. In these circumstances, simple aggregates of federal and state expenditures do not tell us whether governments neglected agriculture or had a beneficial interest in it. The idea that there is necessarily a positive relation between the size of government expenditures on agriculture and agricultural performance is pervasive and unfounded. In some cases, it would have been better if the state had literally "neglected" agriculture. Although it can be argued that more resources should have been devoted to rural roads, water, electricity, and health, it is not clear that they should have been directed to agriculture.

Most of these state interventions affected only a relatively small number of farmers. They did not determine performance. The partial exceptions were the distribution of subsidised fertiliser and the World Bank–sponsored Agricultural Development Projects (ADPs). The equity of these latter projects has been the subject of considerable controversy. As far as infrastructure and output are concerned, their consequences were positive.

The Economic Context and Aggregate Performance

The 1970s and early 1980s are usually seen as a time of agrarian stagnation and crisis in Nigeria.[10] The picture of crisis is associated with the following features: stagnant or declining output, fear of large increases in food price inflation, the virtual disappearance of agricultural exports, and a large rise in food imports. To explain this crisis, the effects of the large increase in oil revenues and state expenditures are invoked together with the drought of 1973–1974. According to the analysis of the oil syndrome that began to appear in World Bank publications in the early 1980s, the massive increase in state expenditure was largely focussed on urban areas and brought about a transfer of labour out of agriculture into trading activities, transport, construction, service industries, and state employment. Agricultural wages rose and more than offset increases in agricultural prices. At the same time, the appreciation of the naira and the reduction of duties on food imports made food imports cheaper relative to domestic staples, thereby bringing about a surge of food imports (wheat, rice, sugar, maize, vegetable oils). The appreciation of the naira also acted as a disincentive to agricultural exports. In these ways, the oil boom acted to undermine domestic agriculture.

In fact, the oil boom eased the burden of extracting a financial surplus from rural areas. It raised the price of food relative to other commodities because of large increases in demand. And it allowed larger agricultural subsidies and more government expenditure in rural areas.

The picture of crisis depends crucially on what happened to output. Most writers, and the World Bank until recently, have claimed that there was a sharp reduction in growth of agricultural output. Agricultural growth was held to be negative or well below 1 percent.[11] In a remarkable revision of its estimates, the World Bank in 1985 estimated agricultural growth at 2.7 percent per annum (3 percent including imports) in the period 1970–1982 and admitted that total production of staple crops had probably kept pace with population growth.[12] Although these figures are still arbitrary, they are more consistent with my view of agricultural growth.

The perils of aggregate output statistics in Africa have been highlighted by Sara Berry who stressed the diversity of performance by crop and by locality.[13] In Nigeria, the argument cannot be settled by recourse to statistics. The chaos of Nigeria's production statistics is well known. We simply have no accurate knowledge of the annual fluctuations in production, and the longer- term trends are subject to wide margins of error. The situation is worst for root crops and tubers, where the differences between the various estimates is simply staggering. Yet the demand for hard statistical data is overwhelming. If, for some reason, a country like Nigeria has no reliable data for its population or agricultural output, figures will nevertheless be invented to fill the gap. They immediately take on a spurious hardness and validity.

The high degree of unreliability surrounding the output performance of individual crops in Nigeria must caution against attempts to build models to "explain" the aggregate data. Data serve many purposes, and one of the reasons for the exaggeration of the food crisis in Nigeria in the 1970s and 1980s was to justify many different forms of intervention in agriculture, both domestic and foreign. Data have been used in Nigeria on several occasions to "project" large food deficits. A target is set for food self-sufficiency within four or five years. The air is then filled with the agitated rhetoric of food crisis, and the government justifies all its activities and expenditures in terms of a drive to food self-sufficiency. For example, both the International Food Policy Research Institute (1977) and the World Bank Food Strategies Mission of 1980 forecast large deficits.[14] The latter study forecast a deficit of 6.6 million metric tons of cereal equivalent by 1985. Nigerian farmers were to confound these experts and undermine their scientific pretensions.

If the production crisis was greatly exaggerated, this does not mean that the effects of oil outlined above were not in operation for some crops in certain areas or that some groups of consumers were not adversely affected. Poorer urban consumers experienced food shortages and a deterioration in diet due to their lack of purchasing power in the wake of the inflation triggered by the Udoji awards. Nor does it exclude the operation of other dynamics. It is scarcely surprising that supply temporarily lagged behind the large increase in urban demand for food associated with the rise of incomes and influx of migrants from abroad. The increase in demand led to a sharp increase in the relative price of food and strong increases in real wages in rural areas, both of which would have acted to stem any large outflow of labour from agriculture. In fact there is little concrete evidence of large loss of labour from food production as distinct from some of the export crops. However, a number of authors placed great emphasis on rural-urban migration to explain what they saw as a poor performance by agriculture.[15] For example, Paul Collier attempted to explain an alleged massive relative decline in food production by a flow of labour out of agriculture that was prompted by increases in government expenditure and attractive wages. I am not convinced by his argument or his methods.[16]

In some rural areas, especially in the northern states, there was a substantial increase in food production, sometimes associated with migration of farmers from other rural areas in response to favourable price increases.[17] The growth of urban food markets in the 1970s under oil boom conditions led to many changes, especially in the vicinity of the new state capitals. Farming families in the urban hinterlands took advantage of the expansion of urban job opportunities to increase their nonfarm incomes. In many cases, it would be inappropriate to describe this as a simple process of labour transfer from agriculture. Seasonal movements, weekend farming, and daily commuting were common. Some urban income was used to expand land holdings and to hire farm labour as migrants from more distant areas were attracted by relatively high wage rates. The cultivation of some less-known crops like soyabean and cowpeas underwent rapid expansion.[18] The production of yams and cassava spread rapidly in the northern states, starting to break down the distinction between southern root crops and northern grains. The point is that Nigerian agriculture and conditions in the rural economy cannot simply be subsumed by one general mechanism. Dubious aggregate figures hide a great deal of variability over time and space and dynamism in production.

The picture of the crisis probably fits best for the labour-intensive export crops of the southern states (cocoa, palm oil, palm kernels, and rubber). Here production was squeezed by high labour costs, by unfavourable export prices, and by the high opportunity cost of nonfarm employment. In the north, the production of both groundnuts and cotton was under the same economic pressures and suffered from more favourable financial returns to sorghum, millet, and maize.

The gap between the burgeoning demand for foodstuffs and the supply was partially filled by imports of wheat, rice, and vegetable oils. These foods were relatively cheap, and consumers switched away from local staples, some of which required laborious processing. The switch in consumption encouraged by the change in relative prices explains the sudden surge of wheat and rice imports, rather than any collapse in the domestic production and supply of foodstuffs. When oil revenues faltered in 1978, import policy was subject to reversal and inconsistency.

Food imports reached a peak by value in 1982. They took a 16 percent share of total imports by value over 1980–1982 (average) compared with about 8 percent a decade earlier. After a peak of 20 percent in 1983, their share then started to fall (see Table 9.1). It is estimated that food imports accounted for about 11 percent of domestic consumption in 1982 (wheat, 7 percent; rice and maize, 4 percent of grain equivalents).[19] Thus the importation of food was not on a scale sufficient to undermine local production. Among the factors accounting for the subsequent decline of food imports were the overall foreign exchange shortage, the start of a decline in the real exchange rate from 1984, and a more protective stance towards domestic food production. As oil revenues declined appreciably, so arguments for self-sufficiency and import bans gained the upper hand. A ban on the import of maize and rice was declared late in 1985 followed by ban on wheat, stockfish, vegetable oil, and day-old chicks.

For what they are worth, aggregate production statistics indicate some improvement in output performance in the 1980s. The U.S. Department of Agriculture estimated growth of grain production at 5 percent per annum over 1982–1985.[20] Drought in 1983, which in some areas was more severe than the 1973 drought, brought a sharp fall in production and a burst of inflation in 1984. In 1985, 1986, and 1988, a combination of good harvests and

TABLE 9.1 Food Imports, 1970–1992 (in 1,000 metric tons)

	Wheat	*Rice*	*Maize*	*Total Grain Index (1980 = 100)*	*Sugar*	*Food Percentage of Total Imports by Value*[a]
1970	267	2	9	16	94	7.6
1972	317	6	2	19	127	9.6
1974	325	5	2	19	72	8.9
1976	745	50	17	47	173	8.5
1977	770	427	37	71	383	10.4
1978	1,166	761	97	116	594	12.4
1979	1,339	488	111	111	555	15.4
1980	1,176	400	168	100	712	15.8
1981	1,517	600	293	138	973	16.4
1982	1,269	539	347	124	692	16.3
1983	870	543	50	84	733	19.8
1984	1,071	213	40	76	439	18.8
1985	1,442	356	77	108	401	17.0
1986	996	320	50	78	442	13.4
1987	141	400	—	31	625	10.5
1988	190	200	—	22	344	7.8
1989	185	200	—	22	303	6.5
1990	252	220	—	27	309	8.2
1991	508	210	—	41	413	8.6
1992	842	270	9	64	695	8.2

[a]Value of food imports is SITC section 0.

Sources: FAO *Trade Yearbooks* (various years) for volumes; Central Bank of Nigeria, *Annual Report* (various years), for value of imports.

better macroeconomic incentives for food crop producers saw rapid increases in output. Gluts were widely reported from the northern states and elsewhere.[21] Here the ban on exports of grains to neighbouring states and the border closure played a part.

The Evolution of Policy

In Chapter 7, I outlined the major changes in policy that occurred in the 1970s. The Marketing Boards were dismantled and the Commodity Boards put in their place. The Agricultural Development Projects were introduced, together with investment in large-scale irrigation projects and the setting up of the River Basin Development Authorities (RBDAs). Subsidies for agricultural inputs increased in scope and scale. There were also various state production schemes promoted by the federal and state governments. Attempts were made to push the introduction of technology packages for specific crops through the National Accelerated Food Production Programme. Finally, there was the effort to promote from above large-scale capital intensive farming by companies and individuals, which only really gathered momentum towards the end of the decade. In the 1980s, pressure on companies to enter agriculture was applied through the allocation of import licences and through targets for the deletion of imported raw materials like sugar, maize, cotton, barley, and vegetable oils.

Under President Shagari (1979–1983), there were no major changes in policy despite the enormous rhetoric devoted to a "Green Revolution" that aimed to reach food self-sufficiency by 1985. There was a rise in the share of federal resources devoted to agriculture, but water resources retained their dominant position, and the RBDAs were lavishly funded.

After 1985, a number of reforms were introduced in the context of the Structural Adjustment Programme with its emphasis on market forces and private enterprise. The World Bank, which had for several years argued against the high exchange rate, high input subsidies, the large-scale irrigation projects and state production schemes, was now in a position to exert more influence over the direction of policy through loan conditionalities. The reforms included the abolition of the Commodity Boards, the withdrawal of federal and state governments from agricultural production, the full-scale or partial privatisation of agricultural parastatals, the commercialisation of fertiliser procurement and marketing (which the Ministry of Agriculture had taken over in 1978), and the reduction of subsidies on agricultural inputs and services. In addition to these changes, the 1986 budget marked a clear priority for the ADPs over the RBDAs and large-scale irrigation. There was also a new, well-funded initiative to improve rural infrastructure through the Directorate of Foods, Roads and Rural Infrastructure (DFRRI).

Prior to the withdrawal of federal and state government agencies from large-scale agricultural production in 1985, the federal government had insisted on government participation in these areas. In the late 1960s it had legislated the United Africa Company (UAC) and Lever Brothers out of palm oil ventures. It had also taken over Tate and Lyle's 33 percent share in the proposed Sunti Sugar Company in 1975. In 1977, the federal government set up the 12,000 hectare Savannah Sugar Company in Gongola state. This project was not very successful despite the commitment of N388 million that included the Kiri Dam.

The Agricultural Development Projects (ADPs)

The ADPs began in the mid-1970s as pilot projects at Funtua, Gusau, and Gombe in areas of rich agricultural potential that were highly commercialised. They then spread to other areas and became statewide projects. The ADPs concentrated on input delivery based on commercially oriented farm service centres. Major chemical companies were represented, and networks of large-scale seed farmers established. The ADPs provided infrastructure and extension services. Where they went statewide, they were responsible for extension services within a state. They had a strong management and financial input from the World Bank.

The original three projects were declared a success by the World Bank and the Nigerian government.[22] However, the projects' own records of output are fraught with problems. In economic terms, it is difficult to assess the impact of the projects with fertiliser subsidies of the order of 90 percent in operation. Yet it would be surprising if, with the favourable prices prevailing, the projects had not been responsible for significant increases in yield and area cultivated.

When looked at more closely, the Gombe and Funtua projects completion reports do not tell a success story.[23] At Gombe, the total gain in crop production was only 35 percent of that anticipated. The major impact of the project was to increase the cultivation of maize and promote the rapid uptake of ox ploughs, which were already widely used in the area. Maize partially replaced sorghum in mixed cropping and also affected millet output adversely. There was no net increase in household grain production. The project, like others in the north, lacked recommendations relevant to mixed-cropping systems. It tried to promote sole cropping and found that most progress could be made with maize. Despite the fact that it was the second most important crop in the area, millet was not in the appraisal report. On the Funtua ADP, where sorghum was the most important crop, covering 58 percent of the cropped area, the sorghum package with new unproven varieties, fertiliser use, and sole cropping made no headway.[24] Sole cropping was clearly inferior to crop mixtures, organic manure, and high levels of family labour.[25] Farmers were right to resist attempts to push them to an unproven higher productivity agriculture based on sole cropping.

One of the original aims of the projects was to boost cotton and groundnut production. Cotton production declined because of higher financial returns to food crops. High wage costs of this labour-intensive crop were reinforced by a decline in access to family labour as parents decided under the Universal Primary Education programme to send children to school.[26] The spread of female seclusion within the Islamic communities that dominate the cotton-growing areas also made female labour less acceptable. Other adverse factors included a demographic shift of pastoralists to the south that brought them into conflict with cotton farmers and, finally, problems in the marketing of cotton that meant that farmers could not be sure of immediate cash payments for their crop after 1977.[27]

Production of groundnuts fell sharply after the 1973 Sahel drought. Purchases by the marketing board fell, and there were negligible exports. After the drought, production shifted south, bringing lower yields because of less suitable soils. The occurrence of aphid infestation and rosette virus was a further problem and was especially severe in 1975 and 1985. Since 1984, data from Bauchi state ADP and from Sokoto indicates that production is locally on a rising trend.

With doubts about the overall cost effectiveness of the ADPs and with failure in terms of their original objectives, the main local benefit of the projects may have come from road building and the multiplier effects of spending public money in rural areas.[28] Yet compared to other state expenditures on agriculture, especially the irrigation schemes and large state farms, the ADPs were undoubtedly a more productive form of investment. They have, however, been rightly criticised for a highly unequal system of input distribution and provision of farm services.[29]

The primary beneficiaries of the projects appeared to be rich village farmers and large-scale farmers. The large-scale farmers were former state officials, rich urban-based traders, and members of the local aristocracy who had access to government and state credit. They often relied on contract labour on a piece-rate basis and located near the main highways, so that labour could be brought in by bus. They also employed farm managers. Local businesspeople, contractors, and rich farmer-traders shade into the rich village-farmer category that cultivated between six and eighty hectares and used family and hired labour (some casual and some permanent).[30] A minority of small village farmers with less land who nevertheless have a net surplus of grain and occasionally hire labour also benefitted.

An Agricultural Projects Monitoring Evaluation and Planning Unit (APMEPU) was established by the World Bank in Kaduna in 1975 to assist the management of the northern ADPs and to produce a data base for planning. It spent N25 million and failed in both these objectives. Its efforts were vitiated by very severe data quality problems involving problems in survey design, lack of control over the generation of data, and the absence of analysis.[31] It could not, for example, show yield responses to fertiliser, a key variable in project strategies. The unit was a major intellectual and financial scandal. It represents a failure of the economists' approach to research and understanding that makes a fetish of quantitative data torn from its social context and largely without meaning. Far more would now be known about the rural economy of Nigeria if only a fraction of the funds absorbed by the unit had been given to investigators working in a more anthropological tradition. The fact that Polly Hill's much more scientific, though less fashionable, empirical and descriptive study, *Rural Hausa*, had been published about the same area in 1972 only highlighted the great gap between the different methodological traditions.[32] The unit's approach was rooted in the utilitarian calculus of neoclassical economics. Large computers were to be used for deductive modelling. The poverty of this approach lay in its obsessive concern with aggregation and quantification, with prediction and prescription, and with commodities and markets. Polly Hill later successfully attacked elements of this tradition in her book, *Development Economics on Trial*.[33]

A political desire to balance the major northern projects with World Bank activity in the southern states in the 1970s led to the establishment of four palm oil projects. They involved nucleus estates and smallholders. The Rivers state and Imo state projects were relatively successful, though the smallholder component in Rivers state failed. The Bendel and Ondo projects had to be cancelled in 1982 with only 44 percent of the combined planting targets met.[34] The main problems were poor management, resulting from political interference from state governments, and inadequate funding. There was an extraordinary unforeseen cost escalation, labour costs rising from N.7 per day in 1974 to N5–10 per day for harvesting in late 1981. Problems of securing additional land for the estates and secure land-user rights for smallholders also set back the projects.

The River Basin Development Authorities (RBDAs) and the Irrigation Schemes

Gunilla Andrae and Bjorn Beckman have shown how in the 1960s three major reports by foreign consultants (the U.S. Agency for International Development, the Food and Agriculture Organization, and the Commonwealth Development Corporation), which were essentially land and water surveys, provided justifications for large-scale irrigation and the production of wheat.[35] These reports made it easier for local supporters of irrigation to push ahead with their schemes. They were later assisted by two major events. The Great Sahelian Drought of 1972–1974 provided ideological support for irrigation, and the dramatic rise in oil revenues enhanced the capacity of the Nigerian government to undertake large-scale, capital- and foreign exchange-demanding projects.

In 1973, the Nigerian government established two River Basin Development Authorities in the Chad and Sokoto basins in the north of the country. In June 1976, a further nine RBDAs were created by federal decree. Although the functions laid down for the RBDAs were very wide (irrigation, flood control, watershed management, pollution control, fisheries and navigation, seed multiplication, livestock breeding, and food processing), the RBDAs concentrated on large-scale irrigation schemes. Some RBDAs went into direct production on a minor scale, and most of them engaged in land clearance, providing access to land for large-scale farmers and corporate enterprises.

The decision to invest in large-scale irrigation projects was as much political as economic. Richard Palmer-Jones has stressed the continuities between the exercise of political patronage and irrigation schemes in the colonial and postcolonial periods.[36] Those at the apex of the traditional political system who allocated land and controlled taxation could use state irrigation schemes as a means of getting access to state resources and enhancing their powers of political patronage. They were later joined by politicians and senior civil servants. In a federal context, the amount of resources devoted to large-scale irrigation demonstrated the political power of northern interests in the allocation of resources. The share of irrigation in total planned federal expenditure on agriculture rose as high as 57 percent in 1983.

The RBDAs presented a facade of integrated planning. Project development preceded integrated appraisal of the water resources of the basins.[37] Definition of the boundaries of the authorities was often on political rather than physiographic grounds. In 1979, nine of the RBDAs were defined wholly in terms of political boundaries rather than water courses and catchment areas. The absurdity of this was compounded in 1984 when it was announced that there was to be one RBDA for each state. Inevitably the RBDAs were seen as a way of channeling party political patronage. The RBDAs were plagued by gross financial mismanagement, low output, huge subsidies, and high foreign exchange costs.

The economic rationale for large-scale irrigation schemes was usually stated in terms of food self-sufficiency, especially for wheat and rice. As Andrae and Beckman in their excellent detailed study of the bread industry and wheat production have shown, the large rise in wheat imports in the 1970s and 1980s was linked to an ever-stronger argument about the need for import substitution.[38] Yet over the years, very little wheat has actually been grown on the large-scale schemes. In 1983, production was estimated generously at 15,000 metric tons, with the area under cultivation at 5,000 hectares. Production of wheat proved to be extremely costly and totally uncompetitive with imported wheat.

Andrae and Beckman demonstrated the fraudulent nature of the early consultancy reports and feasibility studies that provided the legitimation for the efforts of the irrigation lobby, bureaucrats, consultants, and foreign machinery suppliers to promote the schemes. By grossly underestimating the value of preproject production, indulging in fictitious cost-benefit ratios, and ignoring the off-project effects of the schemes, these early reports were able to give a rosy picture of the prospective benefits of the schemes. The technical problems of wheat production in the north of Nigeria were largely overlooked. The schemes generally assumed double cropping and mechanisation, with high demands on water and crop management. Such conditions assumed a high degree of control over peasants by project management. These conditions were not met. Peasants did not become contractual tenants on the Kano and Bakolori projects. At the Bakolori project, they resisted the alienation of their land, crop destruction, and nonpayment of compensation. After a series of protests and blockades that began in August 1978, they were met by armed aggression (in April 1980), resulting in great loss of life, arrests, and the destruction of property.[39]

Wheat production has proved costly and uncompetitive with imported wheat. Andrae and Beckman calculated conservatively that the cost of production of one metric ton of Nigerian wheat delivered in Lagos in the early 1980s was N1030, or some eight times the price of imported wheat at the official exchange rate.[40] If a shadow exchange rate is used to take account of the overvaluation of the naira at that time (N1 = $1), the domestic wheat was still five times more costly than imported wheat.

The growing of wheat on these schemes with their high foreign exchange component involved foreign exchange losses. As regards farmer incomes, a few farmers undoubtedly fared extremely well from the highly subsidised schemes, but farmers' net incomes are only a small fraction of the subsidies involved, and this makes no sense from the perspective of national resource allocation and equity. The overall balance of benefits to the communities affected by the irrigation schemes needs to be considered. Studies have shown that much fertile land was lost upstream from the dams. In the case of Bakolori, forty-three villages were affected involving some 13,000 persons. A similar number of persons was displaced by the Tiga Dam on the Kano River. Over 70 percent of the persons displaced by the Tiga Dam eventually had inadequate farmland in the resettlement areas. Farmers within the irrigation areas also lost land. At Bakalori, it was estimated that such losses were of the order of 20 percent. The consequences for productive activities downstream of the dams and reservoirs also have to be taken into account.

Paradoxically, the publication of the Andrae and Beckman book in 1985, with its strong argument against the continued importation of wheat and espousal of a more viable self-sufficiency strategy of long-term accumulation, may have helped to show that "The Wheat Trap" was not so strongly set or politically entrenched as the authors thought. In May 1986, the Babangida government announced a ban on wheat imports from January 1987. This ban was imposed despite lobbies from the wheat millers and bakers and the fact that organised labour did not support a ban. The ban does not appear to have been successful in preventing the smuggling of about 300,000 metric tons of flour a year. The ban prompted efforts to boost production by state governments, which inflated their production estimates in order to get federal funds. Production of 400,000 metric tons of wheat was claimed. Yet in 1989, millers purchased only 20,000 metric tons of high-cost wheat, demonstrating once again the difficulties of large-scale production in Nigeria.[41]

To conclude this section, I need to place the large-scale irrigation schemes in perspective. It is estimated that the area under double cropping on the formal irrigation schemes is no more than 30,000 hectares.[42] On the most favourable assumptions, this could contribute only a tiny fraction to the country's agricultural output and contrasts with the very heavy expenditure on irrigation. Much more important in terms of output and incomes has been informal water control and supply used by smallholders to supplement rain-fed agriculture. The area devoted to this informal irrigation has undergone rapid expansion and was estimated at over 700,000 hectares.[43]

The Commodity Boards and Marketing

Seven national Commodity Boards were established in 1977, replacing the regional Marketing Boards. The boards, which had a monopoly of exports, acted as buyers of last resort on the domestic market at prices that were set annually and appointed licensed buying agents (LBAs). In practice, their operations would sometimes extend into other forms of intervention. For example, it was often necessary to get clearance from the boards to get an import licence for raw materials. Supplies would sometimes be reserved to meet export contracts even when there were willing domestic buyers.

The boards were not very active in trading because in general the prices they offered local farmers fell well below local market prices. In contrast to the profitable position of the earlier Marketing Boards, the Commodity Boards found themselves gradually squeezed between escalating local production costs and low export prices for which the appreciation of the naira was to a large extent responsible. As export prices at the existing exchange rate were less than costs plus administrative expenses, exports had to be subsidised. By 1981, all exports, including cocoa, were being subsidised by the boards.[44] The parlous financial situation of the boards is underlined by the fact that by 1984 they owed the Central Bank N637 million.[45] The one area where there might have been an opportunity for a board to appropriate a financial surplus from international trade was the grain trade to countries in the Sahel. Fortunately for the farmers, this export trade was unofficial and in private hands.

The Nigerian Grains Board operated a minimum price programme, acting as a buyer of last resort when there were large harvests. It also operated a strategic grain reserve, buying small quantities of sorghum, millet, and maize. The Grains Board proved especially useful to large-scale farmers in times of sudden glut. Farmers could sell in bulk to the board after the excellent maize harvests of 1980, 1982–1983, and 1985–1986 when market prices fell well below the Guaranteed Minimum Price. This activity meant, in effect, subsidising maize from large-scale farmers in the Funtua and Gombe areas. When the dissolution of the boards was announced in 1986, there were protests from groups of large farmers like the National Council of Nigerian Farmers and the Farmers Association of Nigeria.[46]

The Grains Board did not buy directly in the market. It employed LBAs to purchase commodities. Paul Clough has shown how such licences to trade were acquired by virtue of social status and political power.[47] LBAs were often large urban-based merchants or local notables. They could negotiate lucrative buying allowances and other advantages, like guaranteed overdraft facilities with banks. An LBA could collect a large rent, being the difference between the market price at which produce was bought from the farmer and the Guaranteed Minimum Price at which produce was sold to the board. Clough calculated that in 1985 LBAs made a 40 percent profit margin per sack of sorghum sold to the board and 21 percent per sack of maize.[48] These margins were three and one-half to six and one-half times as large as the margins for those in the private grain trade. It would be an error to suppose that LBA activity was always very profitable. Profitability depended on the volume of the commodity purchased and price conditions.

In April 1986, it was announced that the Commodity Boards were to stop trading from 1 June. The idea was that state governments and the price intelligence agency that helped to fix minimum prices would act as buyers of last resort. The federal government would operate a strategic grain reserve and continue to provide grading and quality control services.

In the immediate aftermath of the abolition of the boards, marketing arrangements were in a state of flux. In the case of cocoa, the sharp devaluation of the naira lifted prices offered by private traders up to N8,000 a metric ton as against N1,600 offered by the former Cocoa Board. There was a scramble to harvest and buy cocoa. One result of the speculative rush to buy cocoa was that the preparation of beans was neglected, and poor quality cocoa found its way onto overseas markets. A further problem was that not all foreign exchange proceeds were repatriated by private traders. Cocoa prices were inflated above world prices as exports became a means of capital flight into hard currencies.

Is there a case for government intervention in commodity markets? This question cannot be answered on the grounds of economic logic and equity alone, as the outcome of intervention will invariably depend on political circumstances. The dissolution of the Commodity Boards was a positive step. Clough has shown in the case of the grain trade how private trading was less exploitative of the farmer and consumer than state intervention and licensing. The vigorous private trade, much of it over long distances between surplus and deficit areas, was competitive, albeit imperfectly so. Market competition took place within a trading network made up of patron-client hierarchies and lateral trading friendships between economic equals. Producers got a relatively high share of the final retail price (80 percent).[49]

Clough argued convincingly that the notion of the exploitative middleman is a view fostered by government officials who wish to enhance their bureaucratic powers and employment. It is also promoted by intellectuals who wish to promote their own statist solutions. There can be no doubt that throughout the oil boom period, and later, various types of middlemen did appropriate vast rents from the trading system in Nigeria. The opportunity to gain these massive rents was, however, created by state intervention through management of an overvalued exchange rate and through an extensive licensing system.

In principle, a good case can be made for a crop price-support programme and buffer stock operation in staple food markets that benefit the majority of farmers. Such a programme can offer a reduction in the risks of farming and higher, more stable incomes through the operation of a guaranteed minimum price and interseasonal price stabilisation. Yet in practice, such schemes face major difficulties. As the history of the Marketing Boards demonstrates, the functions that such institutions come to perform may depart radically from their original objectives. The recent experience of the Grains Board showed how the institution favoured large maize farmers and wealthy traders. There is always the danger that such interventions will favour large farmers and become a means of subsidising urban consumers. Second, there are the heavy costs involved not only in running the agency but also in financing the transfer of income to farmers through price interventions in the market. This fiscal burden is easily underestimated. Third, there is the need for a strong administrative capacity and detailed knowledge of market conditions required for decisions about price setting and timely, appropriate methods of intervention.

Large-scale Farming, Land Acquisition, and the Land Use Decree

The Land Use Decree of 1978 abolished the private ownership of land by transferring it to the state. The possessor's interest was reduced to a right of occupancy. Technically this was already the situation in the northern states. Customary systems of land law that governed tenure, inheritance, and land transfer stood, but the decree did introduce uncertainty over how it might be interpreted in relation to local customary systems.

The intention behind the decree was to promote access to land by the state, by companies, and by individuals by clarifying and protecting rights in the use of land. The state itself had often found it difficult to acquire land. There was concern over excessive litigation and the high costs of compensation. There was a great deal of confusion over boundaries and ownership where much land was not formally surveyed and registered. This slowed down land acquisition and made bank loans secured on land more difficult to obtain.

In practice, the decree, by extending state control and regulation, increased the power of the state governors and land use committees in the states. Governors had the power to issue certificates of occupancy and to revoke them and to set rents and approve mortgages. During the period of civil rule, there were many complaints over the use of governors' powers to victimise political opponents and reward supporters. This situation created the expectation that future governors or regimes might change the policy and thus brought a new element of uncertainty.

Paul Francis, working in the cocoa belt, found that the immediate effect of the decree was to introduce uncertainty in relations between tenants and landlords.[50] Customary courts were no longer able to enforce the payment of ground rent in respect of rural land. In Hausaland, Paul Ross has shown how individual rights to land, underpinned by collective memories, have been maintained and extended, allowing great circulation of usufructuary rights within a community, such that almost half of the land is cultivated by resident nonowners.[51] The workings of this local land "market" were under threat both from the Land Use Decree, which denies individual ownership interests in favour of the state, and from official customary land tenure, which assumes that land is commonly owned. In the Sokoto close-settled zone, Ken Swindell and A. B. Mamman have shown how land transfers were unaffected by the decree during the Shagari period.[52] Land brokers acting in association with village heads and local government officials played a very active role in the unregistered transfer of land to city merchants, civil servants, and professionals.

One of the effects of the Land Use Decree was to promote land acquisition on a large scale by those in a position to influence state governors and land use committees. Taken together with a strong federal commitment to large-scale private farming that was communicated to the states, the decree made it easier for individuals to secure large areas of land outside their home states where they would formerly have been regarded as strangers. It would be wrong, however, to attribute to the Land Use Decree much influence on the accumulation of land by the state or individuals. Before the decree, there was plenty of land speculation and the rich and powerful could use their influence at a local level when traditional rulers and local communities decided on the use of land. After the purge of the civil service under Murtala Mohammed, retired bureaucrats used their wealth to collude with traditional rulers and land officers to acquire large areas and fence them off. The expropriation of land by the state accelerated in the 1970s, especially in the vicinity of state capitals, increased the number of landless and land poor.

There is some evidence that the acquisition of land by companies and wealthy individuals and investment in large-scale farming speeded up after 1983. With the decline in government contracts and commercial opportunities, those who had built up wealth through the oil boom period now began to see farming as a more attractive investment. Changes in federal policy also contributed. These changes included the government's import deletion programme, which impelled companies to source their raw materials locally within a specified period, and the withdrawal of the federal government from large-scale agricultural production. The government also put pressure on companies applying for import licences to show their commitment to agricultural production.

Federal agencies and state governments used their powers to lease land to companies and individuals. The Sokoto Rima River Basin Rural Development Authority leased 37,000 hectares under the Niger Valley Project to companies.[53] The Upper Benue River Basin Authority acquired 37,000 hectares and encouraged private companies to move in. The Ogun state government introduced a plantation support scheme under which "idle" land was acquired and then leased out by the government to large-scale corporate farmers for twenty-five years.[54] Some 60,000 hectares was allocated in this manner. Local communities opposed the scheme and physically prevented many companies from taking possession of their lands for fear that the land would be alienated. In 1987, the scheme was suspended.

The enclosure of land by corporate enterprises and leading businesspeople was widespread in some northern states. Among the states most heavily affected were Niger, Plateau, Gongola, Benue, Kaduna, and Kwara. In Plateau state, for example, Inlaks, Cadbury, Union Trading Company (UTC), North Breweries, Brewery Agricultural and Research Company Ltd., and Flour Mills of Nigeria acquired large tracts of land. Prominent among those individuals who established large-scale farms were retired military officers, senior state officials, and businesspeople. In Anambra State, a number of leading businesspeople invested in farms in the Uzo Uwani area.

Swindell and Mamman documented the accumulation of land and deepening of agrarian capitalism in the vicinity of Sokoto.[55] Politicians, bureaucrats, professionals, soldiers, segments of the local aristocracy, contractors, and merchants invested extensively in farms on irrigated *fadama* (low-lying land near water courses)—growing rice in the wet season; vegetables, tree crops, and tobacco in the dry season; cassava and sweet potato in between—and in upland farms of 30 and 200 hectares—growing millet, sorghum, and beans. Smaller-scale commodity producers, however, who financed land acquisition in the 1970s from nonfarm employment, were forced to sell land after 1983 when nonfarm sources of income diminished.

Corporate investment in agriculture was generally undertaken not by new foreign agribusiness, which the government tried, usually unsuccessfully, to attract, but by existing industrial capital. The textile, beer, flour, soft drink, and soap industries were prominent in this movement into farming. Thus Afprint, President Clothing, and Nigerian Textile Mills have gone into cotton production. Other companies planned to establish palm oil plantations. Sometimes the move into agriculture involved the takeover of established Nigerian private companies. UAC bought Marquis Herds in Oyo state, John Holt purchased Ogbemudia Farms in Bendel, and Leventis took over Bendel Farms. Leventis also acquired 10,000 hectares in two other states (Kwara and Niger) for maize production.[56]

Is the large-scale acquisition of land by corporate enterprises and prominent individuals the prelude to a wave of capitalist farming? Here there are grounds for caution. Capitalist farms presently constitute a very small proportion of output and investment in the agricultural economy. Some of the recent land acquisitions were made reluctantly under pressure from government policies. In some cases, farming proceeded no further than land clearance, with the destruction of soil structures and erosion.[57]

Large-scale, capital-intensive farming faced obstacles. There were formidable problems of hiring and disciplining labour where household labour predominated and access to land was relatively easy. The recent fall in real wages made labour-intensive technologies more competitive. In the case of the Texagri cassava plantation, competition from small producers and labour intensive processing of *garri* (cassava) undermined the profitability of the project.[58] Ironically, disease and pest resistant varieties of cassava, which the company had earlier given away free, contributed to its downfall. Since the large devaluation of the naira, the cost of imported capital equipment and foreign management have generally become prohibitive.

Corporate enterprise can avoid some of the difficulties associated with large-scale, capital-intensive production by making some form of contract with smallholders through outgrower schemes. This solution, which avoids the large-scale alienation of land and problems of labour recruitment while allowing company control over the supply of produce, inputs, and credit, was pioneered in Nigeria by the Nigerian Tobacco Company. It has been pursued partially by a large-scale cotton producer in Gongola state (Afcott) and by an agro-industrial enterprise in Plateau state

(Vegfru). Both these producers are vertically integrated and add value through processing.

Policies and Politics

In conclusion, I summarise my position on various policies and try to place them within a broader political context. The withdrawal of the state from large-scale agricultural production and the halt to the expansion of large-scale irrigation schemes are positive steps. Like other recent changes in policy, these measures may stem from the overall fiscal crisis rather than from the recognition of past errors in policy. They may prove to be temporary. There is little evidence that these bureaucratically conceived solutions to a perceived food crisis promoted agricultural development. Very often they provided avenues for bureaucratic corruption. Sometimes they affected smallholders adversely. This is not a blanket argument against state involvement in agricultural production. Both the Bacita sugar estate and the Risonpalm oil palm plantation might show on examination that state initiatives can be productive.

For reasons already advanced, the abolition of the Commodity Boards was a progressive step. State intervention in domestic food markets beyond the storage of a security reserve is hard to justify. As we saw, the record of the Grains Board was not a propitious one. The difficulties of operating marketing agencies in the interests of the majority of farmers are formidable. This is not a free market argument for the reduction of state functions to some kind of residual minimum. It is an argument about certain kinds of intervention at a particular time in one country. State intervention and economic management are subject to conflicting forces and political interests. For example, there is no case for forcing international markets on Nigerian farmers when imported commodities are heavily subsidised in their countries of origin. Protection may well be justified in the national interest.

Since the late 1970s, there has been a sustained attempt by various governments to promote from above large-scale, capital-intensive farming by companies and individuals. The result of this strategy has been some movement by industrial companies into agro-industry and the arrival of a group of large-scale farmers, prominent among whom are retired military officers and civil servants. These enterprises have not been investigated in any detail, and we know little about the accumulation strategies involved or their success, the degree of dependence upon state support, and the extent to which individuals have extended their activities beyond poultry enterprises. We can assume, though, that in terms of output and investment these corporate enterprises are far less important than those larger farms that have evolved from within the rural sector. Rather than continue to support large-scale corporate enterprise, state resources would be better employed assisting smaller-scale village farmers and improving rural infrastructure and services. The alienation of land and state subsidies involved in the large-farm strategy sets up the trajectory for gross inequalities in terms of wealth in the future.

Agricultural policy has not generally been at the centre of the political agenda in Nigeria, nor have rural producers, small or large, mobilised themselves as lobbyists or as part of wider political movements. One reason for this is that policies have not generally had a direct impact on the livelihood of the mass of producers. Another reason is the weakness of agricultural class alignments. Had the government intervened heavily in the procurement of staple crops, the politicisation of state policy would have been much greater. Among the reasons for the absence of intervention have been the sheer size and heterogeneity of farm output, the absence of a politically powerful group of wealthy farmers to actively support it, and the fact that the federal centre, burdened with many other commitments, has lacked the capacity and funds to manage such a commitment. It may intervene in the future as result of greater centralisation of state power and of fiscal pressures that force the government to adopt a more extractive role in the rural economy in order to defend urban living standards. There are plenty of general developmental ideas that go beyond the exploitative middleman syndrome to support large-scale intervention as a means to self-sufficiency and regularity of supply. In this event, food policy would become an instrument of political patronage and a controversial issue like the importation of wheat and rice. By this time, the farm population might have increased its political weight, but it is likely to be split, with large farmers and powerful traders who have privileged access to the state generally supporting and shaping government measures, and making alliances with state officials.

The great physical dispersion of farming communities and the variation in social organisation and culture have also militated against the widespread mobilisation of the peasantry as a class. Differentiation within rural communities does not necessarily follow occupational categories. Nonfarm occupations are often combined with farming. Community identities are strong, and those who are differentiated in terms of wealth and resources can be bound together by kinship, friendship, and clientage. Vertical ties, within the community and those that extend outwards to a wider arena often take the form of patronage ties that cut across horizontal divisions. Political competition for access to the state may dominate and divide those who claim to represent the community at higher levels and those who have economic power to exploit in a wider setting.

In the case of cocoa farmers, low prices and taxation did provide a basis for challenging the state government in the Agbekoya uprisings in 1968 and 1969. Yet this was not a confrontation between a peasantry rooted in the land and an exploitative government. When oil revenues increased, farmers lost their leverage and sought out better opportunities elsewhere.[59] Farmers used cocoa farming as a means to social mobility and gained access to the wider regional political economy.

Land issues and taxation can provide a clear focus for peasant resistance and struggle on a substantial scale. In the case of the state schemes that have displaced large numbers of small farmers, there have been direct and sometimes violent confrontations with the state authorities. Equally, the actual or threatened appropriation of large land holdings by private companies and individuals has been the occasion for resistance by whole communities who fear that land will be permanently alienated. In the northern states, land issues have been an important element in the political struggles of NEPU and the PRP, but they do not necessarily provide an enduring basis for mobilisation among small farmers, who have long adapted to changing circumstances through migration and shifts in their occupational strategies.

Notes

1. R. H. Bates, *Markets and States in Tropical Africa: The Political Basis of Agricultural Policies* (Berkeley: University of California Press, 1981); R. H. Bates, *Essays on the Political Economy of Rural Africa* (Cambridge: Cambridge University Press, 1983).

2. R. H. Bates, "The Politics of Agricultural Pricing in Sub-Saharan Africa," in Z. Ergas, ed., *The African State in Transition* (London: Macmillan, 1987), p. 250.

3. *Times Literary Supplement*, 14 October 1984.

4. K. Hart, *The Political Economy of West African Agriculture* (Cambridge: Cambridge University Press, 1982), p. 165.

5. G. Hyden, *No Shortcuts to Progress: African Development Management in Perspective* (London: Heinemannn, 1983).

6. G. Williams, "Primitive Accumulation: The Way to Progress?" *Development and Change* 18 (1987), pp. 637–659.

7. M. Watts, ed., *State, Oil and Agriculture in Nigeria* (Berkeley: University of California Press, 1987), p. 27–29.

8. G. Williams, "Why Is There No Agrarian Capitalism in Nigeria?" *Journal of Historical Sociology* 1/4, 1988. p. 370.

See also G. Williams, "Inequalities in Rural Nigeria," Development Studies Occasional Paper no. 16, University of East Anglia, 1981.

9. D. K. Fieldhouse, *Black Africa, 1945–1980: Economic Decolonisation and Arrested Development* (London: Allen and Unwin, 1986), p. 159.

10. Shenton writes, "central to a grave socio-economic crisis is the near collapse of the agrarian sector in Nigeria and indeed Africa." R. W. Shenton, *The Development of Capitalism in Northern Nigeria* (London: James Currey, 1986), p. xii.

According to Schatz, the non-oil economy was inert—extremely sluggish and lethargic. S. P. Schatz, "Pirate Capitalism and the Inert Economy of Nigeria," *Journal of Modern African Studies* 22/1 (1984). According to Watts, "The inability of the state to effectively manage the process of capital accumulation resulted in a catastrophic stagnation of the agrarian sector." M. Watts, *Silent Violence: Food, Famine and Peasantry in Northern Nigeria* (Berkeley: University of California Press, 1983), p. 512.

11. *World Development Report,* World Bank, 1981.

12. *Nigeria: Agricultural Sector Memorandum,* World Bank, 1985.

13. S. Berry, "The Food Crisis and Agrarian Change in Africa," *African Studies Review* 27/2 (1984), pp. 59–62.

14. *Nigeria: Agricultural Sector Review,* World Bank, 1979.

15. F. Teal, "Domestic Policies, External Constraints and Economic Development in Nigeria Since 1950," *African Affairs* 87/346 (1988), pp. 79–81. See also, B. Pinto, "Nigeria During and After the Oil Boom: A Policy Comparison with Indonesia," *World Bank Economic Review* 1/3 (1987), p. 432.

16. P. Collier, "Oil Shocks and Food Security in Nigeria," *International Labour Review,* 127/6 (1988), pp. 766–775; P. Collier, "An Analysis of the Nigerian Labour Market," Development Economics Department Discussion Paper, World Bank, 1986. Collier's methods are based on a combination of assumption, aggregation, estimation, and inference. They are used to "explain" changes in indicators that are themselves subject to wide margins of error. For example, his figures for the agricultural labour force in the early 1970s are derived from a residual estimate for 1981. Quite apart from this, the whole conceptual validity of a wage labour force in Nigerian agriculture numbering around 20 million persons needs to be questioned.

17. For southern Katsina, see P. Clough and G. Williams, "Decoding Berg: The World Bank in Rural Northern Nigeria," in M. Watts, ed., *State, Oil and Agriculture in Nigeria* (Berkeley: University of California Press, 1987), pp. 173–174.

Lafia in Plateau state was an area of in-migration and crop expansion in the 1970s. Personal communication from Richard Bruce.

18. P. Clough, "The Production and Marketing of Cash Crops and Grains in Northern Nigeria, 1985: A View based on Village Research," Consultancy Report, Western Africa Regional Office, World Bank, Washington, D.C., 1986, p. 5.

19. *Nigeria: Agricultural Sector Memorandum,* World Bank, 1985.

20. *Agricultural Sector Review,* revised draft, World Bank, 1987.

21. *National Concord,* 16 April 1987; *Guardian* (Lagos), 6 July 1987; *National Concord,* 18 November 1987; *Guardian* (Lagos), 11 March 1987.

22. "Nigeria: Gusau, Funtua, and Gombe Agricultural Development Projects," *Project Performance Audit Report* (Washington, D.C.: World Bank, 1982).

23. *Gombe Agricultural Development Project: Completion Report,* World Bank, Agricultural Projects Monitoring, Evaluation and Planning Unit, Kaduna, 1982.

24. N. G. Daplyn and C. D. Poate, "Some Macro- and Microeconomic Constraints on Agricultural Production and Innovation," paper prepared for the First National Seminar on the Green Revolution in Nigeria, Institute for Agricultural Research, Ahmadu Bello University, 1984.

25. R. Longhurst, "Rural Productivity, Malnutrition and Structural Adjustment," in E. Clay and J. Shaw, eds., *Poverty, Development and Food* (London: Macmillan, 1987), p. 114.

26. G. Andrae and B. Beckman, "Industry Goes Farming: The Nigerian Raw Material Crisis and the Case of Textiles and Cotton," Scandinavian Institute of African Studies, Upsalla, Research Report no. 80, 1987.

27. Clough, "The Production and Marketing of Cash Crops," pp. 6–7.

28. G. Williams, "The World Bank in Rural Nigeria Revisited: A Review of the World Bank's 'Nigeria: Agricultural Sector Review, 1987,'" *Review of African Political Economy* 43 (1988), p. 48.

29. Clough and Williams, "Decoding Berg," pp. 174–176.

30. Clough, "The Production and Marketing of Cash Crops," p. 3.

31. *Agricultural Projects Monitoring, Evaluation, and Planning Unit: Mid-Term Review,* World Bank, 1984.

32. P. Hill, *Rural Hausa: A Village and a Setting* (Cambridge: Cambridge University Press, 1972).

33. P. Hill, *Development Economics on Trial: The Anthropological Case for a Prosecution* (Cambridge: Cambridge University Press, 1986).

34. "Nigeria: Bendel State Oil Palm Project" and "Ondo State Oil Palm Project," *Project Performance Audit Report* (Washington, D.C.: World Bank, 1983).

35. G. Andrae and B. Beckman, *The Wheat Trap: Bread and Underdevelopment in Nigeria* (London: Zed Books, 1985), pp. 80–85. The following paragraphs rely on this work.

36. R. Palmer-Jones, "Irrigation and the Politics of Agricultural Development in Nigeria," in M. Watts, ed., *State, Oil and Agriculture in Nigeria* (Berkeley: University of California Press, 1987), pp. 145–149.

37. W. M. Adams, "River Basin Planning in Nigeria," *Applied Geography* 5 (1985), pp. 297–308.

38. G. Andrae and B. Beckman, *The Wheat Trap*, pp. 77–79.

39. W. M. Adams, "Rural Protest, Land Policy, and the Planning Process on the Bakolori Project, Nigeria," *Africa* 58/3 (1988), pp. 323–327.

40. G. Andrae and B. Beckman, *The Wheat Trap*, p. 125–127.

41. *National Concord*, 5 July 1990.

42. *Nigeria: Agricultural Sector Review*, vol. 1, rev. draft, World Bank, 1987.

43. *Nigeria: Agricultural Sector Review.*

44. *Nigeria: Agricultural Pricing Policy* (Washington, D.C.: World Bank, 1985).

45. *West Africa*, 5 March 1984.

46. *New Nigerian*, 20 December 1985.

47. Clough, "The Production and Marketing of Cash Crops," p. 92.

48. Clough, "The Production and Marketing of Cash Crops," pp. 94–99.

49. Clough, "The Production and Marketing of Cash Crops," p. 83.

50. P. Francis, "For the Use and Common Benefit of All Nigeria: Consequences of the 1978 Land Nationalisation," *Africa* 54/3 (1984), pp. 22–24.

51. P. J. Ross, "Land as a Right to Membership: Land Tenure Dynamics in a Peripheral Area of the Kano Close-Settled Zone," in M. Watts, ed., *State, Oil and Agriculture in Nigeria* (Berkeley: University of California Press, 1987), pp. 223–247.

52. K. Swindell and A. B. Mamman, "Land Expropriation and Accumulation in the Sokoto Periphery, Northwest Nigeria, 1976–86," *Africa* 60/2 (1990), pp. 178–179.

53. *Business Concord*, 5 April 1985.

54. *Sunday New Nigerian*, 18 May 1986.

55. Swindell and Mamman, "Land Expropriation and Accumulation," pp. 179–184. For further evidence of capitalist farming in the Sokoto region, see A. A. Labaran, "Land Appropriation for Capitalised Farming in the Sokoto Region: Some Preliminary Findings," in M. Mortimore, E. A. Olofin, R. A. Cline-Cole, and A. Abdulkadir, eds., *Perspectives on Land Administration and Development in Northern Nigeria* (Kano: Bayero University Department of Geography, 1987), pp. 46–57.

56. *West Africa*, 5 March 1984.

57. *Nigeria: Agricultural Sector Review*, revised draft, World Bank, 1987.

58. *Financial Times*, 3 March 1986.

59. S. Berry, *Fathers Work for Their Sons: Accumulation, Mobility and Class Formation in an Extended Yoruba Community* (Berkeley: University of California Press, 1985), pp. 33, 88, 89.

10

Structural Adjustment and National Accumulation

This chapter examines the economic reforms introduced after the Babangida regime came to power. They are the most important economic reforms in Nigeria since independence and the most comprehensive in Africa. The introduction of the Structural Adjustment Programme in 1986 marked a shift in economic policy towards a strategy that relied more on market forces and private enterprise to promote national accumulation. Through changes in relative prices and a reduction in state regulation, the SAP sought to restructure capital accumulation and achieve closer integration with world markets and international capital. The impetus for these reforms was external and formed part of a worldwide shift towards private enterprise, market forces and tight money that was orchestrated by the IMF and the World Bank. During the 1970s, monetarism and the counterrevolution in development economics made steady progress and provided an intellectual base for the policies of these institutions.[1] When President Ronald Reagan and Prime Minister Margaret Thatcher came to power, the ideological and policy offensive gathered real momentum.

The reforms raise many questions. Some of these cannot be satisfactorily answered until more time has lapsed.

Why did the reforms come so late? How were the reforms introduced and under what political conditions? How far have they been supported and contested through struggles over policy? What are their short- and medium-term economic consequences? What implications do they have for contradictions within Nigeria's relatively weak capitalist order? How far is the economic strategy charted by the reforms compatible with the politics of civil rule?

The growth of state expenditures and the expansion of the public sector in the 1970s might have been expected to occasion a debate between those who favoured a strategy of state-led development and those who favoured a more private enterprise, market-oriented strategy. Yet it was only at the end of the decade that the expansion of the state and its responsibilities began to be questioned. Likewise, fiscal policy was a matter of little concern. Federal funds poured out to cover the deficits of the parastatals and state governments. Why was economic debate so weakly developed? The answer lay partly in the centralisation of the federal system without strong political authority, partly in the nature of the state expansion, partly in the specific character of oil revenues, and partly in the underlying class configuration. We saw earlier that the state expansion was not the product of a strong state-led development strategy. It did not conflict with opportunities for individual or corporate accumulation. On the contrary, the expansion of the state created opportunities for private accumulation. With the enormous expansion of state expenditures and imports, the dominant economic concern was to compete for a share of state expenditures and imports. Such preoccupations did not give rise to differences over policy.

Like fiscal policy, exchange rate policy tended to take the line of least resistance. There was no debate over the sustained appreciation of the naira throughout the 1970s, despite its serious consequences for national development. The radical opposition to the military's economic policies, which had little political weight, tended to leap to a planned socialist alternative and never analysed the exchange rate. The rate was seen as part of a neoclassical concern with relative prices and its adjustment was something that the IMF and World Bank imposed on Third World countries. The appreciation was not the direct result of political pressure from specific interests or groups. Insofar as it was viewed in instrumental terms, it was seen as a means of controlling inflation through cheap imports. The urban middle classes and commercial interests benefitted greatly from the appreciation, but it was only during the early 1980s that they began to actively defend the exchange rate and resist devaluation. By then, import controls and foreign exchange rationing had created their own lucrative opportunities from importing, parallel market activity, and capital flight.

The crisis of 1978, which was provoked by a rapid deterioration in foreign exchange reserves, was a critical moment. It laid bare, with the utmost clarity, the external limits of Nigeria's neocolonial economic order. No changes in policy were forthcoming. There was no hint of a currency devaluation. Instead, policymakers responded by increasing oil company incentives and borrowing heavily abroad to sustain the reserve position and the exchange rate. This borrowing strategy set the pattern for the future and drastically reduced the room for manoeuvre.

Under the Shagari government, political imperatives and prevailing economic opinion completely ruled out serious consideration of economic reform. The National Economic Council's report, which was issued in early 1983, made no reference to the IMF strategy.[2] The report endorsed the April 1982 stabilisation measures. It saw structural adjustment in terms of planning external trade, import licensing, and incentives to assist industry and agriculture.

Under the Buhari regime, the emphasis was on domestic austerity and fiscal probity. Devaluation and trade liberalisation were never accepted. Countertrade was promoted and commercialisation rather than privatisation favoured. In 1984, economic reports in which ministers, civil servants, and academics were involved opposed the dismantling of state controls and a large devaluation.[3]

Thus, when reforms did come, they came very late in the day and were undertaken reluctantly as a last resort. Domestic capital in its various forms had not proved strong enough, as an economic and political force, to promote reform or even pose alternative policies. While oil revenues were abundant, Nigeria was shielded from the influence of the international agencies. Nigerian leaders were under no effective external pressure to undertake economic reform. It was only when international credit finally dried up and threathened international trade that the IMF and World Bank were in a strong enough position to press for domestic policy reform. They then found some domestic allies to support their position.

The IMF Debate and the Introduction of the Structural Adjustment Programme

It was widely held that when President Babangida took power, an agreement with the IMF was imminent. In the months preceding the coup, Babangida appeared to have been convinced of the need for an agreement. One factor here was a gradual shift of opinion among Nigerian corporate managers in favour of an agreement with the IMF.[4] The *Financial Times* held that "it was probably the first time in Africa that a government overthrow has been caused at least in part by failure to reach agreement with the IMF."[5]

Granted that the government wanted an agreement with the IMF, political realities quickly impressed on the president the need for caution on the issue. Majority opinion in the Armed Forces Ruling Council was probably against an IMF loan and close involvement by the IMF in the Nigerian economy. Moreover, under the Buhari administration, anti-IMF rhetoric had been loud. Babangida's solution was to set up a committee on the IMF loan to organise a public debate on the issue and to take memoranda from the public.

If some thought that the debate would provide an opportunity to educate the public on the merits of an IMF loan, they had a rude shock. Once the debate got under way, it was apparent that opposition to the loan was widespread and vocal. Among the groups who opposed a deal were the Nigerian Labour Congress, which threatened a general strike,[6] student bodies, university lecturers, market women, and religious leaders.[7] More generally, urban petty traders, producers, and transporters were opposed to a deal with the IMF.[8] It was through this group that the average consumer would be exposed to the effects of the SAP. The press, too, was generally hostile. Nigerian bankers like Alhaji Umaru Abdul Mutallab (UBA) and Ibrahim Ayagi (Chase Merchant Bank) were also outspoken opponents in a series of public forums organised to promote the debate.[9] The military governors of Kaduna, Gongola,[10] and Imo[11] states also spoke out against a loan. The Manufacturers Association of Nigeria, in its memorandum, rejected a sharp devaluation and described the proposed trade liberalisation as outrageous.[12] Aliko Muhammed, the chairman of the Stock Exchange, saw an agreement with the IMF as a time bomb for social revolution.[13] Opposition to the loan, widespread though it was, lacked coherence. Only the socialists put forward an alternative programme.[14] They called for a planned structural transformation of the economy based on the transfer of political power to working people.

On the middle ground were those who accepted all the IMF conditions but rejected a loan. They included Chief Samuel Falegan[15] (former director of research at the Central Bank) and Oladele Olashore (First Bank).[16] Those in favour of a loan included the Lagos Chamber of Commerce, though it thought that the trade liberalisation conditions should be modified.[17] One of the most prominent advocates of a loan was Chief Ernest Shonekan (managing director of the United Africa Company), who argued his case in terms of a comprehensive shift of economic strategy like that advocated by the World Bank and defended the IMF record in other African countries.[18] Other private sector support for a loan came from Gamaliel Onosode (Dunlop and Cadbury),[19] and Michael Omolaloye (Lever Brothers).[20] Nigerian corporate managers and chairmen constituted the strongest identifiable group in favour of an IMF package. Less visible, though important, were some senior civil servants.

From the outset, the debate centred on the issue of the loan and not on the policy conditionalities involved in an IMF package or the wider questions of economic strategy. This was significant because it diverted attention away from the government's own strategy. Though not widely recognised at the time, many of the IMF conditions had already been agreed to in principle by the government, and some were already in the process of being implemented.[21] Those agreed upon included expenditure controls, project reviews, reductions in grants and subsidies, rationalisation of parastatals, an end to nonstatutory transfers, rationalisation of customs tariffs, a rise in interest rates, removal of the fertiliser subsidy, a review of industrial incentives, a vigorous export drive, adjustment of agricultural producer prices, strict external debt management, and improved operational efficiency of debt revenue collection. The main areas of disagreement outstanding were the petroleum subsidy, trade liberalisation, and above all, devaluation.

How do we account for the very widespread opposition to the loan? Beyond a nationalist response to the infringement of national sovereignty that the dictates of the IMF elicit in all countries and a more specific anti-imperialist opposition to the leading organ of international finance capital from the Left, there was a widespread feeling that additional foreign loans were not the answer to Nigeria's economic problems. It was felt that Nigeria's rulers should not again be given the opportunity to mismanage and waste resources on a grand scale. If the loan was taken, it would only be used to perpetuate the corrupt practices of the past and to service debts of doubtful validity. The revelations of the Johnson Matthey Bank affair at this time served to underline these concerns by exposing fraudulent activities, dubious foreign debts, and massive capital flight from the country.

After three months of debate, negotiations for a loan with the IMF were suspended in December. The outcome was widely seen as a democratic victory for popular forces. Yet, as we shall see, the conclusion of the debate in no way deflected the government from its chosen economic strategy.

The 1986 Budget

On 1 October, President Babangida declared a National Economic Emergency to last for 15 months.[22] Bans on the import of rice and maize were announced. Later, compulsory wage and salary reductions for the armed forces and the private and public sectors were announced. A new ad hoc Presidential Advisory Committee was set up. It was headed by Ojetunji Aboyade. Aboyade's appointment had considerable irony, as he had been in the forefront of earlier drives to promote a planned economy and public sector leadership. The Presidential Advisory Council was heavily involved in the 1986 budget and wielded some influence in the early years of the programme.

When the 1986 budget was announced, it contained a set of measures and commitments that closely followed IMF and World Bank thinking. In fact, it can be argued that the outcome of the IMF debate, by defusing nationalist sentiment, made the 1986 budget politically acceptable. It also allowed the government to claim that the measures were homegrown rather than externally imposed. This claim suited both the government and the international agencies.

The budget marked a compromise between homegrown nationalist forces and the views of those like Finance Minister Kalu Idiku Kalu who were anxious to pursue reforms in line with IMF and World Bank thinking. On the one hand, the budget clearly committed the government to the adoption of a realistic exchange rate, to privatisation, to cuts in public sector subsidies, and tight control of the fiscal deficit. On the other hand, there were a number of homegrown features, like a bureaucratic devaluation (surcharges on imports and export incentives), an Emergency Recovery Fund, more import bans, and a continuing commitment to countertrade to finance large-scale projects. Petrochemicals and steel were singled out as priority areas. Servicing of foreign debt was restricted to 30 percent of foreign exchange earnings.

After the budget, which was well received by Western creditors, an attempt was made to reschedule Nigeria's debts without the agreement of the IMF. This effort foundered on resistance by Western creditors and on the rapid decline of oil prices, which undermined the financial assumptions of the 1986 budget. The Nigerian position was also weakened by the fact that fresh short-term trade arrears were being built up.

The Introduction of the Structural Adjustment Programme

With the political unacceptability of the IMF, the World Bank took the lead in writing and working towards the introduction of a Structural Adjustment Programme that would prove acceptable to the IMF and the Nigerian government and open the way to rescheduling. Key actors in this critical period were Vice-President Ernest Stern from Washington and the Bank's resident representative in Lagos, Ishrat Husain, a former Pakistani civil servant. Since his arrival in Nigeria in December 1983, Husain had adopted a high profile, participating vigorously in various policy debates, feeding up-to-date information to the Nigerian authorities, visiting Dodan Barracks, and establishing links with Nigerians favourable to World Bank policy.[23] Nationalists would never have countenanced such a high profile from a World Bank official in the 1970s. The World Bank office in Lagos was strengthened to increase liaison with Nigerian ministries and improve data collection and analysis. By June 1986, both the Lagos Chamber of Commerce and the Manufacturers Association of Nigeria were openly calling for a substantial devaluation of the naira, and the reluctance of the Nigerian authorities on this critical point had been overcome.[24]

The World Bank took over the role of the IMF by providing credit to fund the SAP. It offered $4.2 billion over three years to fund the SAP, conditional on progress with policy reform. The linchpin of the SAP, which was announced in July, was the introduction of the Second Tier Foreign Exchange Market (SFEM). This was a means of devaluing through the back door and a way of allocating foreign exchange more efficiently. It was only when the SFEM was finally in place in September to the satisfaction of the IMF, which had insisted that government imports be included in the SFEM contrary to the views of some Nigerian officials and advisers, that the programme was endorsed by the IMF. Subsumed within the SAP was a standby agreement with the usual quantitative performance criteria to be met by demand management.

Looking back to the original IMF position, it is clear that the IMF had given little ground. Nigeria had jumped straight to a SAP without first having a standby agreement or Extended Fund Facility. Moreover, it had, for political reasons, concluded an agreement without taking an IMF loan, which was highly unusual. Yet, the outcome of the IMF debate notwithstanding, Nigeria had eventually accepted an agreement with the IMF with all its attendant conditions.

In summary, the objectives of the SAP can be reduced to five elements.

1. Strengthen demand management through monetary, fiscal, and wage policies.
2. Stimulate domestic production by encouraging non-oil exports and by reducing dependence on imported goods through changes in relative prices (notably a lower exchange rate) tariff rationalisation, and export incentives.
3. Reduce public regulation and administrative control by the reduction of subsidies, price decontrol, deregulation of the financial sector, and trade and payments liberalisation.
4. Rationalise the bureaucracy and public sector projects, and commercialise and privatise public corporations and companies.
5. Reschedule the external debt so as to shift the main burden of debt servicing to 1991 and beyond.

The Structural Adjustment Programme Since 1986

The government underestimated the time scale and difficulty of carrying through the reforms. The SAP was introduced in the context of a continued fall in oil revenues, a steep compression of import volumes, and sharp falls in living standards (see Tables 10.1 and 10.2). Although the Babangida regime initially maintained a commitment to the programme, the administration and implementation of the reforms proved fickle and erratic in the face of domestic opposition, limited evidence of success, and political pressures emanating from the transition process. At the core of the reform was the devaluation of the naira and the rationalisation of the foreign exchange market. Other major changes included the deregulation of imports and financial markets, diminished industrial protection, and the relaxation of indigenisation decrees. In other areas, like the withdrawal of subsidies, the adjustment of public sector tariffs, and the reorganisation of parastatals and privatisation, the government was forced to proceed cautiously. For the first time, the ideology of "free market" economists moved out of the classroom and was publicly promoted. The exchange rate and

TABLE 10.1 Selected Economic Indicators, 1980–1993

	1980	1982	1984	1986	1987	1988	1989	1990	1991	1992	1993
Nominal exchange rate[a]	100	81	72	41	14	12	7	7	6	3	2
Real exchange rate	100	114	185	91	29	34	31	28	24	20	22
Consumer price index[b]	100	130	223	249	274	378	534	573	648	937	1,472
Food price	100	134	240	250	271	412	574	595	666	976	1,541
Exports[c]											
Value	100	55	48	24	30	28	33	52	49	48	51
Unit value	100	98	83	49	58	50	59	76	68	68	58
Volume	100	56	58	48	51	56	55	68	72	70	87
Imports											
Value	100	100	39	27	26	26	23	29	60	55	53
Unit value	100	92	87	96	103	110	112	120	119	122	120
Volume	100	109	45	28	25	23	20	24	50	45	44
Naira per $ exchange rate (year end)	0.54	0.67	0.81	3.32	4.14	5.4	7.7	9.0	9.8	19.6	21.8

[a]Exchange rates are period averages.
[b]Price indices are a composite of rural and urban for all income groups.
[c]All trade figures are tentative.

Sources: Exchange rates are from IMF, *International Financial Statistics* (various years); prices are from Central Bank of Nigeria, *Annual Reports* (various years); trade figures are from UNCTAD, *Handbook of International Trade and Development Statistics* (various years).

TABLE 10.2 Index of Real Household Incomes of Key Groups 1980/81–1986/87 (Rural self-employed in 1980/81 = 100)

	1980/81	1981/82	1982/83	1983/84	1984/85	1985/86	1986/87
Rural self-employed	100	103	95	86	73	74	65
Rural wage earners	178	160	147	135	92	95	84
All rural households	105	107	99	89	74	84	74
Urban self-employed	150	124	106	94	69	69	61
Urban wage earners	203	177	164	140	101	101	90
All urban households	166	142	129	109	80	80	71

Sources: National Integrated Survey of Households (NISH), Federal Office of Statistics (FOS) consumer price data, and World Bank estimates. As found in Paul Collier, *An Analysis of the Nigerian Labour Market*, Development Economics Department Discussion Paper (Washington, D.C.: World Bank, 1986).

budget policy became subjects of public debate. In 1988, delays in implementing reforms, together with large budgetary deficits, threatened to block the annual IMF approval upon which further debt rescheduling and fresh credit were dependent. Both the 1989 and 1990 budgets demonstrated a commitment to the SAP strategy, but as the transition to civil rule gathered political momentum, expenditure controls were relaxed.

The slow results of the programme, the deterioration in living standards, and the perception that the burden of the programme was highly unequal combined to fuel the opposition and meant that the government was not free to concentrate its energies on the transition to civil rule. It tried to stifle economic debate by harassing opponents, preventing meetings, and controlling the economic agenda of the new political parties.

The main challenge to the economic reforms came from the trade unions, from the mass of petty producers, traders, and transporters, and from the left intelligentsia. Industrial interests also lobbied strongly against certain measures. Against the background of steep falls in real living standards, which had been experienced well before the introduction of the programme, the Nigerian Labour Congress consistently challenged price increases. This campaign, which drew on a broader undercurrent of support, forced the government to retreat temporarily from its commitment to phase out the fuel subsidy. When the government did implement a small increase in the fuel price in 1988, there were riots in Jos led by students, traders, and transporters. Subsequently there was limited strike action in a number of major cities. Had the government not dismissed the executive of the NLC and its state branches prior to these events, a general strike might have ensued and provided a focus for broader political opposition to the regime. The following year there were further riots in Benin, involving students and workers, which spread to other cities and prompted the closure of universities. There were also scattered and spontaneous riots by urban-based petty producers and traders. As we saw in Chapter 6, these riots were often directed against the police and government property. Although these actions were the result of economic hardship and a groundswell of opposition to the government, they did not present a major threat.

Foreign Exchange Management

The introduction of the SFEM in September 1986 brought with it a large devaluation of the naira (see Table 10.1). At the second auction, the rate was N5.06 to the dollar, implying a devaluation of 69 percent. The rate was generally subject to downward pressure, though it fluctuated with intervention by the authorities. At the end of 1990, the rate stood close to N9.0 to the dollar, and there was the prospect of further decline.

The excess demand for foreign exchange, which exerted downward pressure on the naira, derived from an unsatisfied demand for imports and from the limited supply of foreign exchange on the market. The supply of official funds was reduced initially by a fall in oil earnings and by the existence of external dedicated accounts that had a prior claim to oil revenue. The latter were outside the regular budgetary process and were intended to finance major public projects like steel, aluminium, and gas pipelines and were a constant bone of contention between the Nigerian government and the international agencies.

The flow of foreign exchange into the autonomous market from domiciliary accounts (private capital repatriation), foreign investment, and non-oil exports began slowly but increased with the deregulation of the interbank market exchange rates in January 1987. In 1987 and 1988, funds from these sources accounted for about 30 percent of the foreign exchange allocation under the SFEM.[25] In the case of non-oil exports, there was evidence of underinvoicing and nonrepatriation of foreign exchange receipts, which threatened to undermine the SAP strategy. New direct foreign investment, held by some to be essential to the success of the SAP, remained at a very low level. Much of the positive net flow of foreign investment was made up of the reinvestment of unremitted profits by existing companies.

There was opposition to devaluation from manufacturers, who fought a rearguard action through the press, from urban middle classes accustomed to cheap imports and foreign travel, and from radical nationalists. The virtual absence of any industrial exports provided little political support for devaluation on the export side to counter opposition from importers and those who previously relied on licences. Industrial interests also argued forcibly for reflationary measures and resisted lower levels of protection. They had some success. With demand for foreign exchange exceeding supply, the authorities constantly intervened in the foreign exchange rate market to temper the downward movement of the naira. Yet exchange levels previously thought to be politically unacceptable were breached. The Central Bank intervened by altering the rules of the foreign exchange auction, by changing the method of determining market rate, and by bringing pressure to bear on banks that bid for foreign exchange.

One consequence of this intervention was the opening up of a significant differential between the official rate and the autonomous interbank rate. The spread between the markets was as much as 60 percent in early 1989. This spread created profitable opportunities for banks to trade in foreign exchange, and many new banks were opened, but it did nothing to encourage the productive use of foreign exchange. The explosion of new banks was a major feature of the SAP regime. The rush to set up banks by leading businesspeople had not abated by the end of 1990, when over 100 banks were in operation, a fourfold increase over the decade. It was further encouraged by a fall in the real costs of entry to banking and easier access to licences. Deregulation of the financial system, as controls on interest rates were abolished in 1987, propelled the banks into a more competitive environment. Although the allocation of foreign exchange through the banking system probably improved upon allocation under the old import licence regime, there is a lack of hard evidence on this point.

The devaluation of the naira was a positive measure and long overdue. The sustained appreciation of the naira over a long period of time had encouraged all forms of dependency. It worked against the use of local raw materials and the buildup of local technological capacities. The devaluation encouraged commodity exports and gave local food producers better protection. It reduced the opportunities for importers to make enormous gains from the rents created by the overvaluation of the currency and by trade controls. The importation of rice and sugar during the period of civil rule provided clear evidence of the political exploitation and corrupt practice that such gross margins create. Many companies that existed only in briefcases for the collection of import licences were swept away by the reforms. The adjustment strengthened the weight of the domestic market by bringing consumption more into line with domestically produced goods and services. Lastly, by increasing the price of imports and agricultural exports, the adjustment acted to shift real incomes to rural areas where the majority of the population live.

Monetary and Fiscal Management

With the introduction of the SFEM, demand management became of paramount importance. To avoid a mutually reinforcing currency depreciation and inflation, the programme reduced liquidity in the economy and compressed consumer incomes through a wage freeze and cut in public expenditure. The result of the liquidity squeeze was to moderate the inflationary impact of the SAP. The national composite price index rose by 11.2 percent between March 1986 and March 1987. This increase was lower than the 24 percent inflation target for the first year of the SAP and was much lower than the rate anticipated by most observers and the opponents of the SAP. One favourable factor was the succession of good harvests in 1985 and 1986.

Both monetary and fiscal restraints were relaxed in 1987. The fiscal deficit for 1987 was N11 billion against a budgeted deficit of only N2 billion.[26] Moreover, the 1988 budget was sharply reflationary, and the overall budget deficit was over N6 billion. During 1988, bank credit expansion to the public sector was 21.4 percent against a target of 2.5 percent. Inflation in 1988 was officially estimated at 38 percent, rising to 48 percent in 1989. The reflationary turnabout in the budget was due partly to the political impact of a critical speech by General Obasanjo,[27] which emboldened critics of government policy like the Manufacturers Association and the NLC. The NLC led the opposition to the government's policy of removing the petroleum subsidy. Higher fuel prices would have raised government revenues and reduced the budget deficit.

The removal of the petroleum subsidy was a politically sensitive matter, as an increase in fuel prices would feed through into a rise in transport fares and consumer prices. The origins of this debate lay in the rapid expansion of private road transport in the 1970s and in the appreciation of the naira, which opened up a gap between domestic fuel prices and international prices. Cheap fuel, a massive road building programme, subsidised vehicle loans, and large imports of vehicles had combined to encourage a huge extension of private automobile and bus ownership. The provision of public transport facilities in the cities and the railways were, by contrast, neglected. When the oil-induced recession arrived, transport services rapidly deteriorated. Vehicles and spare parts became expensive, and roads were not maintained.

The government announced its intention of removing the fuel subsidy in 1987. Under pressure from the National Transport Owners Association, the government agreed to raise transport fares in March.[28] This rise was not implemented because of opposition from the Nigerian Labour Congress and the National Union of Road Transport Workers. Nevertheless, the government firmly committed itself to a partial removal of the fuel subsidy later in the year. To persuade the public, it took advertisements claiming that over N6 billion of potential revenue was being lost because of the subsidy. The NLC resolutely opposed this policy, and its leaders were detained at one point. Sensing the political dangers of an increase in transport fares, the government backed down. Subsequently the NLC was dissolved, and a small increase in the fuel price announced.

The 1989 and 1990 budgets marked a rejection of the reflationary stance of the 1988 budget and closely reflected World Bank and IMF policy. In 1991 expenditure controls were loosened and government borrowing from the banking sector increased, inviting stronger inflationary pressure.

Debt Management

A major rescheduling of medium- and long-term debt with the London Club of commercial banks was agreed in principle in early 1987, though the banks remained reluctant to extend fresh credit to Nigeria. Bilateral rescheduling with the Paris Club of official creditors made very slow progress. Early in 1987, Nigeria defaulted on interest payments on promissory notes. In January 1988, terms were finally agreed with uninsured trade creditors for the rescheduling of arrears worth $3.2 billion over a twenty-two year period. Over $2 billion of short-term debt was still unmatched and unverified at the end of this exercise. It was thus effectively disowned by the Nigerian government.

The total external debt continued to rise, reaching over $30 billion at the end of 1988. But the profile of the debt had changed, and it was easier to manage. The share of short-term trade debt had declined sharply from its peak in 1984 (see Table 7.5). There was also a marked fall in the share of the debt held by private commercial banks (the London Club) and a rise in the share of bilateral creditors (the Paris Club) and the World Bank. As a result of rescheduling and refinancing, the debt service, which had peaked under the Buhari government at 38.7 percent (1985), fell to about 30 percent (1988). Periodic disagreements between creditors and the Nigerian government over the use of foreign exchange, policy reform, and fiscal management threatened to disrupt debt rescheduling. In 1992 creditors failed to reach agreement and arrears then increased.

The Effects on Industry

In the short and medium term, the impact of the reforms on industry was very mixed. Industry had to cope with a number of changes at once, including the devaluation of the naira, the abolition of import licencing, a large reduction in the number of banned items, the lifting of ex-factory price controls, the revision of tariffs, and a slump in effective demand. In September 1986, a hurried tariff revision cut duties on finished goods more than on intermediate inputs and raw materials, thereby reducing effective rates of protection and increasing competition. It also introduced a number of anomalies. A new tariff structure was not put in place until the 1988 budget.

Detailed studies of the impact of the recession and the SAP on industry have yet to be made. There was considerable adjustment in distribution and marketing, as industry was forced into sales and marketing promotion. Industries like textiles, which had a steady demand and were less dependent on imports, fared best, and there was considerable new investment. There was new investment in industries that relied on local raw materials like palm kernel, cotton seed, and maize milling; rubber and vegetable oil processing; tanning of hides and skins; sorghum malting; and soya milk. Industries that were dependent on assembly of imported parts, like some of the vehicle assembly plants and electronics, were forced to close down or reduce output. The Nigerian Bottling Company and Seven-Up extended their market shares in soft drinks through acquisitions and new investment. In some industries like furniture and shoes, the decline in demand and the devaluation made large scale, capital intensive producers less able to compete with small artisan production.

Before the introduction of the SAP, there was evidence of a shift towards local material sourcing by industry. Local sourcing of raw materials by industry rose from 38 percent in 1985 to 50 percent by 1988. This shift was prompted partly by increased cost of imports and partly by pressures from government. In 1985, the government set out five-year targets for minimum levels of raw material sourcing. In the case of breweries, there was a ban on imported barley from 1988, which made the construction of sorghum malting plants necessary. The beer industry, flour millers, textile companies, and soft drink manufacturers have all set up agro-industrial enterprises to secure supplies of local raw materials.

For the flour mills, the ban on imported wheat from January 1987 forced some mills to convert to the processing of local grains. Early in 1988, 70 percent of the bakeries in Plateau state and 90 percent of those in Imo state were reported to be closed.[29] The wheat lobby, made up of U.S. and Canadian wheat growers, local flour millers, and bakers, strongly resisted the ban, arguing its case on the grounds of wasteful investment and employment losses. It also attacked the government for not preventing the smuggling of flour on a large scale (estimated at 300,000 metric tons in 1988). These arguments failed to convince the government, which responded by launching a wheat production drive in the northern states.

By early 1989, there was some evidence of a slow diversification of non-oil exports encouraged by the devaluation, by 100 percent retention of foreign exchange proceeds, and by an export-subsidy scheme. The overall share of non-oil exports in total exports rose marginally from 6 percent in 1986 to 12 percent in 1988. Cocoa exports rose initially as producer prices soared from N3,000 a metric ton to over N15,000 in the 1988–1989 season as exports became an avenue for capital flight into hard currencies. The tanning industry in Kano underwent expansion with new investment oriented to exports. Exports of rubber increased. Apart from the traditional exports, there were also exports of yams, fruit, and vegetables. Small exports of textiles, beer, tiles, plastics, carpets, wood products, perfumes, bicycle frames, and tires were recorded.

In the longer term, success or failure in opening West African markets to official exports from Nigeria will test the logic of the SAP strategy and World Bank assistance, as it is premised on an expansion of non-oil exports in the subregion. Circumstantial evidence suggests that unofficial exports are much more important than official ones (textiles, garments, shoes, soap and detergents, cosmetics, motor parts, petroleum products, etc.). Manufactured exports are traded unofficially to bypass the unfavourable official exchange rate and the bureaucracy. Nigerian manufactures have penetrated African markets, especially in the West African subregion, aided by the overvaluation of the CFA franc. Such exports enhance Nigeria's geopolitical position in Africa and give it an economic rationale that was singularly lacking in the ECOWAS initiative. With the development of closer economic ties between France and Nigeria, the penetration of these markets by Nigerian goods is less likely to meet with French opposition.

Wages, Employment, and Labour Policy

Since 1980, there have been severe reductions in real incomes, especially for urban dwellers. It is estimated that between 1980 and 1987 the real income of urban households fell by 57 percent (see Table 10.2). Rural incomes also fell but not so sharply. By 1985/86, rural household incomes were estimated to be higher then those of urban households. The urban self-employed were harder hit than urban wage earners.

The effect of steep falls in real incomes and unemployment on poorer urban households has not been documented. One commentator noted the rise of single female-headed households and the withdrawal of children from school.[30] In the past, children would be sent out as apprentices, but with the closure of many small businesses, this avenue has been restricted. Child malnutrition increased, and the provision of health care services deteriorated. Consumers were forced to switch to less nutritious diets.

At the top, a tiny elite with financial assets and overseas property built up through capital flight during the oil boom and early days of the recession have gained from the SAP, as they could bring in their foreign earnings at favourable rates of exchange without questions being asked. Thus the burden of adjustment to the reforms was very unequally spread, with those at the top gaining through the boom period and through the period of structural adjustment.

Official statistics indicate that urban unemployment rose steadily from 4.7 percent in 1976 to 11.9 percent in June 1986.[31] This conceals radically different experiences for different groups. The hardest hit were those with secondary education and those aged under 25, with rates of 46 percent and over 30 percent, respectively, by mid-1986. Graduate unemployment also accelerated as a consequence of increases in the supply of graduates and the oil slump. Paul Collier suggested that young, urban-born workers may be locked into the urban labour market even if it offers significantly lower returns than agriculture.[32] Evidence suggests that older persons who suffered from retrenchment in the private sector were more likely to take up employment in agriculture and be preferred for new vacancies.

Official concern with unemployment gathered momentum.[33] A National Directorate of Employment was set up and N100 million voted for ad hoc job creation measures. One thousand persons in each state (including 200 graduates) were deployed to the 304 local government areas for a Special Public Works Programme. Under a National Open Apprenticeship Scheme, each state was expected to train 2,000 apprentices annually. A Working for Yourself programme for unemployed graduates was introduced.

After the high point of union militancy in 1981 and the establishment of a national minimum wage, the organised labour movement was gradually weakened by the steady rise in unemployment and the associated fall in union membership. The unions were unable to resist effectively the huge layoffs and the massive decline in real earnings. They were more successful in defending allowances, bonuses, and the existence of a national minimum wage.[34]

Yet the NLC on occasion successfully fought to protect workers and influence government policy. In 1985, under the Economic Emergency, the government introduced compulsory deductions from wages and salaries. The NLC protested, and the government withdrew the deductions for the lower paid. After strong protests, the government also dropped proposals to abolish the national minimum wage for enterprises employing fewer than 500 persons. On the broader political front, the NLC consistently struggled to protect the independent traditions of the trade union movement and to defend human rights.[35]

Privatisation, Commercialisation, and Foreign Investment

The move to privatisation in Nigeria was part of a broader movement that extended beyond the sale of publicly owned assets to private interests. The movement covered distinct and possibly alternative means of changing the relationship between the state and the private sector. It could involve a contraction of the areas reserved for state investment, a relaxation of state licencing of private activity, the dissolution of existing public agencies or parastatals, the sale of shares from the government portfolio, measures to increase the competitive environment for public enterprises, and the outright or partial sale of state companies. Clearly, such measures had different political and economic implications.

Coincident with privatisation, concerted efforts were made to make Nigeria more attractive to foreign investors. These measures included the sweeping away of restrictions on foreign equity participation in areas where 40 percent and 60 percent limits applied. Banking, insurance, petroleum, and mining were excepted. There was also a streamlining of investment procedures and publication of an investment code. All these measures, and the continued decline of the naira notwithstanding, substantial new foreign investment was not forthcoming.

Privatisation was not an obvious process in Nigeria. The distinction between the public and private sectors was blurred in practice. Public funds had been privatised on a large scale through corrupt practices, and opportunities for private gain surrounded all state companies and corporations. Private accumulation was often dependent on state contracts and various forms of state intervention in the economy. The absence of a clear distinction was reflected in attitudes towards the public sector and public funds and in the ideology of the mixed economy that was prominent in the

1970s. It may be argued that the term mixed economy was a misnomer for what was essentially a public-support role for private accumulation, but the term had a real resonance in Nigeria, reflecting the absence of ideological polarity and strong class alignments in Nigerian society.

Another reason why privatisation was not a very obvious process in Nigeria lay in the history of the public sector. Ever since the first major expansion of the public sector under the regional governments in the 1950s, public sector enterprises were subject to high levels of executive interference and control. There was very little delegation of authority. This political control continued despite numerous attempts to give public corporations more autonomy. It hampered the development of technocratic cadres within the state sector. In addition, very few public sector companies were profitable or kept up-to-date accounts, and this limited their appeal to private capital.

It has been argued by Bade Onimode that public enterprises are inherently as efficient as private enterprise and that the problems lie in the general environment in which they operate.[36] They can therefore be reorganised and commercialised so that a viable state capitalism can emerge. In principle, this is correct, but for reasons of political control and executive interference, it must be doubted if public ownership is compatible with greater efficiency and a more competitive environment. Onimode also argued that privatisation increases dependence on foreign capital and imperialist powers. However, the whole history of the public sector in Nigeria suggests that it has not been associated with any enhanced capacity to pursue national goals and development objectives or with self-reliant patterns of economic development. The wasteful expansion of the 1970s contributed heavily to the overall fiscal weakness of the state, laying it open to external pressure.

The main pressure for privatisation arose from the need to reduce public expenditure. There was also some pressure from local private capital, which had grown in scale and was now more likely to perceive state investment and regulation as limiting the opportunities for private investment. This was the case in areas like airlines, hotels, plantations, agroprocessing, petroleum marketing, and banking, where state licencing had become more liberal and where there was a significant Nigerian private presence. There was also some ideological shift among the Nigerian managerial and business elite, who expressed their views in favour of private enterprise more forcibly. Their ranks were swollen by former civil servants and former army officers who earlier profited from the expansion of the public sector and went on to set up their own companies.

A number of concerns prompted the Babangida government to move slowly on the issue. First, there was the worry over the concentration of shares, which had earlier led to the restrictions on individual ownership in the second stage of the indigenisation process. More important was the concern that particular ethnic groups or sectional interests in the country might be favoured by the exercise. The Kano branch of MAN insisted on regional equity and called for quotas and controls in the privatisation process, whereas their southern counterparts defended the case for floating the companies on the stock exchange where the market would determine the allocation of shares.[37] Later it was announced that board membership of privatised companies would be shared among shareholder associations in zones across the country.

In 1985, the federal government announced the withdrawal of federal and state government agencies from large-scale agricultural production. In 1987, the Commodity Boards and the Nigerian National Supply Company were abolished. The government also committed itself to the commercialisation of fertiliser procurement and distribution. In 1988, a privatisation programme involving 135 enterprises was announced by the federal government. Sixty-seven enterprises were to be fully privatised, including hotels, textiles, food, timber companies, breweries, dairies, and insurance. Twenty-one enterprises were to be partially privatised, including development banks, fertiliser, paper, sugar, cement, oil marketing, and steel rolling, together with Nigeria Airways and the National Shipping Line. By the end of 1990, some fifty companies had been sold. Eleven parastatals were to be fully commercialised. They included the Nigerian National Petroleum Corporation (NNPC), Nigerian Telecommunications, and the National Insurance Company. In 1989, the NNPC created ten financially autonomous subsidiaries and sold part of its shareholding in an oil production joint venture for over $2 billion. Fourteen enterprises were to be partially commercialised. These included the Nigerian Railway Corporation, the National Electric Power Authority, and the two major steel operations. Privatisation was also pursued by state governments, but here the strength of state interests tended to preclude full privatisation, and some new state projects were launched.

Conclusion

I have examined the introduction of the reforms, their scope, the nature and extent of the opposition to them, and some of the short- and medium-term consequences. After a brief summary, I will consider some of the political implications and longer-term issues raised by the reform strategy.

The results of the reforms were very mixed. Although foreign exchange reserves had increased by the end of 1990, the exchange rate had not gained greater stability after a long period of devaluation, and the long-term external debt had steadily increased. For industry, confronted with many changes at once, the main adjustment was on the import side with the abolition of import licences and steep falls in import volume. Some industries developed local substitutes for imports and increased the use of local raw materials and inputs. On the export side, the response was slow after many years with an overvalued currency. The reforms have not reduced dependence on oil significantly. In general, the reforms were favourable to the rural economy. Above all, they do not appear to have checked the decline in living standards, especially in urban areas where the provision of services and health care declined.

The economic strategy raises questions about political support and control. In Chapter 6, it was argued that the forces behind the reforms and those behind the return to civil rule were distinct and contradictory. We have seen how during the period of political transition strong opposition to the reforms forced the government to suppress debate. In addition, once the transfer to civil rule had begun, the government started to tolerate higher levels of expenditure to accommodate political pressures and ease the transition.

It may be argued that the economic reforms could contribute to changes in the pattern of political incentives under civil rule. By restricting the scope of state activity in the economy and increasing public accountability, the reforms may reduce the opportunities for the acquisition of wealth based on corruption and privileged access to the state. They may also enhance the power of specifically capitalist interests through the promotion of the market. But these effects are likely to have a very minor impact on the thrust of political activity or the political agenda. Overall, civil rule is likely to increase pressures for state expenditure and enhance the importance of state patronage and political connection in the conduct of business. It should be recalled that the reforms did not derive from political pressures exerted by a domestic class of capital that wished to set limits to the extent of state involvement in the economy and restrict corruption because it held them to be obstacles to corporate and national accumulation. Such a shift in the balance of economic and political power has not taken place. The economic reforms were introduced by a military government under external pressure.

The argument is not that civil rule would lead to the wholesale reversal of policies pursued under the SAP, though there are likely to be pressures for intervention in the foreign exchange market, in agricultural marketing, and public sector tariffs. With a large external debt and the increased influence of international finance capital, there would be less room for manoeuvre than in the Second Republic. Yet immediate expenditure pressures are likely to arise from demands for social justice, from the increased cost of government under civil rule, and from distributive pressures to extend state commitments. How might these pressures be reconciled with the demands of economic management? One response would be an attempt to accommodate these forces and retain support through a more nationalist and populist strategy that involved an extension of state expenditure, deficit financing, protection, and greater state intervention in domestic markets. Another response would be to try to confront and contain these pressures through fiscal discipline and maintain the direction set by the economic reforms. Here the wider dispersion of power and political competition under civil rule may prove to be incompatible with the need for economic control and central political authority. How these contradictions and tensions are resolved through political struggles will affect the future of the reforms.

The reforms highlight contradictions between international capital and national interests. The emphasis on foreign finance and investment in the Structural Adjustment Programme runs counter to a viable path of national accumulation. The policies that are pursued under the SAP are likely to result in increased external debt and increased dependence on flows of foreign finance. According to the beguiling argument of the IMF and World Bank, the SAP is a medium-term strategy aimed at growth and balance-of-payments equilibrium. This assumes speedy adjustment in the appropriate direction. Yet the capital account will not be in equilibrium. There will be negative net transfers to service the debt and an outflow of payments to foreign investors.[38] To finance the outflow of capital, there will be constant pressure to achieve a surplus on trade account, to take fresh loans, and to encourage foreign investment. These pressures will make the achievement of a strategy that takes account of the domestic market and domestic need extremely difficult, for such policies will be resisted by international capital, which places a priority on the servicing of the debt, access to the Nigerian market, and the realisation of profits in a convertible foreign currency.

A further potential source of conflict involves the reduced role of the state and the challenge to industrialisation policy. For example, pressure was exerted by international agencies to reduce the scale of or to abandon the steel and aluminium projects. In the case of the privatisation programme, a revival of the fiscal strength of the state would test the resolve of bureaucrats and state managers. It was the weakness of state finances combined with externally imposed policy conditionalities that ushered in the programme. Sectional and state interests have resisted it and set limits to its scope by initiating new state projects.

Efforts have been made to create conditions more favourable to foreign capital through the relaxation of the indigenisation decree and the streamlining investment procedures. In the longer term, such policies could be reversed by calls for tighter controls over foreign capital.

Another question raised by the reforms, though not directly addressed by them, concerns the overall fiscal character of the state and its dependence on oil revenues. The rich slip through the tax net, and tax collection is ineffective. Since the decline of oil revenues, there is little evidence that the federal or state governments have succeeded in raising the share of non-oil revenues. At the federal level, the improvement appears to be very marginal.[39] Dependence on oil and the top-down distribution of "external" revenue remains acute. At the state level, special levies do not appear to have been successful in reducing the importance of federal transfers. The launching of semiofficial appeal funds in many states for industry, education, and other purposes was really an admission of the failure of income tax collection. "Government by donation," as the appeals came to be known, became widespread in 1986 and 1987. On these occasions, owners of big businesses were invited to make donations in cash and kind. Some of the wealth obtained from the state in the past was then recycled and a claim made on more government patronage in the future.

Finally, the reforms need to be placed in a longer-term perspective. At the time of independence, the organised private sector was identified with foreign enterprise. Indigenous enterprises were small in scale, and businesspeople, as distinct from the older commercial classes, enjoyed little public recognition. Employment in the private sector was ranked below government service and the professions in terms of security, status, and monetary rewards. During the 1970s, there was a shift of material incentives in favour of the private sector, and many responded by leaving public employment. The indigenous private sector also grew in size and in the scope of its activities. National business associations emerged, and greater recognition was given to the business class in the media. A gradual shift in attitudes towards the public sector and private business was underway. With the introduction of the Structural Adjustment Programme, which stirred up debate over economic strategy and led to some realignment of domestic interests, a more marked ideological shift became apparent. It remains to be seen if such private interests have the organisation and political weight to sharpen economic debate and influence economic management and the direction of policy or whether a political economy of distributive patronage will again be dominant.

Notes

1. On the counterrevolution in development economics, see J. Toye, *Dilemmas of Development* (Oxford: Basil Blackwell, 1987).

2. Y. Bangura, "IMF/World Bank Conditionality and Nigeria's Structural Adjustment Programme," paper presented at seminar on the IMF and the World Bank in Africa, Scandinavian Institute of African Studies, Upsalla, 27–29 January 1987, p. 6.

3. (i) "Restructuring of Nigeria's Industrial Sector," Research Department, National Institute for Policy and Strategic Studies, Kuru, 1986.

(ii) Study Group on Industrial Policy under the chairmanship of Chief C. O. Ogunbanjo. See *Nigerian Economic Review*, no. 1, (Lagos: John West, 1986), pp. 33–36.

4. P. Smith, "Nigeria and the IMF," *West Africa*, 9 September 1985.

5. *Financial Times*, 28 August 1985.

6. *Nigerian Newsletter*, no. 175, 19 October 1985.

7. *Nigerian Newsletter*, no. 175, 19 October 1985; *National Concord*, 29 October 1985.

8. Bangura, "IMF/World Bank Conditionality," p. 14.

9. "Reality Takes a Back Seat," *West Africa*, 2 April 1984; *Daily Times*, 18 September 1985.

10. *National Concord*, 27 September 1985.

11. *Guardian* (Lagos), 18 June 1985.

12. *Industry News* 4/5 (September–October), 1985.

13. *Sunday Tribune*, 22 September 1985.

14. Bangura, "IMF/World Bank Conditionality," p. 14.

15. *Daily Times*, 26 September 1985.

16. *Nigerian Newsletter*, no. 176, 3 November 1985.

17. "Strategy for Reviving the Nigerian Economy," mimeo, Nigerian Association of Chambers of Commerce, Industry, Mines, and Agriculture, October 1985.

18. *National Concord*, 6 and 7 March 1985; *Nigerian Tribune*, 1 August 1985; *Punch*, 21 October 1985; *Business Times*, 5 August 1985.

19. *Guardian* (Lagos), 13 October 1985.

20. *Guardian* (Lagos), 13 October 1985.

21. "IMF Negotiation So Far," Cabinet Office Publication, *Sunday Times*, 29 September 1985; "Presidential Committee on the IMF Loan, Press Statement," *Guardian* (Lagos), 5 October 1985.

22. *Daily Times*, 1 October 1985.

23. *Financial Punch*, 20 March 1985. Before he left Nigeria, Husain published a book containing his lectures. See *Perspectives on the Nigerian Economy* (Lagos: Nigerian Institute of International Affairs, 1987).

24. *Business Concord*, 3 June 1986.

25. *Annual Report*, Central Bank of Nigeria, 1988.

26. *Financial Times*, 7 March 1988.

27. A. O. Olukoshi and I. Aremu, "Structural Adjustment and Labour Subordination in Nigeria: The Dissolution of the Nigerian Labour Congress Revisited," *Review of African Political Economy* 43 (1988), pp. 107–108.

28. Y. Bangura, "Crisis and Adjustment: The Experience of Nigerian Workers," in B. Onimode, ed., *The IMF, The World Bank and the African Debt*, vol. 2 (London: Zed Books, 1989), pp. 187–188.

29. *Guardian* (Lagos), 9 March 1988.

30. Molara Ogundipe-Leslie, contribution to Institute of African Alternatives Conference, London, 1987.

31. *Labour Force Survey*, Federal Office of Statistics. Cited in P. Collier, "Oil Shocks and Food Security in Nigeria," *International Labour Review* 127/6 (1988), p. 778.

32. Collier, "Oil Shocks," p. 779.

33. *Guardian* (Lagos), 1 May 1987; *Newswatch*, 2 March 1987; *African Concord*, 5 March 1987.

34. Bangura, "Crisis and Adjustment," p. 177.

35. Bangura, "Crisis and Adjustment," p. 186.

36. B. Onimode, "Privatisation of Public Enterprises," paper prepared for conference on Economic Crisis, Austerity Measures, and Privatisation in Africa, Ahmadu Bello University, Zaria, March 1985.

37. Bangura, "IMF/World Bank Conditionality," p. 20.

38. A capital outflow of more than $14 billion since 1985 has been estimated. *Financial Times*, 12 March 1991.

39. In 1986, the National Economic Recovery Fund raised over N2 billion. This revenue, together with loan recoveries, temporarily raised the share of non-oil revenues in total federal revenue from about 25 percent to 34 percent. *Annual Report*, Central Bank of Nigeria, 1988, p. 84.

PART FOUR

Politics and Economic Development

11

The Failure of the Political Transition and the Demise of the Structural Adjustment Programme: Problems and Prospects

After a brief introduction, this concluding chapter addresses first the complete failure of the political transition and the persistence of military rule. It then turns to economic management and the demise of the Structural Adjustment Programme. A concluding section addresses problems underlying the intensification of the economic and political crises and examines the prospects for change.

In Chapter 6, I suggested that the Babangida regime would be judged by the outcome of the attempt to create a more democratic form of government and by the success of the economic programme. The regime failed badly on both counts. The transition to civil rule never took place: The regime ended with a brief period of dyarchy, followed by full military rule. The economy continued to decline under the regime's gross mismanagement, and living standards fell for the vast majority of people. By comparison, the earlier transition of 1977–1979, under the Obasanjo regime, appears purposeful and exemplary in the pursuit and attainment of its economic and political objectives.

The final years of the Babangida regime were marked by gross manipulation of the transition process. There was a series of unpredictable interventions, rule changes, and postponements, which stretched the life of the regime to eight years and tried the patience of Nigerians to the breaking point. Constant interference in the political process gave rise to acute political uncertainty and raised fears about the future of the country. Among the most spectacular interventions were the disqualification of many of the most capable political candidates; the rejection in October 1989 of all political parties that had been formed, including six shortlisted by the Nigerian Electoral Commission (NEC); and the lifting of the ban on former politicians in 1991. Nothing could prepare Nigerians, however, for the annulment of the 1993 presidential elections, which were fairly conducted and convincingly won by Chief M.K.O. Abiola. Democratic yearnings were alternately inflamed and then dashed to pieces, causing great tension, anger, and despair. The fact that a Yoruba candidate was denied the presidency by a group of northern military officers after a fair election threatened the unity of the country and threw it into the most profound political crisis since 1966. The action appeared to confirm the view that no Yoruba could be elected president.

As if this were not enough, there emanated from the presidency a moral malaise. Equivocation, prevarication, and sudden changes in policy were presented as principled acts, thereby debasing language and authority. A culture of "settlement," or monetary gratification, ate into the social fabric, spreading cynicism, rewarding sycophancy, and condoning corruption. In the end, virtually all claims to leadership, trust, and moral authority were forfeited. Eventually, the president was eased out of office by fellow officers after he attempted to perpetuate his rule through a system of joint military and civil rule.

In the realm of economic management, the regime finally proved itself incompetent. Basic fiscal and monetary discipline were undermined by large federal deficits that were financed by credit from the Central Bank. In addition, the key issues of the petrol price subsidy, the lack of accountability in federal finances, and the growth of the external debt were not addressed. Unlike the Obasanjo regime, Babangida made no discernible effort to leave sound government finances for an incoming civilian regime. The magnitude of the basic responsibilities involved in the management of a large economy towards the end of the twentieth century quite escaped the Babangida regime, with damaging consequences for political and social life.

The Failure of the Political Transition

The two political parties created by the military in 1989 after the rejection of existing parties, the Social Democratic Party (SDP) and the National Republican Convention (NRC), were weak and wracked by factionalism. Both parties lacked strong leadership and organisation, resulting from the manner in which they were created and an attempt to ensure that no powerful politicians emerged. There was little ideological difference between the parties, the NRC leaning to the right and the SDP tending to the left. The SDP drew supporters from the People's Front, led by retired Major-General Shehu Yar'Adua; from the People's Solidarity Party, with strength in the south-west; and from the Middle Belt. The NRC's strength lay in the far north, and it attracted former members of the NPN. In terms of support, the parties were fairly evenly matched.

The SDP won majorities in most state assemblies and, after July 1992, in both houses of the National Assembly. The NRC emerged with more governors than the SDP. After the failure and cancellation of the first presidential primaries in August and October 1992, twenty-three candidates from both parties were barred from standing on grounds of bribery and corruption. The date for a return to civil rule was shifted back to August 1993. The electoral rules were changed in favour of a knockout contest among the presidential candidates, starting at the ward level and progressing upwards with final decisions made at the national party conventions.

In an attempt to shore up the credibility of the regime after the delays and rule changes, a civilian Transitional Council was formed in early 1993 with a civilian chairman, Chief Ernest Shonekan. Shonekan, former chief executive and chairman of the United Africa Company, was a staunch supporter of the SAP. The Transitional Council was given an impossible timetable of five months to bring some semblance of order to the economy. At the same time, key legislative powers, like budget and security, were removed from the National Assembly to the presidency, which was already exercising some influence over the Central Bank and the NNPC. The Armed Forces Ruling Council was replaced by a National Defence and Security Council and filled with officers loyal to the president.

1993 Presidential Elections

Two wealthy businessmen, Alhaji Bashir Tofa, 46, and Chief M.K.O. Abiola, 56, emerged as candidates for the NRC and SDP respectively. Far from being "new breed" politicians, both had been prominent members of the discredited NPN and both were friends of the president. Tofa was a weak candidate. Though he was born in Kano state, his family was from Borno and he was not widely known in Kano. He had returned to Nigeria from studies abroad in 1976 and had traded crude oil. His appeal was tarnished by the fact that he was widely perceived as Babangiba's preferred candidate. His opponents highlighted the fact that he had written a newspaper article in 1990, arguing that the military should stay on until 2000.[1] In his campaign, he avoided issues of economic policy and through silence condoned the SAP. His running mate, Sylvester Ugoh, an Igbo, was a respected economist and former governor of the Central Bank of Biafra.

Chief Abiola was an altogether more substantial and well-known figure. He was formerly a vice-president of International Telephone and Telegraph (ITT) for Africa and the Middle East.[2] Since the late 1960s, he had developed links with the military, beginning when he succeeded in collecting debts owed to ITT by the military; he later secured lucrative contracts for ITT and his own telecommunications company from military governments. Abiola's running mate was Babagana Kingibe, a Muslim from the north-east. Abiola selected Kingibe, a former diplomat, member of the People's Front, and chairman of the SDP, because he had a significant following of his own among the SDP governors. Abiola's position, though short on policy specifics, drew on social democratic and free market policies with an emphasis on the eradication of poverty.[3] Through his *Concord* newspaper, he attacked SAP and the deployment of Nigerian troops in Liberia.

Observers agreed that the election was very well conducted. The SDP won nineteen out of thirty states, including Kaduna and Kano with the support of former governors Balarabe Musa and Abubakar Rimi and three states in the south-east. The NRC suffered from high abstention rates in the northern states where well-known candidates like Adamu Ciroma, Umaru Shinkafi, Shehu Yar'Adua, and Bamanga Tukur had earlier been barred from contesting.[4] In Kano, only 12.5 percent voted. The SDP captured 58 percent of the overall vote with substantial support in all regions. Only 36 percent of the SDP vote came from Yorubaland. The nationwide spread of support for Abiola was far greater than that achieved by Chief Obafemi Awolowo, the Yoruba politician who had for years tried and failed to gain significant support outside Yorubaland. This shift away from political support based on ethnic constituencies was remarkable and was widely seen as a step towards a more national political consciousness. Religious allegiances played little part and the double Muslim ticket of Abiola and Kingibe secured strong support in Christian areas. These positive features of the election only served to heighten the feeling of betrayal and despair following the annulment.

Abiola's victory can be partly explained by the fact that he was already widely known and popular for his philanthropy.[5] Reservations about the way in which Abiola's candidacy emerged through the disqualification of others and the shadow cast by his reliance on military contracts to accumulate wealth counted for little. He had assiduously courted various constituencies, including the military.[6] He put a great deal of effort into his campaign. His opponent, in contrast, was virtually unknown. Most importantly, a vote for Abiola was a vote for change, and he drew strength from the unpopularity of Babangida, who was perceived to support the NRC.

According to retired General Olusegun Obasanjo, Babangida acted virtually alone in cancelling the election but was able to cultivate the support of substantial numbers of senior military officers for his action.[7] The seeds of Chief Abiola's unacceptability to some northern military officers lay in a number of factors. As a southern Yoruba candidate, Abiola threatened to bring about a shift in power away from dominant northern interests. There was also the probability that the military under civil rule would suffer a sharp reduction in its power and privileges. There were strong doubts, too, whether the corrupt practices of the military, and other skeletons in the cupboard of the regime, would have remained undisturbed in the euphoria of a regime change. In short, Abiola was too strong, independent, and unpredictable for the kind of managed transition Babangida and his supporters had in mind. They wanted to retain their power through some form of dyarchy with compliant civilian elements.

Prior to the election, the Association for a Better Nigeria (ABN), led by Chief Francis Arthur Nzeribe,[8] had campaigned for the military to stay on in power in violation of the transition programme and had attempted to get the 12 June election suspended. The ABN was an unregistered organisation and was widely perceived as a front for the president. Initially, the NEC ignored a court injunction aimed at preventing the elections. But the ABN later succeeded in getting the declaration of the election results suspended halfway (but not before the overall result had leaked out), through a second court injunction from the Abuja High Court that the NEC accepted. Such interference in the electoral process could only have been initiated with the prompting, support, and encouragement of the president. General Obasanjo tried to get the labour unions out in protest, but the Nigeria Labour Congress had been emasculated as an independent force.[9] The leadership, which was sympathetic to the president, refused to act. The way was then open for the elections to be annulled on 23 June, on the totally unconvincing grounds that the reputation of the judiciary needed to be protected.

Babangida then began to pressurise the parties and National Assembly members, oscillating between the idea of fresh elections and the appointment of an interim government. If there were no elections, he threatened to dissolve the parties and all elected bodies and appoint an interim administration. He was able to play on divisions between the NRC and SDP and exploit north-south divisions. Chinua Achebe was forthright in his condemnation: "What we can and do hold against him is a willingness to play on our deep divisions more flagrantly than any other leaders we have had."[10]

Neither party took a strong democratic stand. As Peter Lewis argued, the absence of strong countervailing pressures from a divided and weak civil society and an easily co-opted, or manipulated, political elite that was divorced from any base of popular support allowed the military to set the political agenda.[11] Babangida dangled the prospect of gaining power in a second round of elections in front of the NRC, while threatening to dissolve the SDP if it stood by its decision to boycott fresh elections. Yoruba support for Abiola remained strong, and this precluded fresh credible elections in the south-west of the country. Divisions within the SDP became more serious, the national leadership distancing itself from Abiola as the faction led by Shehu Yar'Adua increased its power over party structures. Key members of both parties in the House of Representatives and the Senate received favours from the presidency as incentives to persuade their colleagues to maintain support.[12]

The most effective opposition to the annulment of the elections came not from the parties but from extra-parliamentary opposition groups that originated in Lagos, though they had wider support. They included the Campaign for Democracy (CD), a coalition of forty-two human rights organisations;[13] the June 12 Movement; and the Association for Democracy and Good Governance in Nigeria (ADGN). They insisted on the installation of Abiola as president. The CD called for a one-week demonstration beginning 5 July. Three days of anti-government protest paralysed economic activity in the western states and led to the deaths of between 30 and 100 people. Fears for personal safety triggered a movement of Igbo populations from Lagos to their home areas. Despite a strong clamp-down on the press and the detention of pro-democracy supporters by the security services, these organisations were able to maintain a vocal opposition to the government and played a key role in sealing Babangida's demise. A series of reasoned attacks by retired General Obasanjo damaged what was left of the regime's credibility.

International reaction to the annulment was very negative. Nigeria's image abroad continued to decline and its claims to leadership on the continent were undermined at a time when the credentials of South Africa rose dramatically. There was little prospect of the emergence of a South African–Nigerian axis when Nigeria was enfeebled by acute domestic political problems and economic decline. Yet the signals given by the major powers to Nigeria's rulers were weak and mixed. Nigeria suffered a few minor punitive measures. The United States suspended aid programmes. Later, the United States suspended direct air links with Nigeria because of the security situation at the Lagos airport and declared Nigeria a major drug-trafficking country.[14] Britain suspended visas for military officers and ended military training programmes; but it continued to sell Vickers tanks to the military and maintained its small aid programme. Japan, which gave aid worth $830 million in 1992/93, suspended aid in 1994.[15] If Nigeria had been the recipient of a major aid programme, there is little doubt that leverage for a more democratic government would have been applied. A move to prevent oil sales by Nigeria would have been far more difficult to organise and was not seriously considered.

At the beginning of August, Chief Abiola went abroad to drum up international support in the United States and Britain on a trip that was to last fifty-four days. Tactically, this was an error and his attacks on the regime from abroad resulted in a loss of support at home. Abiola never became an effective opposition leader and seemed not to know how to mobilise popular support. He had to be persuaded to leave America and come to London to address a rally of his supporters.[16] Apparently, he still expected to get power through his military connections and spent much time lobbying generals and traditional rulers. Strategies that had helped him advance his political and business careers proved liabilities when he was in opposition.

Within the military, support for Babangida began to erode after the 12 June fiasco and the blatant manipulation of the political process. A number of military officers were reported to have resigned their commissions in protest over the cancellation of the elections.[17] Among them was Colonel Abubakar Umar, son of the Emir of Birnin Kebbi and former military governor of Kaduna state. Service chiefs and field commanders insisted that the military hand over power on 27 August and keep existing elected bodies.

A proposal for an Interim National Government (ING) with representatives of both parties to replace the Transitional Council finally gained acceptance among politicians and the military as a way out of the morass. This allowed for the removal of Babangida, who left office on 26 August, and the continuation of the military in power. Existing elected bodies would stay and the National Assembly would get back its powers. Ernest Shonekan, the chairman of the Transitional Council, became chairman of the ING and commander-in-chief of the Armed Forces. The sole military representative to the interim government was General Sani Abacha as defence secretary. General Abacha from Kano, who was an important player in the coups of 1983 and 1985 and an ally of Babangida, had been promoted to chief of defence staff and chairman of the joint chiefs in 1990.

The ING solved none of the fundamental problems and was at best a temporary improvisation. Like the Transitional Council, it was a body suspended in a political vacuum without legitimacy or support for its policies. The ING never reached accommodation with Abiola supporters. The economy was given priority, with pledges to tackle corruption, close dedicated accounts, and reduce the petroleum price subsidy. A probe of the NNPC was initiated and in November a petrol price rise of 700 percent was announced. A court ruling declared the ING illegal because the relevant decree establishing it had not been properly signed. As strike action spread and the threat of action by junior officers mounted, General Abacha forced Shonekan to resign on 18 November after eighty-two days in office.[18]

The Abacha Government

General Abacha swiftly reached a settlement with the NLC by reducing the increase in the petrol price and created the Provisional Ruling Council and the Federal Executive Council of 33 ministers. All elected bodies and the two parties were dissolved and state governors dismissed, effectively ending the transition to civil rule. The Federal Executive Council consisted of a patchwork of individuals culled from a variety of sources and recycled from previous governments in an attempt to appease various constituencies and abide by the rudiments of federal character. Only in the military was there a clear pattern of renewal, as supporters of Babangida were retired and young officers were brought in as state governors. The appointment of General Oladipo Diya, a Yoruba, as chief of defence staff was aimed at restoring a semblance of non-partisanship to the military.

The civil appointments indicated the absence of any particular strategic resolve and showed how easily the military could co-opt and manipulate members of the political class. Former ministers, governors (Lateef Jakande, Soloman Lar, Samuel Ogbemudia, and Abubakar Rimi), and pro-democracy activists were brought in and some technocrats retained. Babagana Kingibe, Abiola's running mate, was appointed foreign minister. Dr Olu Onagoruwa, secretary of the National Movement for Reformation and long-time critic of the Babangida regime, became attorney general. Kalu Idiku Kalu, a former finance minister with sound money views and a free-market philosophy, regained his position in order to please the IMF and the World Bank.

No date was announced for a handover of power to civilians, though a return to party politics was promised for 1995. After much delay, the regime eventually set up a national constitutional conference in an attempt to give legitimacy to the idea of another transition. The mandate of this body was heavily circumscribed. It came nowhere near meeting the demands of those who had called for a sovereign national conference that would discuss the basis and structure of national unity. Calls for a national conference had first come to the fore in the wake of the 1990 coup attempt, when they were pressed by a group of nationalists led by Philip Asiodu and then by the National Consultative Forum headed by Alao Aka-Bashorun and Beko Ransome-Kuti. Among the 90 members out of 360 who were nominated by the federal government were key supporter's and members from the ruling party of the Second Republic, the NPN. They included Umaru Dikko, former NPN patron and boss of the Rice Task Force; Sunday Adewusi, former police commissioner; and Uba Ahmed, party secretary. Umaru Dikko, who had been in exile in London following the 1983 military coup and a failed attempt to smuggle him back to Nigeria to face corruption charges, thus completed the kind of spectacular rehabilitation so common in Nigerian politics.

In May, opposition groups formed the National Democratic Coalition (NADECO), which called for a boycott of the constitutional conference, the return of elected persons, and the installation of Abiola as president. These actions were in response to the fact that Abiola lacked a political organisation. NADECO, though primarily based in the southern states, received support from some prominent northern figures, including the former federal permanent secretary, Ahmed Joda; retired Lt-General T. Y. Danjuma; and former governors Jonah Jang and retired Air Commodore Dan Suleiman. The government responded by arrests and a clampdown on the press. On the eve of the 12 June anniversary, Abiola declared himself president and promply went into hiding without announcing a cabinet. He was later arrested and charged with treason.

Support for Abiola came from the trade unions in the oil industry, the National Union of Petroleum and National Gas Workers (NUPENG) and the Petroleum and Natural Gas Senior Staff Asoociation (PENGASSAN), which unilaterally started strike action early in July. By mid-August, crude oil production had been cut by 20 percent and fuel distribution severely disrupted. The umbrella trade union body, the NLC, whose leadership had been emasculated by the Babangida government, was far less effective. It suspended or delayed general strike action three times. The government responded by dismissing the executives of the NLC and its two affiliates in the oil sector and appointing new administrators. The strike was called off after nine weeks. Later, the government detained the leading officials of the oil unions, Frank Kokori and Wariebi Agamene, and announced that they were to be tried for financial misappropriation.

In August, the government began to take a harder line, ruling out hope of dialogue and compromise with the opposition. There were signs of a coordinated campaign of intimidation, including violent attacks on the residences of opposition leaders.[19] NADECO officials were arrested. Moderate military officers, who wanted a more restricted, professional role for the military, were replaced and board members of all public companies dismissed. Further measures included a decree banning legal challenges to government actions, an extension of the period of detention without trial, and the proscription of three southern-based newspapers, including the *Guardian*, the most influential and respected independent newspaper. In March 1995, an alleged coup plot led to the detention or house arrest of retired General Olusegan Obasanjo, retired Major-General Shehu Yar'Adua, and a number of serving officers. Pressures for an early return to civil rule within the Assembly were rebuffed by the military, opening the way to an indefinite period of transition under military rule.

The Demise of the SAP

The Structural Adjustment Programme was comprehensively undermined after 1990 by a failure to control expenditures in the face of a surge in oil revenues and by political pressures emanating from the transition programme and the general unpopularity of the reform programme. Large increases in government expenditure were financed by borrowing from the Central Bank, resulting in rapid inflation and sustained depreciation of the naira (see Table 7.2). Central Bank credit to the government sector rose by a staggering 529 percent between December 1991 and December 1993.[20] The naira suffered a real depreciation of 76 percent between 1986 and 1993 (see Table 10.1). The commitment to economic reform and leadership, which was never strongly entrenched, faded away. Even where there was a political will, the underlying lack of governmental legitimacy and the decline in the authority of the state made the pursuit of particular measures like the removal of the fuel price and fertiliser subsidies, which involved immediate economic sacrifices, much more difficult to undertake.

The effects of the economic reforms, which began in 1986, were evident initially in higher overall growth of GDP at 4.7 percent between 1986 and 1992.[21] Manufactures grew at 4.9 percent before tailing off; industrial output fell by a quarter between 1991 and 1994.[22] Small initial gains in official exports of manufactured goods were not sustained. Manufactured exports were worth only $40 million in 1994, under half their 1991 level.[23] Total agricultural output was estimated to rise by 3.8 percent a year over the same period, responding to liberalisation of trade and markets. The fastest area of growth was the service sector at 6.3 percent a year; finance, which grew at 23.3 percent in response to deregulation, led the way.[24]

There was no consistent improvement in the external balance, which at first strengthened and then declined sharply after 1990. External debt rose from $23.4 billion to $30.9 billion at the end of 1992 (see Table 7.5). With the failure to reach agreement with international creditors in 1992, debt was not rescheduled. Arrears of interest and principal on foreign debt exceeded $8 billion by 1995.[25] Thus, the country has sunk deeper into a debt trap.

The economic reform programme failed to act as a magnet for fresh foreign investment. The positive factors of a large domestic market, low wages, and natural resources were more than offset by persistently weak economic management, monetary instability, and low endogenous growth. There was evidence of divestment by European, American, and Japanese companies. A study of 46 firms with Japanese equity that invested in Nigeria between 1964 and 1991 showed that 4 divestments occurred between 1980 and 1985 and 13 divestments between 1986 and 1992.[26] This suggests that devaluation of the naira, which accelerated after 1986, encouraged divestment. The negative international image of Nigeria also played a part in discouraging foreign investors.[27] In a credit-risk rating published in the *Economist* in 1994, Nigeria was ranked third in the world with 75 percent, after Iraq and Russia.[28] A contributory factor was the persistent adverse publicity given to the involvement of Nigerians in attempts, sometimes successful, at international financial fraud, popularly known as "419" activity after a section of the colonial penal code.

There was stagnation or, at best, very modest improvements in health and education indicators. Cuts in health expenditures were dramatic; federal health expenditures in 1990 were about 40 percent of their value in 1981.[29] Life expectancy edged only marginally upwards in the 1980s to stand at 52 years in 1992.[30] Infant mortality improved slightly to 97 deaths per 1,000 live births in 1992. Adult illiteracy rates fell during the 1980s and then suffered a reversal. Primary and secondary school enrollment both fell sharply during the 1980s, reversing the gains associated with the universal primary education programme.[31]

We now examine four critical issues in the political economy of economic reform in Nigeria, all of which reflect low state capacities and have negative consequences for economic growth: (1) the instability of economic policy; (2) the weakness of elementary macro-economic management and regulation; (3) the presence of an inefficient and unproductive public sector that has been heavily subsidised by oil revenues; and (4) problems in the strategic oil industry, where the lack of accountability and poor performance of the NNPC, the hostility of communities in the oil-producing areas to the activities of the oil companies, and problems associated with the low price of domestic fuel have all posed serious threats to the viability of the industry.

The Instability of Economic Policy

Economic policy in Nigeria has suffered from instability and inconsistency, with no clear sense of economic strategy. These problems have eroded credibility and adversely affected investor confidence. With the demise of the SAP, two conflicting positions emerged. On the one side were those who favoured market-based reform, budgetary discipline, and attractive conditions for foreign investment. They were most clearly represented by the Economic Summit Group, which led a concerted effort by the private sector to influence policy. On the other side were those who favoured greater state regulation and control and appealed to nationalist and populist sentiments. These contending forces can be seen at work in policy shifts exemplified in the 1994 and 1995 budgets and in controversy that erupted over government plans to retake a controlling interest in four major commercial banks, which had been privatised in 1993/94.

The Economic Summit Group, a broad, private-sector coalition, transcended sectoral interests and largely superseded the Manufacturers Association of Nigeria and the Chamber of Commerce movement as the main forum for dialogue with the government. Its origin can be traced back to conferences in Nairobi (1986) and Abuja (1989) and the founding of the Enabling Environment Forum in 1990.[32] The Group aimed to evolve a common position on economic policy, developing a more consensual approach that would overcome the inconsistency and instability of economic policy.

The Economic Summit Group first came to prominence in 1993 through a failed attempt to put the reform programme back on course under the short-lived Transitional Council. This episode was insutructive, for it showed that the business community and technocrats could deliver, on paper, a long-term, market-oriented strategy with a detailed economic agenda for immediate action.[33] The problem was that they were operating in a political vacuum: Military leaders gave rhetorical support but had a conflicting political agenda. Rather than co-opting the business community, the military simply ignored its views.[34]

After General Sani Abacha came to power, the 1994 budget deliberately reversed some central policies of the reform programme and introduced a fixed exchange rate. The sound money, free-market views of Finance Minister Kalu Idiku Kalu and Paul Ogwuma, the Central Bank governor, lost out to more populist, interventionist views. The result was a return to foreign exchange regulation and centralisation through the Central Bank. The naira was revalued and pegged at $1 to N22.0. Ironically, the move came very soon after the announcement of a devaluation by one-half of the CFA franc against the French franc, the first parity change since 1948. The combined effect of the two measures was to temporarily reduce official Nigerian exports to West African countries from an already low base to a paltry level. Other measures included a reduction in the interest rate, withdrawal of export incentives, greater industrial protection, and a ban on some imports. The budget succeeded only in encouraging economic rent-seeking behaviour, in pushing goods into the parallel market, and in increasing the gains from currency round-tripping for those able to get foreign currency at the official rate. Middlemen intervened and charged large sums for access to foreign exchange at the official rate.

It is possible to discern a very loose coalition of interests and economic opinions behind the reversal of economic policy. Northern sponsors of

Abacha, including military officers, traders, bureaucrats, and a few emirs, who support government patronage and regulation, joined forces with former Action Group and UPN welfarists and regulators, who thrive on a populist nationalism. The latter were brought in to appease vociferous Yoruba critics of the annulment. They included Lateef Jakande, Housing and Works minister, who was the governor of Lagos state during the Second Republic. He chaired a ten-man economic committee set up in the federal executive council. Another prominent figure was Sam Aluko, long-time populist Action Group economist and fierce critic of IMF/World Bank orthodoxies in Africa, who was appointed chairman of the National Economic Intelligence Committee, a panel set up to monitor the budget. Important northern supporters of economic regulation included Aminu Saleh, secretary to the federal government and former permanent secretary at the ministry of defence, and Abubakar Rimi, former governor of Kano state. This coalition of interests could never gain any lasting ascendancy and the 1995 budget saw a partial retreat to more market-oriented policies. This retreat owed more to the patent failure of the 1994 budget measures than to any positive conviction as to the merits of deregulation.

The 1995 budget partially liberalised the foreign exchange system, creating an autonomous market. However, the official exchange rate (N22 to $1) was maintained for government transactions. The budget scrapped the Nigerian Enterprises Promotion Decreee of 1989, which had constrained foreign investment by restricting foreign shareholding in existing Nigerian companies to between 40 and 60 percent. It was to be replaced by the Nigeria Investment Promotion Council, a body controlled by the private sector with a facilitating rather than a regulatory role. The budget also repealed the Exchange Control Act of 1962, thereby freeing the import and export of capital. However, privatisation was abandoned and the policy of commercialisation reaffirmed, together with the leasing of parastatals. Finally, dedicated accounts were to be closed and all oil revenues placed in a federal account at the Central Bank.

During 1995, the federal government declared its intention to reacquire control of the four largest commercial banks. This announcement provoked warnings from the World Bank and foreign governments that it could jeopardize future agreements with international creditors. The move was prompted by successful boardroom coups in which Nigerian entrepreneurs took control of the United Bank for Africa (UBA) after a proxy battle. In one view, this was creative, efficient capitalism of a kind that was anathema to northern vested interests in business, politics, and the army, who relied on state patronage.[35] These interests generally distrusted free enterprise and reliance on the market because they were thought to enhance the relative prosperity of areas in the south. In another, very widespread view, such business people were short-term adventurers solely interested in personal gain without any concern for building up an effective corporate enterprise. This populist, anti-capitalist sentiment could draw strength from great disparities in private wealth that were made all the more visible by the limited development of a middle class.

A further test of the government's political will and economic strategy was the outstanding question of whether distressed banks and associated finance houses would be allowed to go under. Many of these banks were speculative ventures, attracted by trading in foreign exchange, that had obtained licences through the political connections of powerful individuals in the military.

Fiscal Failures and Extra-Budgetary Spending

Figures for public expenditure and domestic credit creation show that macro-economic control began to break down in 1990. The money supply accelerated dramatically and the federal budget deficit as a percentage of GDP increased to over 9 percent by 1992.[36] Strong inflationary pressures were evident and a wide gap between official and parallel foreign exchange markets opened up. By September 1993, the parallel market rate stood at $1 to N68, three times the official rate. Inflation was estimated at nearly 70 percent.[37] The enormous gap between the annual budget statements and actual fiscal outcomes showed that there was no budgeting in the true sense of the term. Instead, there was a series of ad hoc, short-term responses, some outside the budget framework, to the fluctuations of oil revenues and expenditure pressures. It was in the area of macro-economic management and stabilisation, which was a precondition for structural reform in other areas, that a lack of commitment to the SAP became strikingly evident.

Among the factors that played a part in the loss of control and expansion of expenditure was the abortive coup attempt of April 1990, which shook the regime severely and brought a loss of confidence, coherence, and direction. It prompted costly, hasty political palliatives like the creation of nine new states and poorly-planned new local government areas. The expenditure surge was assisted by the Gulf War crisis which brought additional windfall revenues of about $5 billion from a 6 percent increase in production and a 31 percent increase in price.[38] For the third time in Nigeria's recent history, a revenue windfall had proved destabilising and controversial. A confidential World Bank report of November 1991 asserted that "public expenditures are used more to distribute oil revenues and generate lucrative business and employment opportunities for selected groups than to ensure efficient delivery of goods and services to the public at large."[39]

Symptomatic of the absence of budgetary control was the remarkable increase in federal revenues and expenditures that were outside the budget. Federal oil revenues were placed in various dedicated accounts and stabilisation funds. Thus, revenues that could have accrued to the Federation Account and could have been distributed through it were diverted to accounts in the Central Bank and the Nigerian National Petroleum Corporation. Both these institutions lost power to the presidency, the Central Bank having formally lost its autonomy in 1991.[40]

The extraordinary scale of spending from these sources is indicated by estimates that extra-budgetary spending increased from 4 percent of GDP (22 percent of total spending) in 1986 to 17 percent of GDP (65 percent of total spending) in 1992.[41] Some of these funds were used to finance public sector projects like steel, aluminium, and natural gas. Expenditure on the political transition programme increased with allocations of N1.7 billion to the National Electoral Commission over two years (1990–1991) and N200 million to the Directorate for Social Mobilisation (1990–1991).[42] Over the same period, the National Population Commission absorbed N835 million.[43] Other areas of expenditure included the new capital at Abuja and ECOWAS Ceasefire and Monitoring Group (ECOMOG) peacekeeping forces in Liberia.

The result of the absence of control and much wasteful expenditure was a weak and unstable currency and low reserves. The IMF withdrew its endorsement of economic policy in early 1992, thereby ruling out debt rescheduling and possible debt relief. Without rescheduling, interest payments on Nigeria's external debt would average around $5 billion a year, consuming 36 percent of total export revenue.[44] Since Nigeria is now officially classified as a heavily indebted low-income country, it is theoretically eligible for concessionary debt relief under enhanced Toronto or the more generous Trinidad terms.[45]

The Public Sector and Wasteful Investment

The overall impact of the economic reform programme on public enterprises was limited. The public sector continued to be dogged by the presence of large capital-intensive projects with high costs and low returns. For the Ajaokuta steel plant, capital expenditures were expected to be four times higher than those of new, competitive plants.[46] Costs for the aluminium plant smelter at Ikot Abasi were estimated by the World Bank to be 60 percent above those elsewhere.

Many of the problems identified by the Onosode report in 1984 persisted. Among these were a lack of clear priorities; uncoordinated, ad hoc financing through budget and non-budget channels; a lack of accountability; and an inherent tendency to start projects and not complete them.

The key parastatal body, the NNPC, had no published accounts. The much-delayed liquified natural gas project and the petrochemical projects were not included in the budget. In addition, neglect of operations and maintainence led to underperformance. This was especially evident in power generation and petroleum refining, where the problems lay not in the lack of existing capacity but in the ineffective use of plant and delivery of services. A further feature was the high turnover of senior executives and board members, as parastatals were subject to political interference and patronage that reflected wider power struggles and factional shifts. Frequent changes in management and policy prevented long-term planning and the buildup of a technocratic cadre that could learn from experience.

By March 1992, the privatisation programme had raised N1.6 billion from fifty-eight affected enterprises at the federal level.[47] This sum was relatively small and extensive state involvement in enterprises continued. There was fresh capital investment in steel, aluminium, fertilisers, machine tools, liquified natural gas, and sugar. Some larger enterprises, like the National Electric Power Authority and the Nigerian Railway Corporation, were largely unaffected. Commercialisation was slow, with many companies still in receipt of transfers from the federal government.

Crisis in the Oil Sector

It was noted above that the NNPC, the most important parastatal in the country, was not properly accountable. Other oil-producing countries like Venezuela, with a stronger sense of nationalism to underpin a proprietary attitude to natural resources, would never have tolerated such lack of financial transparency with its potential for corrupt leakages. Large revenues did not pass into the federal budget to be shared but were held in various dedicated accounts. Decisions affecting the size of these funds and their use were often taken in the presidency and not in the ministry of finance. Quite apart from the fact that this practice tended to undermine the system of federal revenue allocation, the lack of accountability created fertile ground for rumour and suspicion of financial irregularity. In early 1993, auditors were unable to trace funds of $1,000 million from the sale of equity in a joint venture company.[48] Later, the NNPC made unauthorised payments worth $64 million, ostensibly to fund a controversial project to store oil products in tankers anchored off Lagos to alleviate Nigeria's fuel shortages.[49] The funds were made available through a company involved in smuggling fuel; this company was also closely linked to the military regime.[50]

The NNPC suffered from underfunding and was starved for capital. It could not pay its share of oil production costs in joint-venture companies where it owned well over 50 percent of the equity. This led to arrears of some $800 million and to cutbacks in drilling and development programmes in the oil industry.[51]

There was increased resentment and hostility to the activities of oil companies and the policies of the federal government among groups and communities in the oil-production areas of the Niger Delta. Over the years, these groups have seen their relative share of oil revenues steadily reduced through the application of political power by the non–oil producing majority of the country.[52] This was a corollary of the more even distribution of oil revenues effected in the 1970s through the decline of the principle of derivation and the rise of the Federation Account, noted in Chapter 3. Disaffection and protests became more vocal after the failure of the Orkar coup attempt in 1990. As the legitimacy and authority of the state diminished, so the very right of the federal goverment to exploit resources in the Niger Delta was challenged. As a sop to local communities, the government set up the Oil Mineral Producing Areas Development Commission (OMPADEC) in 1992 with 3 percent of the revenues from the Federation Account and a mandate to provide infrastructure, jobs, education, and better environmental conditions.[53] This move was dismissed as mere tokenism by locals, and many observers thought the sums inadequate.[54] It is unclear how far OMPADEC has gained the trust of local communities and assuaged their feelings of bitterness and neglect.

The most strident voice was that of Ken Saro-Wiwa, author and leader of the Movement for the Survival of the Ogoni People (MOSOP), who succeeded in raising the plight of the Ogonis onto an international stage through extensive media coverage.[55] Communities in oil production areas felt that their resources were taken away and wasted or used elsewhere in ways that did not ultimately benefit them or the country as a whole. They were also aggrieved that they did not get a greater share of oil revenues. State creation did not solve this problem because smaller groups in new states often found themselves in a less advantageous position, dominated by their neighbours. Furthermore, they were victims of environmental degradation through oil spills and flaring of natural gas and were not given adequate compensation. MOSOP demanded that Shell Oil Company pay royalties directly to half a million Ogonis, beginning with $6 billion in back pay.[56] In the face of rising hostility, Shell withdrew from the area in mid-1993. A series of unprovoked attacks on Ogoni villages led to the loss of hundreds of lives.[57] The Nigerian government claimed that the attacks were the outcome of disputes between neighbouring communitites. However, the use of sophisticated weaponry, and the fact that all Ogoni police were removed from the area prior to the attacks, suggested the involvement of the military.[58]

The groundswell of opposition led to attacks on oil installations and disruption of oil supplies. Oil companies estimated that losses in production and equipment because of civil disruptions and protests against loss of land, pollution, and inadequate living conditions amounted to $200 million in 1993.[59] Shell Nigeria, which produced a half of Nigeria's quota of 1.8 million barrels per day (b/d), recorded 168 incidents affecting production, lost 1,400 project days, and deferred production of 14 million barrels of oil.[60] Half of Shell's 5,000 staff members were employed in security positions, at a cost of $18 million a year.

A third unresolved problem, with serious fiscal consequences for the NNPC and the federal budget, that had first become a major issue in 1987 was the existence of very low, heavily subsidised, petrol prices. Enormous revenues were foregone from 300,000 b/d of crude oil that was allocated for domestic refining and consumption. Crude oil was priced at levels far below the technical cost of production, let alone international oil prices.[61] In addition, processing, refining, and transport costs to the NNPC were estimated at N21.3 billion, but it only received N4.7 billion in revenue.[62] The total revenue foregone was estimated at N57.5 billion based on international crude oil prices. One result was decapitalisation and decay of oil facilities. In addition, revenue was lost on the estimated 100,000 b/d of refined products that was smuggled out to take advantage of the enormous differential between pump prices in Nigeria and those in neighbouring countries. In 1993 petrol pump prices were N0.7 a litre, or the equivalent of $.03. In neighbouring Cameroon, pump prices were the equivalent of N10.93. This price disparity, and the consequent oil smuggling, contributed to shortages of refined petroleum products countrywide. The shortages were compounded by the inability to effectively manage and maintain the four refineries, which worked well below capacity. As a result, refined products had to be imported.

Problems and Prospects

From Federal to Unitary State

One of the arguments of this book has been that the attempt to create a stronger national centre and increase the pace of economic development through the use of oil revenues has, to a large extent, failed because underlying political and institutional conditions have been unfavourable. The two objectives, which arose in the aftermath of the civil war, were linked in the sense that the effective management and use of oil revenue required a strong central authority. The latter could, in principle, be strengthened and consolidated by centralised oil revenues. However, this benign model of mutually supportive interaction was very far from being realised. There are a number of reasons why, despite greater political and economic centralisation, the centre has been weak and its capacity for government and economic management poorly developed. Among these are a lack of coherence or agreement among the political, military, and bureaucratic elites; political instability and a decline in the authority of state institutions.

The political vacuum at the centre, which I noted existed at the time of decolonisation, was not filled by a coherent indigenous class or by a secure military-bureaucratic alliance. The result was that no stable political community with a sense of national identity has emerged. As the focus of politics shifted to the federal level, so the prospect of controlling centralised oil revenues created intense competition for power at the centre. Shifting coalitions and regime changes have resulted from an unstable structure of national power in which elites of various ethnic and regional groups struggle for power. In this arena, northern-dominated military governments have generally prevailed. The legitimacy of the political leadership has been constantly questioned. Thus, military and civilian regimes have been liable to coups, though the difficulty of effectively organizing coups across the country with a sufficiently broad base of support has acted as a deterrent and foiled some attempts to seize power.

The weakness of the centre was not the only factor that militated against purposeful administration and effective command over resources. The move to centralise also set in motion other forces emanating from regional, sectional, and community bases, which affected centre-local relations. The shift away from genuine federalism to a unitary system, which has occurred indirectly under military governments, has created its own tensions. The original creation of 12 states in 1967 broke down the regional blocs and corrected imbalances in the federal system. It achieved the difficult feat of strengthening allegiance to the centre and promoting sub-national loyalties to the states at the same time. Subsequent state creation started to undermine federalism.[63]

The proliferation of states diminished the power of individual units relative to the centre. Acute dependence on federal funding from the centre reinforced this trend. Local governments, which the states have begun to resemble, also came to depend directly on federal funds.[64] The decline in the power of states was accentuated by the military practice of appointing relatively junior officers as state governors. The states are no longer units of sufficient scale to possess the economic resources and political constituencies required for political decentralisation and the devolution of powers characteristic of a federal system. Subdivision into smaller units has also spread administrative talent very thinly and created inefficient bureaucracies. It has imposed a high economic cost in terms of administrative overheads and undermined the viability of individual units.

The pressure for new states has not abated. A national cake syndrome continues to be fuelled by centralised oil revenues. Nigerians commonly perceive the state as a national cake to be divided and distributed. There are no limits in principle either to the size of the cake or to its subdivision. The larger the cake, the more there is to share, and subdivision can immediately enhance the share of a particular area or ethnic group through the system of revenue allocation.[65] Yet the creation of new states and local government areas only introduces new imbalances lower down the hierarchy of communities, which opens up fresh distributive claims from the newly disadvantaged. Capitulation to the national cake syndrome through the creation of states and local governments often appears to be an easy way of winning political support and diverting energies, but it is actually a sign of weak government.

Dissatisfaction and disagreement over the distribution of power and the organisation of the federal system have led to calls for reform. Thus, there have been demands for the presidency to be rotated on a regional basis; for the principle of federal character, which southerners see as impeding their progress in education and the bureaucracy, to be abolished; and for the federal system to be restructured into six zones or regions. Among minority groups, strong disaffection has been linked to calls for changes in the system of revenue allocation.

The authority of the state, never widely recognized or firmly entrenched, declined during the 1980s and early 1990s. Legitimacy of and respect for state institutions, including the military, the police, and the judiciary, were steadily eroded by partisan interventions and corruption. The military presided over an erosion of nationalist sentiment and an ethical collapse in many areas of public life as illegal appropriation and self-aggrandisement intensified. With the partial exception of the Buhari regime, there was a failure to check, investigate, and punish corruption in high places. Disorder and violence increased. A failure to provide elementary security was evident in the spread of armed robbery, confrontations between the police and the people, and religious disturbances that brought large loss of life. State-sponsored violence was suspected in the assassination of the journalist Dele Giwa and in attacks on Ogoni villages and the homes of activists who opposed the annulment of the 12 June elections. There were many abuses of civil rights.[66] Freedom of the press was regularly violated, with harassment of editors and outright closure of papers being common.[67]

The Military, the Bureaucracy and the Political Class

The military in Nigeria failed to capitalise and build on the nationalist impulse engendered by the civil war. The military was responsible for few successful national projects of socio-economic development, and it presided over enormous waste. The alliance of the military with the bureaucracy in the aftermath of the civil war proved short-lived. The civil service was purged and demoralised. Merit, initiative, and a sense of purpose were not rewarded. The effectiveness of the bureaucracy was undermined, leading the way to instability, a lack of accountability, and a long-term increase in institutional corruption in the public sector.[68] No coherent technocratic group emerged from the bureaucracy to augment state capacities and give a sense of direction. The military came to rely on the short-term recruitment of outsiders, including academics.[69] Turnover of top personnel in key positions throughout the public sector was high. This instability worked against consistent policy-making and learning from experience. The civil service became more vulnerable to political interference.

The advent of a presidential system in 1979 centralised power within the presidency and diminished the influence of the ministries and other state bodies. Since then, governments have tended to create parallel institutions that bypass the ministries and reduce their influence. Earlier in this chapter, I noted that during the Babangida regime, the Ministry of Finance and the Central Bank lost power in relation to the presidency. There is no doubt that this concentration of power without responsibility had serious consequences. It did not lead to better government or greater accountability—rather, the reverse. It created the conditions for rapid growth of extra-budgetary expenditures, unaccountability on a grand scale, and a loss of macroeconomic control.

We have seen how the military itself has steadily become more politicised and partisan as its rule persisted; this politicisation in turn affected the distribution of power within the state and claims to state resources. The role of nationalism, which initially bound the military to the broader purposes of the state, has diminished. Instead of holding the ring for a transfer of power to civilians and making a pact with incoming leaders, the military constantly intervened and eventually refused to give up power. If there once was an autonomous sphere of politics distinct from the armed forces, it no longer exists.

The military did not launch its own party or attempt to incorporate interest groups within the government. Rather, it exercised a loose form of control through decrees, patronage, and preferment; sponsorship of rival factions within civil associations; a resourceful intelligence network;

and bouts of intimidation. The need for a highly authoritarian form of rule was obviated both by the weak, fragmented nature of the opposition and by the control over the top-down distribution of resources. These factors allowed opponents to be bought off and supporters, including the officer corps, to be rewarded. Meanwhile, military officers used their positions to aggrandise themselves at the expense of the public purse. Serving and retired military officers became more involved in business. This involvement often took the form of individual rentier interests that were dependent on state regulation and patronage for their access to wealth; Nigeria has not evolved a collective military presence in the private sector or state corporations. Because of these practices and the persistence of military rule, distrust of the military has grown.

During the Babangida regime, the military was able to manipulate, confuse, and recycle a vulnerable political class, which could mount no effective challenge. The political class had no popular base or mass appeal from which it could draw support. Successive governments had prevented the development of links between trade unions and political parties. And, as we have seen, agrarian political movements, which could provide another potential basis for party mobilisation, did not exist. The political class remains incoherent, insecure, and divided in its loyalties to community, region, and section. It has little economic security of its own and tries to gain wealth through control of state resources. Since electoral defeat would cut off these opportunities, it attempts to retain power at all costs. There is no consensus and very little commitment to ideology, policy, or party. Individuals are readily co-opted by the military. The ease with which party officials and national assembly members have become ministers in the Abacha regime is indicative.

A return to civil rule, though it may constitute a step on the road to democracy, does not secure democracy; no political community exists with agreement on the fundamental rules and institutions that could shape and give direction to society and underpin the state with a sense of national community and identity.[70] Until a community begins to emerge from challenges to the elite by new class forces, which constrain the uses and extent of state power through constitutional government, the prospects for democracy remain tenuous in the extreme.

The Prospects for Economic Development

It is remarkable that from 1971 to 1992, two decades when large oil revenues became available to the government, real per capita GDP declined by 10 percent.[71] The political system and institutional conditions outlined above have not been favourable to economic development. Competition for oil rents among elites has led to weak economic control and management and unstable policies. State capacities for undertaking core accounting functions, macro-economic control and stabilisation, resource allocation in the public sector, and the pursuit of a coherent economic strategy were never strongly developed. Large oil revenues exposed these weaknesses and accentuated them. I have noted on several occasions in this work how easily the management of the economy became subordinated to political imperatives, how quickly oil windfalls created macro-economic instability, how oil revenues have not been properly accounted for, and how public resources have been allocated to a series of unproductive or low-return projects.

I argued earlier that the introduction of the Structural Adjustment Programme did not indicate any shift in the underlying political and social context within which state power is exercised. Rather, it was the product of external pressures and resource constraints. I also argued that the reform would not itself change the balance of political forces by removing opportunities for state patronage, promoting capitalist interests, or creating a supportive domestic constituency. These views have been borne out by the undermining of the commitment to SAP and later a reversal of key elements of the reforms under a new military government. The populist, nationalist, and sub-nationalist currents that were identified earlier in this chapter as lying behind the resurgence of state regulation in the 1994 budget have been challenged by a more determined, private-sector initiative, but they retain their appeal to Nigeria's military-bureaucratic rulers. In addition, the forces I identified most clearly in the National Party of Nigeria—a political economy that combined distributive patronage with opportunities for the commercial political class to profit from rent-seeking through personal connections—remain strong. They provide no check to the further expansion of the state in the economy, nor do they press for transparency and accountability in public finances in order to check corruption.

Peter Lewis has sought to explain the poor economic performance in general, and the lack of a supply response to SAP in particular, in terms of a neopatrimonial state and a rentier economy in which a very unproductive rentier class pursues access to state created rents and prevents the emergence of an independent capitalist class.[72] My own work suggests that this view of the business class equates it too readily to a rentier class and incorporates it too closely with the political and military elites who exercise state power.[73] A distinction needs to be made between those whose accumulation strategies are dependent on access to the state and rental opportunities, including the political/commercial class, and those with more independent trajectories of accumulation, including large corporate interests. Under very adverse political and economic conditions, independent capitalists have made advances in scale and organisation and in managerial and technical capacities, but their collective influence on those who exercise state power and the general environment in which business operates remains limited. Their impact is diluted by a strong commercial and service component, which tends not to align itself on matters of economic policy. Although national private-sector organisations like the Economic Summit Group and the Manufacturers Association of Nigeria have emerged, there has been little co-operation or understanding between business and government.

To explain Nigeria's limited economic success, I would put more emphasis on weakness, instability, and lack of direction at the centre, where no coherent political class has emerged. These factors give rise to failures of management and economic instability. In addition, the complete dominance of centralised oil rents imparts an extreme distributive twist to federal economic policy, undermining its managerial functions. The form, weakness, and limited capacities of domestic capital have some effect, but they are more a consequence, than a cause, of rentier bias, mismanagement, and slow growth.

The dominance of oil in the Nigerian economy for more than 20 years has reduced the chances of political changes that would, in turn, enhance the prospects for economic growth in the longer term. The inability to use oil revenues and manage the oil economy in ways that would encourage economic diversification and end the vice-like grip of the rentier economy has ensured the maintenance of political incentives associated with centralised oil wealth. My argument is not that large oil revenues determine the course of political and economic development but that they do help explain the persistence of certain features in the Nigerian political economy. They allow the state to continue to distribute largesse, heightening distributive struggles among military and political elites and placing a premium on the exercise of power at the centre. The concomitant neglect of personal taxation has long-term negative consequences for political mobilisation and representation and the use of public resources. Less reliance on centralised oil wealth would weaken these political incentives, promote a healthier system of government, and begin to undermine the distributive basis of politics and economic management.

Notes

1. *Daily Times*, 11 May 1990.

2. For details of Abiola's business career, see T. G. Forrest, *The Advance of African Capital: The Growth of Nigerian Private Enterprise* (Edinburgh: Edinburgh University Press for the International African Institute, 1994), pp. 98–102.

3. I. Campbell, "Nigeria's Failed Transition: The 1993 Presidential Election," *Journal of Contemporary African Studies* 12/2 (1994), p. 184.

4. Campbell, "Nigeria's Failed Transition," pp. 185–186.

5. According to Abiola, "One thing God has done for me is the fact that in every community I am local. I have 235 chieftaincy titles from all over Nigeria. There are three ways you can become a native in any locality in Nigeria: either you are born there, or you marry from there, or you are a chief. And it was easier for me to become a chief because I gave a lot of scholarships: secondary schools, polytechnics, universities, about 3750 scholarships in all so far. I helped to build mosques, build churches, boreholes in arid areas and so on. And I went to see them in every local government. We went through all that. We covered four times the distance covered by the NRC during the entire campaign." O. Oguibe, ed., *Democracy in Nigeria: The June 12 Mandate* (London: African Research and Information Bureau, 1993), p. 31.

6. According to Abiola, he was connected with the army for twenty-five years and was the only civilian member of the mess committee for a very long time. "I settled the bills over the years. They would invite me as chairman at their weddings, naming ceremonies and house warming. I would spend five minutes here, ten minutes there, over the years for twenty-five years. I have done that over the years in their constituency. It is a very important constituency too." Abiola claimed that "we collated the figures from military cantonments; the army, the air force and the navy, throughout Nigeria. Out of the 129,711 votes cast by the army, navy and air force, I got over 124,000; about 97%." Oguibe, ed., *Democracy in Nigeria: The June 12 Mandate,* p. 33.

7. O. Obasanjo, "A Note to a Friend," *Sunday Tribune,* 31 October 1993, p. 19.

8. For details of Chief Francis Arthur Nzeribe's career, see T. G. Forrest, "The Advance of African Capital," pp. 262–263.

9. Obasanjo, "A Note to a Friend."

10. C. Achebe, "A Call to All Nigerians," *Nigeria Now* 2/7-8 (1993), p. 13.

11. P. M. Lewis, "Endgame in Nigeria? The Politics of a Failed Democratic Transition," *African Affairs* 93/372 (1994), pp. 332–336.

12. *Africa Confidential,* 30 July 1993, p. 7.

13. The Campaign for Democracy was incorporated in November 1991. It was jointly initiated by the Civil Liberties Organisation (CLO), the Committee for the Defense of Human Rights (CDHR), the National Association of Democratic Lawyers (NADL), the Gani Fawehinmi Solidarity Association (GFSA), the National Consultative Forum (NCF), the National Association of Nigerian Students (NANS), Women in Nigeria, Lagos branch (WIN) and the Nigerian Union of Journalists (NUJ). Its main objectives were to work for an end to military rule and the convening of a sovereign national conference.

14. Under the terms of the Foreign Assistance Act, the drug declaration meant that the United States ended Export-Import Bank financing and opposed loans to Nigeria from multilateral banks. According to U.S. officials, Nigerian drug couriers accounted for 35 to 40 percent of the heroin entering the United States. *Financial Times,* 5 April 1994.

15. Economist Intelligence Unit, "Country Report, Nigeria," 2d quarter 1994, p. 24.

16. Oguibe, ed., *Democracy in Nigeria: The June 12 Mandate,* p. 26.

17. Campbell, "Nigeria's Failed Transition," p. 192.

18. The strikes had widespread support. Among the unions involved were the

Senior Staff Consultative Association of Nigeria and, for the first time, the Association of Senior Civil Servants of Nigeria.

19. Among them were Gani Fawehinmi; retired Air Commodore Dan Suleiman; G.O.K. Ajayi, counsel to Abiola; and Segun Osoba, former governor of Oyo state.

20. *Annual Report,* Central Bank of Nigeria, 1993, p. 23.

21. World Bank, *Nigeria: Structural Adjustment Programme, Policies, Implementation, and Impact* (Washington, D.C.: World Bank, 1994), p. 54.

22. *Financial Times,* 26 May 1995.

23. *Financial Times,* 26 May 1995.

24. World Bank, *Nigeria: Structural Adjustment Programme,* p. 69.

25. *Financial Times,* 26 May 1995.

26. I owe this information to Kweku Ampiah. The scale, causes, and consequences of foreign divestment from Nigeria are in need of research.

27. For concern over Nigeria's image, see *West Africa,* 4–10 April 1994, pp. 582–588.

28. *The Economist,* 21 May 1994.

29. R. Faruqee, "Nigeria: Ownership Abandoned," in I. Husain and R. Faruqee, eds., *Adjustment in Africa: Lessons from Country Case Studies* (Washington, D.C.: World Bank, 1994), p. 280.

30. Education and health data are taken from the UNDP, *Human Development Report 1994* (New York: Oxford University Press, 1994) and Faruqee, "Nigeria: Ownership Abandoned," p. 279.

31. Gross enrollment at primary level as a percentage of age group was 32 in 1965, rising to 98 over 1978/80 and falling to 72 in 1990. *World Development Report,* World Bank, 1986, p. 236; Farquee, "Nigeria: Ownership Abandoned," p. 279; UNDP, *Human Development Report 1994,* p. 157.

32. *The Enabler (Journal of the Enabling Environment Forum)* 2/1 and 2 (1992), p. 8.

33. P. Dozie and O. Bickersteth, eds., *Report on the First Nigerian Economic Summit* (Ibadan: Spectrum Books, 1993); P. Dozie and O. Bickersteth, eds., *The Economic Action Agenda* (Ibadan: Spectrum Books, 1993).

34. Peter Lewis argued that business groups were incorporated into the clientalist orbit of the military. Lewis, "Endgame in Nigeria?" p. 338.

35. *Financial Times,* 26 May 1995.

36. World Bank, *Nigeria: Structural Adjustment Programme,* p. 17.

37. *Financial Times,* 15 September 1994.

38. T. M. Callaghy, "Political Passions and Economic Interests: Economic Reform and Political Structure in Africa," in T. M. Callaghy and J. Ravenhill, eds., *Hemmed In: Responses to Africa's Economic Decline* (New York: Columbia University Press, 1993), p. 493.

39. *Financial Times,* 16 March 1992. Cited in Callaghy, "Political Passions," pp. 493–494.

40. Central Bank of Nigeria Decree No. 24 of 1991 subjected the bank to the authority of the president.

41. World Bank, *Nigeria: Structural Adjustment Programme,* p. 23.

42. Privileged sources cited in T. Olagunju, A. Jinadu, and S. Oyovbaire, *Transi-*

tion to Democracy in Nigeria, 1985–1993 (Ibadan: Spectrum Books, 1993), pp. 257, 261.

43. Privileged sources cited in Olagunju, Jinadu, and Oyovbaire, *Transition to Democracy in Nigeria*, p. 258.

44. *Financial Times Survey, Nigeria*, 1 April 1993, p. 5.

45. The enhanced Toronto terms were agreed upon by the Paris Club in December 1991. They allow for a 50 percent reduction (in net present value terms) of debt service payments on non-concessional official debt. The World Bank estimated that rescheduling using the enhanced Toronto terms would reduce Nigeria's debt service ratio to 21 percent in 1993–1996 and cut the debt stock to $16 billion. The Trinidad terms were proposed by the UK in 1991 but have never been applied by the Paris Club. They imply a one-off reduction of two-thirds of the eligible debt and an extended repayment period. They would halve the dollar value of Nigeria's external debt by 1998. *Financial Times Survey, Nigeria*, 1 April 1993, p. 5.

46. Faruqee, "Nigeria: Ownership Abandoned," p. 251.

47. World Bank, *Nigeria: Structural Adjustment Programme*, p. 32.

48. *Africa Confidential*, 18 February 1993.

49. *Financial Times*, 4 December 1993.

50. *Financial Times*, 3 November 1993.

51. *Financial Times*, 17 March 1994.

52. P. Asiodu, "Petroleum Resources and National Development," in A. Mahadi, G. A. Kwanashie, and A. M. Yakubu, eds., *Nigeria: The State of the Nation and the Way Forward* (Kaduna: Arewa House, 1994), p. 205.

53. The entitlement of mineral-producing states was raised in May 1992 from 1.5 percent to 3 percent of the Federation Account. *West Africa*, 4 October 1992, p. 1619. In its first year, OMPADEC had a budget of $90 million. *Financial Times*, 13 January 1994.

54. Philip Asiodu argued that funds should be increased and private sector projects be included. Asiodu, "Petroleum Resources and National Development," p. 207.

55. See K. Saro-Wiwa, *Genocide in Nigeria: The Ogoni Tragedy* (Port Harcourt, Nigeria: Saros International Publishers, 1992).

56. *Financial Times*, 7 June 1994.

57. Greenpeace, *Shell-Shocked: The Environmental and Social Costs of Living with Shell in Nigeria*, London, July 1994.

58. Greenpeace, *Shell-Shocked*, p. 20.

59. *Financial Times*, 26 January 1994.

60. *Financial Times*, 7 June 1994.

61. In November 1993, petrol prices were raised from 70 kobo to N3.5 a litre, which covered production costs.

62. *Financial Times*, 1 April 1993.

63. For an eloquent and forceful critique of state creation, see J. Ellah, *Nigeria and States Creation* (Port Harcourt, Nigeria: Chief J. W. Ellah, Sons & Co., 1983). Ellah, who resigned from the Senate during the Second Republic because he was prevented from finishing his motion on state creation, argues for a limited number of states, ideally twelve, based on ethnic, linguistic, and historical criteria.

64. A new federal Ministry of States and Local Government has been created. This is a contradiction in terms.

65. In order to reduce the incentives for further subdivision, Rotimi Suberu suggested the following measures: reduce the proportion of federal funds shared equally among all units; give greater rewards to the major contributors to national wealth; compel all units to raise half their revenues internally. R. T. Suberu, "The Travails of Federalism in Nigeria," *Journal of Democracy* 4/4 (1993), p. 52.

66. See Civil Liberties Organisation, *Executive Lawlessness in the Babangida Regime*, Lagos, March 1991; Civil Liberties Organisation, *Human Rights in Retreat: A Report on Seven Years of Human Rights Violations by the Military Regime of General Ibrahim Babangida, August 1985 to August 1992*, Lagos, 1993.

67. Constitutional Rights Project, *The Crisis of Press Freedom in Nigeria*, Lagos, 1993, pp. 34–46.

68. D. Olowu, "Ethical Violations in Nigeria's Public Services: Patterns, Explanations, and Remedies," in S. Rasheed and D. Olowu, eds., *Ethics and Accountability in African Public Services* (Nairobi: Icipe Science Press, 1992).

69. Y. Bangura, "Intellectuals, Economic Reform, and Social Change: Constraints and Opportunities in the Formation of a Nigerian Technocracy," *Development and Change* 25/2 (1994).

70. Three political scientists who were closely involved with the Babangida regime (two became ministers) attempted to justify the long transition period to civil rule. In their book, the transition is seen as an opportunity for learning and social engineering in which liberal democracy would be institutionalised and the political class taught the values of a participatory political culture. The idea that democracy could be created from above, by an unelected military government, is not questioned. No case is made for the existence of political and social forces that are prepared to struggle for democracy and limit the powers of the state. See Olagunju, Jinadu, and Oyovbaire, *Transition to Democracy in Nigeria*.

71. World Bank, *Nigeria: Structural Adjustment Programme*, p. 73.

72. P. M. Lewis, "Economic Statism, Private Capital, and the Dilemmas of Accumulation in Nigeria," *World Development* 22/3 (1994).

73. T. G. Forrest, *The Advance of African Capital: The Growth of Nigerian Private Enterprise* (Edinburgh: Edinburgh University Press for the International African Institute, 1994).

Bibliography

Abdulraheem, T., and A. Olukoshi. "The Left in Nigerian Politics and the Struggle for Socialism, 1945–1985." *Review of African Political Economy* 37 (1986).

Abernethy, D. B. The Political Dilemma of Popular Education. Stanford: Stanford University Press, 1969.

Aboyade, O. "The Economy of Nigeria." In P. Robson and D. A. Lury, eds., *The Economies of Africa*. London: Allen and Unwin, 1969.

______. "The Development Process." In A. A. Ayida and H.M.A. Onitiri, eds., Reconstruction and Development in Nigeria. Ibadan: Oxford University Press, 1971.

______. "The Management of Intellect." *Quarterly Journal of Administration* 11/3 (1977).

Aboyade, O., and A. A. Ayida. "The War Economy in Perspective." *Nigerian Journal of Economic and Social Studies* 13/1 (1971).

Achebe, C. *The Trouble with Nigeria*. London: Heinemann, 1984.

Adams, W. M. "River Basin Planning in Nigeria." *Applied Geography* 5 (1985).

______. "Rural Protest, Land Policy, and the Planning Process on the Bakolori Project, Nigeria." *Africa* 58/3 (1988).

Adeboye, T. O. "Public Sector Participation in Manufacturing." Mimeo, Annual Conference of the Nigerian Economic Society, 1978.

Afigbo, A. E. *The Warrant Chiefs: Indirect Rule in Southern Nigeria*. London: Longman, 1972.

Akeredolu-Ale, E. O. "Private Foreign Investment and the Underdevelopment of Indigenous Entrepreneurship in Nigeria." In G. Williams, ed., *Nigeria: Economy and Society*. London: Rex Collings, 1976.

Andrae, G., and B. Beckman. *The Wheat Trap: Bread and Underdevelopment in Nigeria*. London: Zed Press, 1985.

Asiodu, P. "Petroleum Resources and National Development." In A. Mahadi, G. A. Kwanashie and A. M. Yakubu, eds., *Nigeria: The State of the Nation and the Way Forward*. Kaduna: Arewa House, 1994.

Ayida, A. A. "Contractor Finance and Supplier Credit in Economic Growth." *Nigerian Journal of Economic and Social Studies* 7/2 (1965).

______. "The National Revolution, 1966–76." Presidential address to the Nigerian Economic Society, 1973.

Bangura, Y. "IMF/World Bank Conditionality and Nigeria's Structural Adjustment Programme." Paper presented to seminar on the IMF and the World Bank in Africa, Scandinavian Institute of African Studies, Uppsala, 27–29 January 1987.

______. "Crisis and Adjustment: The Experience of Nigerian Workers." In B.

Onimode, ed., *The IMF, the World Bank and the African Debt.* Vol. 2. London: Zed Books, 1989.

______. "Intellectuals, Economic Reform, and Social Change: Constraints and Opportunities in the Formation of a Nigerian Technocracy." *Development and Change* 25/2 (1994).

Banjo, A. "The Principal Problems of Indigenisation." *Management in Nigeria.* September 1976.

Barber, K. "Popular Reactions to the Petro-Naira." *Journal of Modern African Studies* 20/3 (1982).

Bates, R. H. *Markets and States in Tropical Africa: The Political Basis of Agricultural Policies.* Berkeley: University of California Press, 1981.

______. *Essays on the Political Economy of Rural Africa.* Cambridge: Cambridge University Press, 1983.

______. The Politics of Agricultural Pricing in Sub-Saharan Africa. In Z. Ergas, ed., *The African State in Transition.* London: Macmillan, 1987.

Bauer, P. T. *West African Trade: A Study of Competition, Oligopoly and Monopoly in a Changing Economy.* Cambridge: Cambridge University Press, 1954.

Beckman, B. "Neocolonialism, Capitalism and the State in Nigeria." In H. Bernstein and B. Campbell, eds., *Contradictions of Accumulation in Africa.* Beverly Hills: Sage, 1985.

______. "The Post Colonial State: Crisis and Reconstruction." *Institute of Development Studies Bulletin* (Brighton, Sussex) 19/4 (1988).

Berry, S. *Fathers Work for Their Sons: Accumulation, Mobility and Class Formation in an Extended Yoruba Community.* Berkeley: University of California Press, 1985.

______. The Food Crisis and Agrarian Change in Africa. *African Studies Review* 27/2 (1984).

Bevan, D., P. Collier, and J. W. Gunning. *Nigeria: Policy Responses to Shocks, 1970–1990.* San Francisco: International Center for Economic Growth, 1992.

Biersteker, T. *Multinationals, the State, and Control of the Nigerian Economy.* Princeton: Princeton University Press, 1987.

Bray, M. *Universal Primary Education in Nigeria: A Study of Kano State.* London: Routledge and Kegan Paul, 1981.

Burghart, Richard. "Ministerial Emoluments in Nigeria." *Nigerian Opinion,* no. 8. Reprinted in *Nigeria 1965: Crisis and Criticism.* Ibadan: Ibadan University Press, 1966.

Callaghy, T. M. "The State as Lame Leviathan: The Patrimonial Administrative State in Africa." In Zaki Ergas, ed., *The African State in Transition.* New York: Macmillan, 1987.

______. "The State and the Development of Capitalism in Africa: Theoretical, Historical and Comparative Reflections." In D. Rothchild and N. Chazan, eds., *The Precarious Balance: State and Society in Africa.* Boulder: Westview Press, 1988.

______. "Political Passions and Economic Interests: Economic Reform and Political Structure in Africa." In T. M. Callaghy and J. Ravenhill, eds., *Hemmed In: Responses to Africa's Economic Decline.* New York: Columbia University Press, 1993.

Campbell, I. "Army Reorganisation and Military Withdrawal." In K. Panter-Brick, ed., *Soldiers and Oil*. London: Frank Cass, 1978.

______. "Nigeria's Failed Transition: The 1993 Presidential Election." *Journal of Contemporary African Studies* 12/2 (1994).

Civil Liberties Organisation. *Executive Lawlessness in the Babangida Regime*. Lagos, March 1991.

______. *Human Rights in Retreat: A Report on Seven Years of Human Rights Violations by the Military Regime of General Ibrahim Babangida, August 1985 to August 1992*. Lagos, 1993.

Clough, P. *The Production and Marketing of Cash Crops and Grains in Northern Nigeria, 1985: A View Based on Village Research*. Consultancy Report, Western Africa Regional Office, World Bank, 1986.

Clough, P., and G. Williams. "Decoding Berg: The World Bank in Rural Northern Nigeria." In M. Watts, ed., *State, Oil and Agriculture in Nigeria*. Berkeley: University of California Press, 1987.

Coleman, J. S. *Nigeria: Background to Nationalism*. Berkeley: University of California Press, 1958.

Collier, P. "An Analysis of the Nigerian Labour Market." Development Economics Department Discussion Paper, World Bank, 1986.

______. "Oil Shocks and Food Security in Nigeria." *International Labour Review* 127/6 (1988).

Constitutional Rights Projects. *The Crisis of Press Freedom in Nigeria*. Lagos, 1993.

Cooper, F. "Africa and the World Economy." *African Studies Review* 24/2 and 3 (1981).

Corden, W. M. "Booming Sector and Dutch Disease Economics: Survey and Consolidation." In W. M. Corden, ed., *Protection, Growth and Trade: Essays in International Economics*. Oxford: Basil Blackwell, 1985.

Diamond, L. "Nigeria: Pluralism, Statism and the Struggle for Democracy." In L. Diamond, J. L. Linz, and S. M. Lipset, eds., *Democracy in Developing Countries: Africa*. Boulder: Lynne Rienner, 1988.

Dozie, P., and O. Bickersteth, eds. *Report on the First Nigerian Economic Summit*. Ibadan: Spectrum Books, 1993.

______. *The Economic Action Agenda*. Ibadan: Spectrum Books, 1993.

Dudley, B. J. *An Introduction to Nigerian Government and Politics*. London: Macmillan, 1982.

Elaigwu, J. I. *Gowon*. Ibadan: West Books, 1985.

______. *The Economic Action Agenda*. Ibadan: Spectrum Books, 1993.

Ellah, F. J. *Nigeria and States Creation*. Port Harcourt, Nigeria: Chief J. W. Ellah, Sons & Co., 1983.

Erivwo, S. U. "The Church in a Changing Nigeria." In M. O. Kayode and Y. B. Usman, eds., *The Economic and Social Development of Nigeria*. Vol. 2, *1985*. Proceedings of the National Conference on Nigeria Since Independence, Zaria, March 1983.

Falola, T. "Lebanese Traders in Southwestern Nigeria, 1900–1960," *African Affairs* 89/357, 1990.

Falola, T., and J. Ihonvbere. *The Rise and Fall of Nigeria's Second Republic, 1979–84.* London: Zed Books, 1985.

Faruqee, R. "Nigeria: Ownership Abandoned." In I. Husain and R. Faruqee, eds., *Adjustment in Africa: Lessons from Country Case Studies.* Washington, D.C.: World Bank, 1994.

Fieldhouse, D. K. *Black Africa, 1945–1980: Economic Decolonisation and Arrested Development.* London: Allen and Unwin, 1986.

Forrest, J. "The Contemporary African State: A Ruling Class?" *Review of African Political Economy.* 38 (April 1987).

Forrest, T. G. "Agricultural Policies in Nigeria 1900–78." In J. Heyer, P. Roberts, and G. Williams, eds., *Rural Development in Tropical Africa.* London: Macmillan, 1981.

———. "Brazil and Africa: Geopolitics, Trade and Technology in the South Atlantic." *African Affairs* 81/322 (January 1982).

———. "The Political Economy of Civil Rule and the Economic Crisis in Nigeria, 1979–84." *Review of African Political Economy.* 35 (1986).

———. "State Capital, Capitalist Development and Class Formation in Nigeria." In P. M. Lubeck, ed., *The African Bourgeoisie: Capitalist Development in Nigeria, Kenya and the Ivory Coast.* Boulder: Lynne Rienner, 1987.

———. "The Advance of African Capital: The Growth of Nigerian Private Enterprises." In F. Stewart, S. Lall, and S. M. Wangwe, eds., *Alternative Development Strategies in Sub-Saharan Africa.* London: Macmillan, 1992.

———. *The Advance of African Capital: The Growth of Nigerian Private Enterprise.* Edinburgh: Edinburgh University Press for the International African Institute, 1994.

Francis P. "For the Use and Common Benefit of All Nigeria: Consequences of the 1978 Land Nationalisation." *Africa* 54/3 (1984).

Freund, W. M. *The Making of Contemporary Africa.* London: Macmillan, 1984.

Friedman, M. R. *Capitalism and Freedom.* Chicago: University of Chicago Press, 1962.

Gboyega, A. "Choosing a New Cabinet." In O. Oyediran, ed., *The Nigerian 1979 Elections.* London: Macmillan, 1981.

———. "The 'Federal Character' or the Attempt to Create Representative Bureaucracies in Nigeria." *International Review of Administrative Science* 84/1 (1984).

Gelb, A. H. "Adjustment to Windfall Gains: a Comparative Analysis of Oil Exporting Countries." In P. J. Neary and S. van Wijnbergen, eds., *Natural Resources and the Macroeconomy.* Oxford: Basil Blackwell, 1986.

Greenpeace. *Shell-Shocked: The Environmental and Social Costs of Living with Shell in Nigeria.* London, July 1994.

Guyer, J. "Representation Without Taxation: An Essay on Democracy in Rural Nigeria, 1952–1990." *African Studies Review* 35/1 (1992).

Hart, K. *The Political Economy of West African Agriculture.* Cambridge: Cambridge University Press, 1982.

Hastings, A. *A History of African Christianity, 1950–1975.* Cambridge: Cambridge University Press, 1979.

Hay, A. M., and R.H.T. Smith. *Interregional Trade and Money Flows in Nigeria, 1964.* Ibadan: Oxford University Press, 1970.

Hayek, F. W. *The Constitution of Liberty*. London: Routledge and Kegan Paul, 1960.
Held, D. *Political Theory and the Modern State*. Oxford: Polity Press, 1989.
Helleiner, G. K. *Peasant Agriculture, Government and Economic Growth in Nigeria*. Homewood, Ill.: Irwin, 1966.
Hill, P. *Rural Hausa: A Village and a Setting*. Cambridge: Cambridge University Press, 1972.
______. *Dry Grain Farming Families: Hausaland (Nigeria) and Kanakata (India) Compared*. Cambridge: Cambridge University Press, 1982.
______. *Development Economics on Trial: The Anthropological Case for a Prosecution*. Cambridge: Cambridge University Press, 1986.
Hoogvelt, A. "Indigenisation and Foreign Capital: Industrialisation in Nigeria." *Review of African Political Economy* 14 (1979).
Husain, I. *Perspectives on the Nigerian Economy*. Lagos: Nigerian Institute of International Affairs, 1987.
Hutchful, E. "Oil Companies and Environmental Pollution in Nigeria." In C. Ake, ed., *Political Economy of Nigeria*. London: Longman, 1986.
Hyden, G. *No Shortcuts to Progress: African Development Management in Perspective*. London: Heinemann, 1983.
Ibrahim, J. "The Political Debate and the Struggle for Democracy in Nigeria." *Review of African Political Economy* 37 (1986).
______. "The Politics of Religion in Nigeria: The Parameters of the 1987 Crisis in Kaduna State." *Review of African Political Economy* 45/45 (1989).
Igue, J. O. "Le Nigeria et ses périphéries frontalières." In D. C. Bach, J. Egg, and J. Philippe, eds., *Le Nigeria: Un pouvoir en puissance*. Paris: Karthala, 1988.
Ihonvbere, J. O. "A Critical Evaluation of the Failed 1990 Coup in Nigeria." *Journal of Modern African Studies* 29/4 (1991).
Ikoku, S. G. *Nigeria's Fourth Coup d'État*. Enugu: Fourth Dimension, 1985.
Jamal, V., and J. Weeks. "The Vanishing Rural-Urban Gap in Sub-Saharan Africa." *International Labour Review* 127/3 (1988).
Joda, A. "Education in Nigeria 1971–75." In M. O. Kayode and Y. B. Usman, eds., *The Economic and Social Development of Nigeria*. Vol. 2, Proceedings of the National Conference on Nigeria Since Independence (March 1983). Zaria, 1985.
Joseph, R. *Democracy and Prebendal Politics in Nigeria*. Cambridge: Cambridge University Press, 1987.
Kastfelt, N. *Religion and Politics in Nigeria: A Study in Middle Belt Christianity*. London: British Academic Press, 1994.
Kilby, P. *Industrialization in an Open Economy: Nigeria, 1945–1966*. Cambridge: Cambridge University Press, 1969.
______. "Manufacturing in Colonial Africa." In P. Duignan and L. H. Gann, eds., *Colonialism in Africa, 1870–1960*. Vol. 4, *The Economics of Colonialism*. Cambridge: Cambridge University Press, 1975.
Kirk-Greene, A.H.M. "Ethnic Engineering and the 'Federal Character' of Nigeria: Boon of Contentment or Bone of Contention." *Ethnic and Racial Studies* 6/4 (1983).
Kukah, M. *Religion, Politics, and Power in Northern Nigeria*. Ibadan: Spectrum Books, 1993.

Labaran, A. A. "Land Appropriation and Capitalist Farming in the Sokoto Region: Some Preliminary Findings." In M. Mortimore, E. A. Olofin, R. A. Cline-Cole, and A. Abdulkadir, eds., *Perspectives in Land Administration and Development in Northern Nigeria.* Kano: Bayero University Department of Geography, 1987.

Lewis, P. M. "Economic Statism, Private Capital, and the Dilemmas of Accumulation in Nigeria." *World Development* 22/3 (1994).

———."Endgame in Nigeria? The Politics of a Failed Democratic Transition." *African Affairs* 93/372 (1994).

Leys, C. "African Economic Development in Theory and Practice." *Daedalus* 3 (1982).

Longhurst, R. "Rural Productivity, Malnutrition and Structural Adjustment." In E. Clay and J. Shaw, eds., *Poverty, Development and Food.* London: Macmillan, 1987.

Lubeck, P. M. "Islamic Protest Under Semi-Industrial Capitalism: 'Yan Tatsine Explained," *Africa* 55/4 (1985).

———. *Islam and Urban Labour in Northern Nigeria: The Making of a Muslim Working Class.* Cambridge: Cambridge University Press, 1986.

Lubeck, P. M., and M. J. Watts. "An Alliance of Oil and Maize? The Response of Indigenous and State Capital to Structural Adjustment in Nigeria." In B. J. Berman and C. Leys, eds., *African Capitalists in African Development.* Boulder: Lynne Rienner, 1994.

Luckham, R. *The Nigerian Military: A Sociological Analysis of Authority and Revolt, 1960–67.* Cambridge: Cambridge University Press, 1971.

———. "The Military, Militarization, and Democratization in Africa: A Survey of Literature and Issues." *African Studies Review* 37/2 (1994).

Marenin, O. "The Anini Saga: Armed Robbery and the Reproduction of Ideology in Nigeria." *Journal of Modern African Studies* 25/2 (1987).

Marshall, R. "Power in the name of Jesus." *Review of African Political Economy* 52 (1991).

Martin, S. M. *Palm Oil and Protest—An Economic History of the Ngwa Region of South-Eastern Nigeria, 1800–1980.* Cambridge: Cambridge University Press, 1988.

Mazrui, A. "African Islam and Competitive Religions: Between Revivalism and Expansion." *Third World Quarterly* 10/2 (1988).

Mba, N. "Women and Khaki: Women and the Militarized State in Nigeria." In J. Parpart and K. Staudt, eds., *Women and the State in Africa.* Boulder: Lynne Rienner, 1988.

Mohammed, A. S. "The Struggle for Democratic Rights and Socialism in Nigeria, 1979–1986." Review of African Political Economy Conference, Liverpool, 1986.

Mortimore, M. "Shifting Sands and Human Sorrow: Social Responses to Drought and Desertification." Lecture, University of Durham, 1985.

———. *Adapting to Drought: Farmers, Famines and Desertification in West Africa,* Cambridge: Cambridge Unviersity Press, 1989.

Nigeria. *Report of the Working Party on Statutory Corporations and State-Owned Companies.* Federal Ministry of Information, Lagos, 1967.

———. *Second National Development Plan, 1970–74.* Federal Ministry of Economic Development, Lagos, 1970.

———. *Report of the Public Service Review Commission.* Lagos, 1974.

______. *Third National Development Plan, 1975–80.* Central Planning Office, Lagos, 1975.

______. *Federal Government's Views on the Report of the Panel on Creation of States.* Federal Ministry of Information, Lagos, 1976.

______. *Federal Military Government's Views on the Report of the Federal Assets Investigation Panel, 1975.* Federal Ministry of Information, Lagos, 1976.

______. *Federal Military Government's Views on the Report of the Tribunal of Inquiry into the Activities of Trade Unions.* Federal Ministry of Information, Lagos, 1977.

______. *Report of the Technical Committee on Revenue Allocation.* Mimeo, Lagos, 1978.

______. *The Constitution of the Federal Republic of Nigeria.* Federal Ministry of Information, Lagos, 1979.

______. *Report of the Tribunal of Inquiry into Crude Oil Sales.* Federal Government Printer, Lagos, 1980.

______. *Views of the Government of the Federation on the Report of the Crude Oil Sales Tribunal.* Lagos: Federal Government Printer, 1980.

______. *Report of the Presidential Commission on Revenue Allocation.* Lagos: Federal Government Printer, 1980.

______. *Guidelines for the Fourth National Development Plan, 1981–86.* Federal Ministry of National Planning, Lagos, 1981.

______. *Report of the Tribunal of Inquiry on Kano Disturbances.* Lagos, Federal Government Printer, 1981.

______. *National Economic Council Expert Committee Report on the State of the Nigerian Economy.* Federal Ministry of National Planning, Lagos, 1983.

______. *Government's Views and Comments on the Findings and Recommendations of the Political Bureau.* Lagos: Federal Government Printer, 1987.

______. *Report of the Political Bureau.* Lagos: Federal Government Printer, 1987.

______. *Presidential Task Force on the Implementation of the Civil Service Reforms.* Lagos: Federal Government Printer, 1988.

Nnoli, O. *Ethnic Politics in Nigeria.* Enugu: Fourth Dimension, 1978.

Nolutshungu, S. "Fragments of a Democracy: Reflections on Class and Politics in Nigeria." *Third World Quarterly* 12/1 (1990).

Nwabueze, B. O. *The Presidential Constitution of Nigeria.* London: Hurst, 1982.

______. *Nigeria's Presidential Constitution, 1979–83.* London: Longman, 1985.

Nzeribe, F. A. *Nigeria: Another Hope Betrayed. The Second Coming of the Nigerian Military.* London: Kilimanjaro, 1985.

Obasanjo, O., and F. Shyllon. "The Demise of the Rule of Law in Nigeria under the Military: Two Points of View." Institute of African Studies, Ibadan, 1980.

O'Connell, J. "Political Integration: The Nigerian Case." In A. Hazlewood, ed., *African Integration and Disintegration.* London: Oxford University Press, 1967.

______. "The Political Class and Economic Growth." In P. Kilby, *Industrialization in an Open Economy: Nigeria, 1945–1966.* Cambridge: Cambridge University Press, 1969.

Offe, C. *Contradictions of the Welfare State.* London: Hutchinson, 1984.

Oguibe, O., ed. *Democracy in Nigeria: The June 12 Mandate.* London: Africa Research and Information Bureau, 1993.

Ojo, M. A. "The Contextual Significance of the Charismatic Movements in Independent Nigeria." *Africa* 58/2 (1988).

Olagunju, T., A. Jinadu and S. Oyovbaire. *Transition to Democracy in Nigeria, 1985–1993*. Ibadan: Spectrum Books, 1993.

Olowu, D. "Ethical Violations in Nigeria's Public Services: Patterns, Explanations, and Remedies." In S. Rasheed and D. Olowu, eds., *Ethics and Accountability in African Public Services*. Nairobi: Icipe Science Press, 1993.

Olukoshi, A. O. "Some Remarks on the Role of the Levantines in the Capitalist Industrialisation of Kano." *Nigerian Journal of Political Science* 4/1 and 2 (1985).

Olukoshi, A. O., and I. Aremu. "Structural Adjustment and Labour Subordination: The Dissolution of the Nigeria Labour Congress Revisited." *Review of African Political Economy* 43 (1988).

Onimode, B. "Privatisation of Public Enterprises," Mimeo, Conference on Economic Crisis, Austerity Measures and Privatisation in Africa, Zaria, 1985.

Osoba, S. "The Nigerian Power Elite, 1952–65." In P.C.W. Gutkind and P. Waterman, eds., *African Social Studies: A Radical Reader*. London: Heinemann, 1977.

Othman, S. "Classes, Crises and Coup: The Demise of Shagari's Regime." *African Affairs* 83/333 (1984).

Oyediran, O., ed. *Survey of Nigerian Affairs, 1975*. Nigerian Institute of International Affairs. Ibadan: Oxford University Press, 1978.

______. *Survey of Nigerian Affairs, 1976/77*. Ibadan: Nigerian Institute of International Affairs and Macmillan, 1981.

Oyediran, O. *Essays on Local Government and Administration in Nigeria*. Lagos: Project Publications, 1988.

Oyediran, O., and A. Agbaje. "Two-Partyism and Democratic Transition in Nigeria." *Journal of Modern African Studies*, 29/2 (1991).

Oyovbaire, S. E. "The Politics of Revenue Allocation." In K. Panter-Brick, ed., *Soldiers and Oil*. London: Frank Cass, 1978.

Paden, J. N. *Religion and Political Culture in Kano*. Berkeley: University of California Press, 1973.

______. *Ahmadu Bello, Sardauna of Sokoto*. London: Hodder and Stoughton, 1986.

Palmer-Jones, R. "Irrigation and the Politics of Agricultural Development in Nigeria." In M. Watts, ed., *State, Oil and Agriculture in Nigeria*. Berkeley: University of California Press, 1987.

Panter-Brick, K., ed. *Soldiers and Oil: The Political Transformation of Nigeria*. London: Frank Cass, 1978.

Pearson, S. R. *Petroleum and the Nigerian Economy*. Stanford: Stanford University Press, 1970.

Peel, J.D.Y. *Ijeshas and Nigerian: The Incorporation of a Yoruba Kingdom*. Cambridge: Cambridge University Press, 1983.

______. "Social and Cultural Change." In M. Crowder, ed., *The Cambridge History of Africa*. Vol. 8, *c. 1940–c. 1975*. Cambridge: Cambridge University Press, 1984.

______. "The Cultural Work of Yoruba Ethnogenesis." In E. Tonkin, M. McDonald, and M. Chapman, eds., *History and Ethnicity*. London: Routledge, 1989.

Pinto, B. "Nigeria During and After the Oil Boom: A Policy Comparison with Indonesia." *World Bank Economic Review* 3 (1987).

Pittin, R. "Selective Education: Issues of Gender, Class and Ideology in Northern Nigeria." *Review of African Political Economy* 48 (1990).

Ross, P. J. "Land as a Right to Membership: Land Tenure Dynamics in a Peripheral Area of the Kano Close-Settled Zone." In M. Watts, ed., *State, Oil and Agriculture in Nigeria*. Berkeley: University of California Press, 1987.

Rothchild, D., and N. Chazan. *The Precarious Balance: State and Society in Africa*. Boulder: Westview Press, 1988.

Sandbrook, R. *The Politics of Africa's Economic Stagnation*. Cambridge: Cambridge University Press, 1985.

Saro-Wiwa, K. *Genocide in Nigeria: The Ogoni Tragedy*. Port Harcourt, Nigeria: Saros International Publishers, 1992.

Schatz, S. P. "Pirate Capitalism and the Inert Economy of Nigeria." *Journal of Modern African Studies* 22/1 (1984).

Seymour, T. "Housing Policy and Income Distribution in Kaduna." *Nigerian Journal of Public Affairs* 7 (1977).

Shenton, R. W. *The Development of Capitalism in Northern Nigeria*. London: James Currey, 1986.

Suberu, R. T. "The Struggle for New States in Nigeria." *African Affairs* 90/361 (1991).

______. *State and Local Government Reorganizations in Nigeria*. Ibadan: Institut Français de Recherche en Afrique, 1991.

______. "The Travails of Federalism in Nigeria." *Journal of Democracy* 4/4 (1993).

Swindell, K., and A. B. Mamman. "Land Expropriation and Accumulation in the Sokoto Periphery, Northwest Nigeria, 1976–86." *Africa* 60/2 (1990).

Tamuno, T. N. "Patriotism and Statism in the Rivers State, Nigeria." *African Affairs* 71/284 (1972).

Teal, F. "Domestic Policies, External Constraints and Economic Development in Nigeria since 1950." *African Affairs* 87/346 (1988).

Teriba, O. "Development Strategy, Investment Decision and Expenditure Patterns of a Public Development Institution: The Case of the Western Nigerian Development Corporation, 1949–1962." *Nigerian Journal of Economic and Social Studies* 8/2 (1966).

Toye, J. *Dilemmas of Development*. Oxford: Basil Blackwell, 1987.

Tseayo, J. I. *Conflict and Incorporation in Nigeria: The Integration of the Tiv*. Zaria: Gaskiya Corporation, 1975.

Turner, T. "Commercial Capitalism and the 1975 Coup." In K. Panter-Brick, ed., *Soldiers and Oil*. London: Frank Cass, 1978.

______. "The Working of the Nigerian National Oil Corporation." In P. Collins, ed., *Administration for Development in Nigeria*. Lagos: African Education Press, 1980.

Udo, R. K. *Migrant Tenant Farmers of Nigeria*. Lagos: African Universities Press, 1975.

UNDP, *Human Development Report 1994*. New York: Oxford University Press, 1994.

Usman, Y. B. *For the Liberation of Nigeria: Essays and Lectures, 1969–1978*. London: New Beacon Books, 1979.

———. *Political Repression in Nigeria.* Zaria: Gaskiya Corporation, 1982.

———. *The Manipulation of Religion in Nigeria, 1977–1987.* Kaduna: Vanguard Publishers, 1987.

Van Hear, N. "Recession, Retrenchment, and Military Rule: Prospects for Nigerian Labour in the 1980s." In R. Southall, ed., *Trade Unions and the New Industrialisation in the Third World.* London: Zed Books, 1988.

Watts, M. *Silent Violence: Food Famine and Peasantry in Northern Nigeria.* Berkeley: University of California Press, 1983.

Watts, M., ed. *State, Oil and Agriculture in Nigeria.* Berkeley: University of California Press, 1987.

Williams, G. "Inequalities in Rural Nigeria." Development Studies Occasional Paper No. 16, University of East Anglia, 1981.

———. "Primitive Accumulation: The Way to Progress?" *Development and Change* 18/4 (1987).

———."Why Is There No Agrarian Capitalism in Nigeria?" *Journal of Historical Sociology* 1/4 (1988).

———. "The World Bank in Rural Nigeria Revisited: A Review of the World Bank's 'Nigeria: Agricultural Sector Review 1987.'" *Review of African Political Economy* 43 (1988).

World Bank. *Options for Long Term Development.* Baltimore: Johns Hopkins Press, 1974.

———. *Nigeria: Agricultural Sector Review.* 3 vols. Washington, D.C.: 1979.

———. *World Development Report.* New York: Oxford University Press, 1981.

———. *Nigeria: Macro-Economic Policies for Structural Change.* Washington, D.C., 1983.

———. *Nigeria: Agricultural Pricing Policy.* Washington, D.C., 1985.

———. *Nigeria: Agricultural Sector Memorandum.* Washington, D.C., 1985.

———. *World Development Report.* New York: Oxford University Press, 1987.

———. *Nigeria: Agricultural Sector Review.* Revised draft, 1987.

———. *The Nigerian: Structural Adjustment Programme: Policies, Impact and Prospects.* Washington, D.C., 1988.

———. *Adjustment in Africa: Reforms, Results, and the Road Ahead.* Oxford: Oxford University Press, 1994.

———. *Nigeria: Structural Adjustment Programme, Policies, Implementation, and Impact.* Washington, D.C., 1994.

Yahaya, A. D. "The Creation of States." In K. Panter-Brick, ed., *Soldiers and Oil.* London: Frank Cass, 1978.

———. "Nigerian Public Administration Under Military Rule: The Experience of the Northern States." In O. O. Adamolekun, ed., *Nigerian Public Administration, 1960–1980.* Ibadan: Heinemann, 1985.

About the Book and Author

Since the end of civil war in 1970, Nigeria has struggled to build a stronger federal center and to reduce conflicts resulting from uneven development and from ethnic, regional, class, and religious differences. This book provides a comprehensive account of the dynamic interplay between the political and economic forces that have shaped government policies, institutions, and the patterns of development in Africa's most populous country.

Tom Forrest identifies the major issues and challenges in Nigerian politics, giving particular attention to the evolution of the federal system, aspects of political competition, and the nature of ruling groups. He examines the links among political demands and incentives, economic strategy, and capitalist development and analyzes the evolution of economic policy and performance, looking specifically at the impact of large oil revenues, agrarian policies, and the program of economic liberalization.

In a completely new chapter for this edition, Forrest examines the annulment of the presidential elections in 1993 and explores the persistence of military rule, the demise of the economic reform program, and the intensification of the economic crisis. Assessing the prospects for economic and political change, Forrest considers whether enough political coherence and legitimacy at the center can be reestablished to allow for effective economic management and more productive use of oil wealth in the years ahead.

Tom Forrest is research associate at Queen Elizabeth House, Oxford University.

Index

For Product Safety Concerns and Information please contact our EU representative GPSR@taylorandfrancis.com Taylor & Francis Verlag GmbH, Kaufingerstraße 24, 80331 München, Germany

Batch number: 10726013

Printed by Printforce, the Netherlands